The Life and Work of Teachers

Bringing together the work of researchers from across the world, this unique collection links policy, school leadership and teachers' lives, the three factors that are arguably the most influential in creating quality learning opportunities for students.

Each chapter provides contemporary insights and represents a range of original empirical and conceptual research focusing upon the ideological, social and educational policy contexts, national and global trends and their impact upon leadership, and the quality of teachers' work in schools. These related international perspectives provide an analysis of the current and future challenges of raising standards of achievement in the third millennium.

The chapters collectively show that although the vision for reconstructing education has been so far flawed, there is scope for considerable optimism for the future; and that the key to the successful fulfilment of such a vision is the teacher.

Contributors: Ivor Goodson; Gary McCulloch; Paul Morris, K.K. Chan and Lo Mun Ling; David F. Labaree; Judyth Sachs; Gill Helsby; Shirley Grundy and Stewart Bonser; Kirsti Klette; Ibrahim Bajunid; Gunnar Berg; Colin Biott and Franz Rauch; Brian J. Caldwell.

Editors: Christopher Day is a Professor of Education, Co-Director of the Centre for Teacher and School Development, and Head of Humanities Division, Graduate School, University of Nottingham. **Alicia Fernandez** is the current Professional Actions and Cultures of Teaching Group Administrator at the Ontario Institute for Studies in Education, University of Toronto. **Trond E. Hauge** is Professor of Education at the Department of Teacher Education and School Development, University of Oslo. **Jorunn Møller** is an Associate Professor at the Department of Teacher Education and School Development at the University of Oslo.

The Life and Work of Teachers

International Perspectives in
Changing Times

**Edited by Christopher Day,
Alicia Fernandez, Trond E. Hauge
and Jorunn Møller**

2000

London and New York

First published 2000
by Falmer Press
11 New Fetter Lane, London EC4P 4EE

Simultaneously published in the USA and Canada
by Falmer Press
Garland Inc., 19 Union Square West, New York, NY 10003

Falmer Press is an imprint of the Taylor & Francis Group

© 2000 Christopher Day, Alicia Fernandez, Trond E. Hauge and
Jorunn Møller selection and editorial matter; individual chapters,
the contributors

Typeset in Times by
BC Typesetting, Bristol
Printed and bound in Great Britain by
Biddles Ltd, Guildford and King's Lynn

British Library Cataloguing in Publication Data
A catalogue record for this book is available from the British Library

Library of Congress Cataloguing in Publication Data
The life and work of teachers: international perspectives in changing
    times/edited by Christopher Day . . . [et al.].
        p.   cm.
    Includes bibliographical references and index.
    I. Teachers.   2. Teaching.   3. Educational change.   I. Day,
Christopher, ACP.
LB1775.L45   1999
371.102–dc21   99-36838
                                                       CIP

ISBN 0–750–70944–8 (pbk)
ISBN 0–750–70945–6 (hbk)

Contents

Contents

Figures and Tables

Figures

Tables

Introduction

This book brings together the work of researchers from many different countries, all of whom are committed to enhancing the lives and work of teachers and the changing contexts in which they work through association with the Professional Actions and Cultures of Teaching (PACT). Organized in April 1992, PACT is a project which aims at bringing together international scholars in the fields of teaching, teachers' work and teacher professionalism to exchange and develop new research in a community of common interest and shared experience. The contributions in this book were presented originally as part of an international Nordic research conference.

The titles of the chapters characterize schools and teachers in these countries as being in transition as they struggle to manage the challenges of the 'new work order' of conflicting expectations, curriculum reform and restructuring which result in 'contested realities' of the meaning of professionalism confronting them in their daily work. In 1975 Dan Lortie described the work of teachers as 'fraught with uncertainties'. Since then there have been a plethora of reform efforts aimed at improving educational systems perceived to be lagging behind in preparing students for the economic, social and technological changes in society. However, despite such reform and restructuring attempts, the position of teachers within the educational hierarchy has essentially remained the same. They were and still are the front-line workers charged with implementing policies created from above.

These new policies have put a heavy demand on teachers' personal and professional lives. The constant stream of change, especially in curriculum, pedagogy and evaluation, has exacerbated rather than alleviated the already relentless pace of teachers' daily work. Changes in the educational system have created shifting images, interpretations and perceptions of roles and goals, thus bringing more uncertainties which have eroded the fixed realities of traditional roles, responsibilities and accountabilities. Increasing governmental concern over whether the adults of tomorrow will be well equipped to compete in a global economy have drawn schools into the arena of accountability. The perceived failure of schools to produce responsible, literate and skilled citizens has also diminished the traditional support, respect and trust accorded to teachers by parents and the public at large. Thus, not only do they have to cope now with the changing internal contexts of their work, they also have to battle against negative criticism and publicity from the outside. This is the current setting in which calls for increased teacher professionalism are located. In effect, the call for professionalism in teachers' work is a call for competence. In the last decade, issues about the training, ability and skill of teachers to 'deliver' results have dominated both policy decisions and studies of school effectiveness and improvement.

According to most research studies internationally, leadership which promotes empowerment, collaboration, organizational learning, continuing professional development and participatory decision making is a key characteristic of effective schools. Taken together, these concepts are expected to bring about change in teachers' behaviours, attitudes and beliefs about their work. The rhetoric is that this will transform practice and thus improve student learning and achievement. Yet in terms of systemic reform, these ideas often come in conflicting packages. While enthusiasm for empowerment is generated, there might be increased prescription in curriculum, pedagogy and assessment. While time is reorganized to provide for collaborative work, there might be increased demands for meetings and paperwork which address managerial, bureaucratic concerns rather than teachers' pedagogical issues and problems. While continuous learning is advocated, teachers' opportunities for professional development may be curtailed by the heavy demands of additional duties and responsibilities. The focus has been upon system rather than individual, teaching rather than learning.

In Part I, 'Teacher Professionalism and Conditions of Change', the authors examine how reforms are impacting upon teachers' knowledge, identity and professional self-understanding, and the development of professional knowledge among teachers. Chapter 1, 'Professional Knowledge and the Teacher's Life and Work', identifies the central issue for those who wish to enhance the quality of teachers' work. 'The way we study teachers reflects the value we put on them. It confirms what sort of people we think teachers are and should be.' By these words Ivor Goodson profiles an important agenda for teacher research. He is particularly concerned about how we constitute our understandings of teachers and their work. The question of how teachers' voices may be heard is at the heart of his analysis. He recommends research on teachers' life and work that may evoke a counter-culture against the tendency to return teachers to the 'shadows' or the instrumental places of teaching that too often are preferred by politicians and administrators. According to Goodson, a focus on teachers' voices will provide a valuable range of insights both into the new restructuring and reform processes in education and into new policy concerns and directives.

In 'The Politics of the Secret Garden: Teachers and the School Curriculum in England and Wales', Gary McCulloch examines how curriculum changes in England and Wales have affected teachers' freedom and autonomy since 1950. He questions the 'myth' and 'memory' of teacher freedom in the curriculum often evoked by both supporters and critics of the National Curriculum introduced by the Education Reform Act of 1988; and he concludes that teachers' work in England and Wales has for a long time been regulated by prescribed syllabuses in the public examinations.

In 'Curriculum Reform and Education Change', Paul Morris, K.K. Chan and Lo Mun Ling focus on the introduction in 1990 of a 'Target Oriented Curriculum' by the Hong Kong government in primary and secondary schools. They evaluate the impact of this curriculum at three levels: the policy level, the school or organizational level and the classroom level. In the initial phase, the years 1990–94, the study reveals that the government failed to justify the reform adequately to schools and teachers. It was a political top-down initiative without the necessary understanding of what brings about changes at school and classroom levels. Studies of the implementation phase of the reform from 1995 and onwards show that schools and teachers have interpreted the reform in terms of prior experiences and understandings that are not necessarily in accordance with the intentions of the reform. According to this research, policy makers in Hong Kong know too little about translating policy into practice so that schools may improve.

David F. Labaree follows by critically analysing forms of knowledge in Schools of Education. In 'Educational Researchers: Living with a Lesser Form of Knowledge', his main thesis is that because education schools in America are living with an applied form of knowledge, they are easy targets for attacks from outside as well as from counterparts within the university structure. He claims that educational knowledge is more soft than hard, more applied than pure and that it has 'low exchange' but 'high use' value. The consequence is a weak authority base of knowledge in education with low resistance to changing political winds. Schools and teachers are seen as easy targets for change from a political and administrative level. This problem is also a part of the crisis in teacher education. In the final, more optimistic chapter from Australia, 'Rethinking the Practice of Teacher Professionalism', Judyth Sachs highlights the benefits of action research when extended beyond the walls of the school, where expertise is viewed as a two-way street by the network of partners rather than the sole possession of just one group. She introduces the notion of 'activist' professionalism in which teachers take control by providing moral and intellectual leadership in order to ensure a high quality of student learning.

The chapters in Part II, 'The Lives and Work of Teachers', demonstrate how the numerous changes affect teachers' work and teachers' lives. The experiences of teachers portrayed in the examples from Australia, the United Kingdom and Norway parallel those of almost every western industrialized country. The results of the studies illustrate that the impact of change on teachers' work is neither simple nor straightforward. Time and structure, agency and personality, leadership and culture, history and context are all factors that interact in complex and novel ways to produce varying experiences of change and innovation amongst different individuals, groups and schools. They also highlight the parameters of teachers' work. Innovation in education hardly resembles the free atmosphere for experimentation characteristic of most private industries. As public servants engaged in providing a social service, teachers are bounded by bureaucratic imperatives. New ideas frequently emanate from those outside the school system and changes are often mandated from the top. A typical pattern of change has been for policy makers and administrators to mandate those who work in schools to make a new policy work, often without adequate or appropriate support and assistance. Furthermore, hardly has a new innovation been institutionalized when a change in the political wind may bring a different policy. It is not uncommon to find several non-complementary innovations being implemented within the education system at the same time. These generate feelings of anxiety, stress and frustration and create an atmosphere of uncertainty, confusion and insecurity. Energies are often focused on simply coping with change and keeping up with new developments, so inhibiting teachers from creative and risk-taking pedagogic endeavours.

But while the studies cited in this part of the book display the common theme of intensification of work, deskilling and even proletarianization, there are also examples of innovative and novel ways that create structure and opportunity for professionalism to flourish. In 'Multiple Truths and Contested Realities: The Changing Faces of Teacher Professionalism in England', Gill Helsby illustrates how some teachers have found manoeuvrability within the structure of the National Curriculum in Britain. Given time to learn and master its contents, they have been able to build upon their skills and acquire new ones in the process of finding ways of implementing the curriculum. This may well illustrate that reflection is the heart of good teaching and may alter the thinking that professionalism can only occur if teachers have autonomy and power over the trio of curriculum, pedagogy and assessment. Likewise, Christopher Day in 'Stories of Change and Professional Development: The Costs of Commitment', suggests that after the initial shock, innovation fatigue and sometimes disillusionment of imposed reforms, some teachers have been able to redefine their personal and professional identities so that their work has continued to fit their closely held values and the moral purposes of teaching and learning.

In their research on reforms which shift the responsibility of developing the agenda of professionalism onto teachers themselves, Shirley Grundy and Stewart Bonser, in their work, 'The New Work Order in Australian Schools', and Kirsti Klette, in 'Working-Time Blues: How Norwegian

Teachers Experience Restructuring in Education', demonstrate the dilemmas of participative work. They illustrate that collaboration and shared decision making can easily become a control mechanism aimed at manipulating people, giving them the illusion of voice, rather than a device which can enhance and develop teacher professionalism.

Learning to teach is a complex task. It is highly personal, contextual and content oriented. Trond E. Hauge illuminates this learning problem through analyses of student teachers' professional growth during a teacher education programme in Norway. Case studies are presented of three student teachers in a university-based programme in 1993. The study underlines the necessity to design teacher education programmes that are far more sensitive to students' preconceptions of learning and teaching and their personal learning histories. At the same time it reveals that practice teaching in school is a vulnerable learning arena for student teachers, and one which sometimes may be counter-productive to students' professional growth as teachers and to the overall intentions in teacher education programmes.

The chapters in the final part, 'Dilemmas of School Leadership', provide an analysis of leadership for change and the contexts within which school leadership is exercised. A major element of current reform in almost all western democracies is the self-managing school, and so it is important to understand how some of the main features of the changing landscape affect governing structures, both defining and influenced by the work of principals, who, arguably, are in key positions to influence the culture and achievements of the schools they lead.

Chapter 11, the first chapter of Part III, 'Rethinking the Work of Teachers and School Leaders in an Age of Change', provides a timely reminder of the need to re-evaluate purposes and practices. Writing from a Muslim perspective, Ibrahim Bajunid explores the meaning of being a teacher and leader in an age of change from within an ethical framework. The chapter raises issues of spirituality and highlights concerns about the omission of, for example, attention to 'emotional intelligence' in the curricula of pre-service and continuing professional development.

In Chapter 12, 'Steering in and Steering of the School', Gunnar Berg provides a synthesis of a number of key concepts currently being used in the field of organizational and curriculum theory in order to deepen our understanding of school governing and school development. A conceptual framework, based on relations between different forms of steering and politics and bureaucracy in general, and between school politics and school bureaucracy in particular, is constructed, discussed and applied to the Swedish school system. The traditional Swedish model can be described in terms of an active welfare state based upon industrialization and democratization. Its decline can be viewed as a process towards a more reactive welfare state based upon post-industrialization and market orientation. These overall societal changes have affected steering *of* the school as an institution, and steering *in* the school as an organization. When it comes to steering *of* school as an institution, centralization and steering by rules has been replaced by decentralization and steering by goals. When it comes to steering *in* school as an organization, the room for professional manoeuvre and scope of action has become more ambiguous. The change in the relationship entailed by decentralization appears to represent a shift of power from the state to society. However, it is an empirical question whether decentralization does result in a weak state, because the power which the state gives up via decentralization can be – and often is – taken back, and even strengthened, by means of various control measures.

An empirical analysis of the tensions between steering *of* the school versus steering *in* the school is continued in Chapter 13, 'School Principals in Transition: Conflicting Expectations, Demands and Desires', in which Jorunn Møller attempts to capture some of the foremost dilemmas confronting principals as they try to cope within a context characterized by devolution of greater responsibilities to schools. Her analysis is based on data from a two-year action research project among principals, and focuses on how a group of Norwegian principals experience contradictory orientations and often find themselves engaged in coping strategies to comply with legal mandates which sometimes seem impossible to implement. Møller reveals how decentralization to a large degree has come to mean an opportunity to manage dwindling budgetary resources, an increase in paperwork as a result of greater emphasis on accountability and evaluation, and a tendency for the state to exert more control over teachers' work and teachers' time. At the same time Møller emphasizes that there are many ways to resist top-down control, and that the scope of action is ambiguous. It is, however, clear that the tension between control and autonomy within schools seems to be accentuated with decentralization, and that principals are involved in a struggle to negotiate and maintain their legitimacy as leaders. Møller argues that in this process, action research as an approach to professional development seems to have a great potential for strengthening the educational agenda in schools.

Although the effectiveness and roles of teachers and principals are defined partly by the structures and cultures in which they find themselves, they will always have some power to influence. This is a theme in the next chapter where the proactive role principals may play in the improvement of schooling is addressed. In a case study, Colin Biott and Franz Rauch explore a local and personal response to broad structural changes. Their chapter, 'Preparing for External Inspection: School Leadership as a Continuing Project in Identity Construction', is based on field work in a large urban primary school in England during a six-month period prior to an external inspection by the Office for Standards in Education (OFSTED). It traces the interplay between a headteacher's attempt to cling to her preferred identity as a leading professional and her urgent concern to present the school favourably according to externally imposed criteria. The case study shows how the headteacher transformed external regulation into a resource to reduce her own uncertainty. In their analysis the authors have captured the constant interplay between the kind of person the principal wants to be and the kind of person she feels she has had to become during the build-up to a critical event. They have uncovered ways in which structure, power, personal agency and identity are interrelated and shaped in subtle and changing ways, and suggest that school leadership can be understood as a continuing project of identity construction in the face of contradictory demands.

How leadership is a primary mediating variable influencing the successful implementation of educational change in general, and improved teaching and learning in particular, is a concern in Chapter 15 by Alicia Fernandez, based on a grounded study of teacher professionalism in Canada. In 'Leadership in an Era of Change: Breaking Down Barriers of the Culture of Teaching', teachers from five schools were interviewed during the implementation of a restructuring policy aimed at improving education through the development of its teachers. All five schools had principals who were known for being proactive in setting the tone of discipline in their school and seeking ways to improve the quality of learning and teaching. Based on teachers' perceptions of principals' behaviours, Fernandez argues that principals have the potential to influence the quality of student learning in the school by supporting the growth of teacher professionalism and that they achieve this largely through their visibility, modelling, support, high expectations and decisiveness and courage. Teachers appreciated principals who were always ready to help them with problems and facilitate their work. It helped them to stay in focus. Modelling, leading by example or 'walking the talk' seemed to be one of the best mechanisms for building trust among staff and for creating exemplary standards of practice. She concludes that it was leadership that created a professional community of teachers who were committed to continuous learning, and who worked in collaborative ways to create and develop shared goals and visions for their school.

In the final chapter of the book, aptly entitled 'Reinventing School Leadership for Lasting Reform in the Third Millennium', Brian Caldwell complements Fernandez's perspective by providing an account of 'Schools of the Future'. Victoria, Australia, has the largest system of public education anywhere to have decentralized as much as 90 per cent of its budget to schools within a centrally determined framework of goals, policies, priorities, standards and accountabilities. Findings from several research projects reveal the effects of a capacity for self-management on improved learning outcomes for students. The effects on outcomes seem laden with an increasing number of roles and responsibilities for school leaders. The study also reports, however, that the overwhelming majority of principals would not wish their schools to return to previous arrangements, despite unfulfilled expectations and intensification of work due to devolution of authority and responsibility. In a forward-looking chapter, Caldwell pays particular attention to what lies beyond the 'self-managing school', discussing the implications for the future work of school leaders. He looks to schools of the third millennium, and argues that major change lies ahead, largely owing to the effects of information and communication technology.

Teaching has been described by numerous studies as complex, immediate, strongly oriented to action rather than reflection, reactive rather than proactive, and full of activities characterized by brevity, variety and discontinuity. Altering teachers' work is therefore challenging and calls for strategies that go beyond merely espousing the rhetoric of collaboration, empowerment, shared decision making and continuous learning. It needs a restructuring of time, space and opportunity. It needs to extend and expand teachers' parameters of practice beyond those of the classroom or the school. Rather than establishing partnerships or collaborative teams moving towards shared visions and goals, there is a need to develop a community in which professionalism is underscored by respect for each individual's contribution to the betterment of its members; in which networking goes beyond merely reaching out to experts outside the system; in which problems are owned and solved collectively; and in which accountability is not confined to just one group but is a shared responsibility of all involved.

The call for teacher professionalism in an atmosphere of constant change is an aspect of the idea that teachers are our heroes. The demands of constant change create fatigue of the mind and spirit that makes martyrs out of them instead. The choice of redefining professionalism cannot and should not belong only to those who do not teach. Teachers themselves have to be active in creating the work conditions, the opportunities and the spaces in which competence, creativity, risk taking and learning may thrive. This cannot be done in isolation. A professional community has to be built upon the shared insights and the collective experiences of those from within the community. Many of the chapters in this book present the results of empirical research which reveal that far from being 'proletarianized', passive victims of imposed reforms, teachers, principals and teacher educators are actively engaged in making sense of them within their own professional values and practices in organizational and classroom contexts. Nor are the principals and teachers in this research stubbornly resisting change at all costs. They are acting with courage and integrity in what are often adverse circumstances. What is fascinating in this collection is the similarity, not only of the changes in conditions of work in schools, but also the ways in which they are being managed in different countries, and the continuing tensions between the visions of those who are responsible for policy and policy implementation and those who work in classrooms.

It is how teachers manage and ride the waves of change which will determine the success of reform efforts and, ultimately, the learning and achievement of the students with whom they work.

Christopher Day
Alicia Fernandez
Trond E. Hauge
Jorunn Møller
June 1999

Part I

Teacher Professionalism and Conditions of Change

1 Professional Knowledge and the Teacher's Life and Work

Ivor Goodson

In this chapter Ivor Goodson claims that the kind of research knowledge we generate about teachers and for teachers is crucial in order to understand and define what sort of professionals teachers are and might become. He argues against conceptualizations of the teacher as researcher which focus upon pedagogical practice only, arguing instead that the parameters of practice cover a very wide terrain which extends beyond the classroom. Research, then, should focus more broadly on the teacher's life and work. A range of strategies are identified and discussed. Goodson argues that focusing on teachers' voices will provide a valuable range of insights into the new restructuring and reform processes in education, and into new policy concerns and directives.

This chapter begins with a short introduction detailing some of my views about the way global developments in this field are progressing. I have two suspicions, possible interpretations, about emergent patterns. First, the arguments of Alan Wolfe (1996) carry considerable weight with me. Wolfe has argued that what we are seeing globally is an attack on what he calls the 'median level'. By this he means the public institutions: schools, universities, public broadcasting, libraries, hospitals and so on. In most countries, these institutions are coming under attack; this is evidenced by the fact that less and less is being spent on them. Lest we accept that it is a problem of shortage of money, it is worth pointing out that the opposite is happening to the police, the army and expenditure on military weapons and private developments like private shopping malls and private housing. Here there is a huge growth in expenditure and in expanding developments. Overall then, we are obviously not short of money. What is happening is that we are consistently choosing the private over the public at nearly all levels and this is playing through into an attack on the 'median level'.

Wolfe argues that the median levels of professional life are a confusing nuisance between the direct relationship of the state and its subjects and industry and its customers. In the median-level critique, social criticism, theory building and arguments against inequality still reside. The attempt, therefore, at the global level, is to weaken this level and move the centre of action for knowledge construction to other levels. Michael Gibbons et al. (1994) have recently written about the distinction between mode 1 and mode 2 knowledge. Mode 1 knowledge is essentially disciplinary knowledge, normally developed in the traditional universities. Mode 2 knowledge is applied knowledge, increasingly developed in the R & D sectors of the private industrial base, together with the think tanks associated with this sector of the economy. Whilst mode 1 knowledge is under sustained attack, mode 2 knowledge is being sponsored. This is merely a version of the changing priority from the public to the private that I mentioned earlier.

A second line of inquiry concerns how we would test if some of these dark suspicions that I have detailed are in any way true. Well, one way is to look at *workplace knowledge*. Again, there is increasing evidence that the knowledge that workers and professionals are being given in training is, in spite of globalization, less and less general and theoretical and more and more context-specific, local and utilitarian.

Now, of course we can all think of examples that do not fit this pattern, but in terms of the teaching profession, how would we test this hypothesis? It would mean we would be looking for evidence that teachers are being turned from intellectual workers who control their own curriculum and pedagogy into technicians who define the curriculum designed by other people. They are less and less planners of their own destiny and more and more deliverers of prescriptions written by others.

So that is my long introduction of suspicions – to let you know where I stand. For it is at this point in the chapter that a discussion of the research about teachers and the kind of way we research teachers comes into the frame. My central point is that *the way we study teachers reflects the value we put on them*. It confirms what sort of people we think teachers are and should be. Crucially, the kind of research knowledge we generate helps in defining what sort of professionals teachers are and whether there is any real teacher professionalism at all, since the kind of knowledge base that is generated feeds back into the kind of professionalism which is legitimized. In short, the sort of research we do about teachers and on the teacher's life and work is one of the areas of struggle in which the whole range of issues I have detailed about professionalism and policy are decided. So in asking what sort of knowledge is generated about teachers and for teachers, I want briefly to review the place of the teacher in research literature.

The Teacher's Life and Work

Dan Lortie summarized the relationship between teachers and educational research studies in the United States in his book *Schoolteacher* (1975):

Schooling is long on prescription, short on description. That is nowhere more evident than in the case of the two million persons who teach in the public schools. It is widely conceded that the core transactions of formal education take place where teachers and students meet. . . . But although books and articles instructing teachers on how they should behave are legion, empirical studies of teaching work – and the outlook of those who staff the schools – remain rare.

(Lortie 1975: vii)

The general point that Lortie makes with regard to knowledge/power has been a continuing one in the research discourse as related to teachers: a good deal of prescription and implicit portrayal but very little serious study of, or collaboration with, those prescribed to or portrayed. Yet whilst there is continuity, there are also changes over time which exist at the intersection with social, political and economic history.

Introducing the book *Teachers' Lives and Careers*, Ball and I (writing in 1985) argued that British research on teachers had moved through a number of contemporary phases. 'In the 1960s teachers were shadowy figures on the educational landscape mainly known or unknown through large-scale surveys or historical analysis of their position in society; the key concept in approaching the practice of teaching was that of role' (Ball and Goodson, 1985). Teachers, in short, were present in aggregate through imprecise statistics or were viewed as individuals only as formal role incumbents, mechanistically and unproblematically responding to the powerful expectations of their role set.

In the late 1960s and early 1970s this approach changed somewhat (but from the point of view of the teacher not necessarily for the better). Case study researchers began to examine schooling as a social process, particularly in the manner through which school pupils were 'processed'. 'The sympathies of the researchers lay primarily with the pupils, working-class and female pupils in particular, who were the underdogs in the classroom: teachers were the villains of the piece.' By the late 1970s we discerned a further shift: 'attention began to be directed to the constraints within which teachers work. . . . Teachers were transformed from villains to victims and, in some cases, "dupes" of the system within which they were required to operate' (ibid.: 7).

But this latter characterization of teachers finally opened up the question of 'how teachers saw their work and their lives'. Writing in 1981, I argued that researchers had not confronted the complexity of the school teacher as an active agent making his or her own history. Researchers, even when they had stopped treating the teacher as numerical aggregate, historical footnote or unproblematic role incumbent, still treated teachers as interchangeable types unchanged by circumstance or time. As a result new research methods were needed:

> The pursuit of personal and biographical data might rapidly challenge the assumption of interchangeability. Likewise, by tracing the teacher's life as it evolved over time throughout the teacher's career and through several generations the assumption of timelessness might also be remedied. In understanding something so intensely personal as teaching it is critical we know about the person the teacher is. Our paucity of knowledge in this area is a manifest indictment of the range of our sociological imagination. The life historian pursues the job from his [*sic*] own perspective, a perspective which emphasises the value of the person's 'own story.'
>
> (Goodson 1981: 69)

In the event, whilst the argument for studies of teachers' lives and careers now began to be more generally pursued in the educational research community, political and economic changes were moving sharply in the opposite direction. The changes in the patterns of political and administrative control over teachers were enormous in the 1980s. In terms of power and visibility, in many ways this represents 'a return to the shadows' for teachers in the face of new curriculum guidelines (in some countries like Britain an all-encompassing national curriculum), teacher assessment and accountability, a barrage of new policy edicts and new patterns of school governance and administration.

Developing a Counter-Culture: Rationales for Studying the Teacher's Life and Work

In one sense the project of 'studying the teacher's life and work' represents an attempt to generate a counter-culture that will resist the tendency to return teachers to the shadows; a counter-culture based upon a research mode that above all places teachers at the centre of the action and seeks to sponsor 'the teacher's voice'. 'The proposal I am recommending is essentially one of reconceptualising educational research so as to assure that the teacher's voice is heard, heard loudly, heard articulately' (Goodson 1991: 36).

Butt, Raymond, McCue and Yamagishi (1992) have argued that:

> The notion of the teacher's voice is important in that it carries the tone, the language, the quality, the feelings, that are conveyed by the way a teacher speaks or writes. In a political sense the notion of the teacher's voice addresses the right to speak and be represented. It can represent both the unique individual and the collective voice; one that is characteristic of teachers as compared to other groups.
>
> (Butt et al. 1992: 57)

The sponsoring of the teacher's voice (if sponsoring can be accepted with its paternalist overtones) is thus counter-cultural in that it works against the grain of power/knowledge as held and produced by politicians and administrators.

Yet if the economic and political times are inauspicious, on the other side, the current 'postmodernist movement' provides an emergent climate of support, certainly at the level of research. Foucault has been hugely influential in encouraging researchers to retrieve and represent the voices of their 'subjects'. Likewise, Carol Gilligan's superb body of work exemplifies the power of representing the voices of women previously unheard. Above all, the postmodern syntagm sponsors 'the idea that all groups have a right to speak for themselves, in their own voice, and have that voice accepted as authentic and legitimate' (Harvey 1989: 48).

Beyond the general sponsorship of the teacher's voice there are a range of other rationales for studying the teacher's life and work. First, such work will provide a valuable range of insights into the new moves to restructure and reform schooling and into new policy concerns and directives. A number of authors have addressed this 'crisis of reform' or more specifically 'crisis of prescription'. I have recently examined the importance and salience of the belief in curriculum as prescription (CAP).

CAP supports the mystique that expertise and control reside within central governments, educational bureaucracies or the university community. Providing that nobody exposes this mystique, the two worlds of 'prescriptive rhetoric' and 'schooling as practice' can coexist. Both sides benefit from such peaceful coexistence. The agencies of CAP are seen to be 'in control' and the schools are seen to be 'delivering' (and can carve out a good degree of autonomy if they accept the rules).

However, there is a substantial downside to this 'historic compromise'. There are costs of complicity in accepting the myth of prescription: above all these involve, in various ways, acceptance of established modes of power relations. Perhaps most importantly the people intimately connected with the day-to-day social construction of curriculum and schooling – teachers – are thereby effectively disenfranchised in the 'discourse of schooling'. To continue to exist, teachers' day-to-day power must remain unspoken and unrecorded. This is one price of complicity: day-to-day power and autonomy for schools and for teachers are dependent on continuing to accept the fundamental lie (Goodson 1990: 300).

In addressing the crisis of prescription and reform, it becomes imperative that we find new ways to sponsor the teacher's voice. As a particularly generative example, Kathleen Casey's (1992) work provides a valuable rationale for studying teachers' lives to understand the much discussed question of 'teacher drop-out'. She notes that a certain set of taken-for-granted assumptions control the way in which the problem of teacher attrition has normally been defined; one which presumes managerial solutions.

She notes how the language confirms this direction, referring to 'teacher defection', 'teacher turnover' and 'supply and demand'.

This belief in managerialism and prescription is underpinned by the research methods employed within the academy. She finds that former members of the teaching profession have often been traced statistically, rather than in person, and information has typically been collected from such sources as district files and state departments of public instruction, or through researcher-conceived surveys. The results of the research paradigms employed in the academy have powerful implications for our understanding of the management of educational systems.

> The particular configuration of selectivities and omissions which has been built into this research frame slants the shape of its findings. By systematically failing to record the voices of ordinary teachers, the literature on educators' careers actually silences them. Methodologically, this means that even while investigating an issue where decision-making is paramount, researchers speculate on teachers' motivations, or at best, survey them with a set of forced-choice options. Theoretically, what emerges is an instrumental view of teachers, one in which they are reduced to objects which can be manipulated for particular ends. Politically, the results are educational policies constructed around institutionally convenient systems of rewards and punishments, rather than in congruence with teachers' desires to create significance in their lives.
>
> (Casey 1992: 188)

Again and again, teachers' testimonies expose the shallowness of the managerial, prescriptive view of schooling. It is, in truth, not difficult to see in whose interests the teacher's voice has been suppressed and in whose interests academics have embraced less 'curious' research modes.

Perhaps the most eloquent epitaph for the believers in managerialism and prescriptions comes from the case study of 'Glenda' by Butt et al. The teacher's guide was closed and the students' workbooks were returned to the bookroom. The culture and knowledge within the classroom was infinitely more exciting (Butt et al. 1992).

A further rationale for studying the teacher's life and work develops out of the literature on teacher socialization. One major tradition in this literature has designated the period of pre-service training and early in-service teaching as the most formative socializing influence. An alternative tradition, however, has insisted with accelerating force that it is really far more complicated than this. Many studies in the 1970s and 1980s focused on teachers' own experiences as pupils, which are seen as being not only as important as the training periods but in many cases more important. (It should be noted that although this chapter focuses on teachers it argues for future work to also be conducted on pupils' lives and their relationship to their school experiences.) Dan Lortie refers to this pupil period as an 'apprenticeship of observation'. Teacher socialization then occurs through the observation and internalization of particular models of teaching experienced as the recipient pupil. Lortie argues that these latent models, are activated during the training period, having often been, so to speak, 'carried in suspension' over a period of time, particularly the undergraduate years. One way to follow up this alternative tradition in teacher socialization research requires that we examine those socializing influences relevant to the formation of the teacher over the full life experience.

Another rationale for studying the teacher's life and work comes out of the range of feminist work most excitingly exemplified in Sue Middleton's work. Work on teachers' lives provides vital and generative insights into teaching as a gendered profession (Middleton 1992). Other work pursues the issue of women's lives in teaching: Margaret Nelson's attempt to reconstruct the experiences of women teachers in Vermont in the first half of the twentieth century (Nelson 1992) and Kathleen Casey's investigation of why progressive women activists leave teaching (Casey 1992). Nelson's work provides a fascinating vindication of the oral history approach. She notes that:

> Numerous studies have shown that there is a gap between what we can discover when we rely on published accounts of some historical event and what we can discover when we ask questions of the on-site participants of those same events. This gap looms larger when we are looking at women's history because of the private nature of so much of women's lives.
>
> (Nelson 1992: 168)

She adds later, 'Public history often ignores minority views. But women's lives are further hidden because important information is overlooked, consciously avoided, or distorted' (ibid.: 185).

Middleton argues that 'Writing one's autobiography becomes, in this framework, in part a process of deconstructing the discursive practices through which one's subjectivity has been constituted' (Middleton 1992: 20). This work reflects a fourth rationale for studying the teacher's life and work, which relates to the earlier discussion about managerialism: namely the desire to produce teacher-centred professional knowledge. I have pursued this argument at length elsewhere but, put briefly, the issue is to develop a modality of educational research which speaks both of and to the teacher (Goodson 1991). This will require a major reconceptualization of educational research paradigms, but the emerging work on teacher thinking, teacher journalling, teacher's practical knowledge, as well as the new corpus of work on reflective practitioners and action research, is, I think, a harbinger of new modalities of research.

To date, much of the educational research employed in teacher training has been developed from a foundational disciplinary discourse – philosophical, psychological, historical, sociological – far removed from teachers. It has been produced by scholars writing within their own contexts and resonates with their own career concerns in a 'publish or perish' environment. The audience is mainly their academic peers, who are addressed through scholarly journals. In the profoundest sense, the knowledge they produce is, from the teachers' point of view, decontextualized. As Woods has argued, 'such knowledge is not under their control. It is produced "out there" and "up there" on an apparently superior plane in forms and terms with which they cannot engage. Further, much of this knowledge appears to be critical of teachers' (Woods 1987: 121).

Teachers' Lives, Teacher Development and the Nature of Collaboration

Studies of the teacher's life and work develop structural insights which locate the teacher's life within the deeply structured and embedded environment of schooling. (Goodson, forthcoming.) This provides a prime 'trading point' for teachers as researchers (insiders) and the external researchers (outsiders). One of the significant aspects of collaboration between insiders and outsiders is that it is collaboration between two parties that are differentially located in structural terms. As a result, each sees the world through a different prism of practice and thought. Such a valuable difference may provide the external researcher with a possibility of backing goods in 'the trade'. The insider offers data and insights; the outsider, in pursuing glimpses of structure in different ways, may now also bring data and insights. The terms of trade, in short, look favourable. In such conditions collaboration may at last begin in a genuine spirit of 'give and take'. We have the prospect of genuinely reciprocal research.

As a possible route to collaboration, this does not suspend issues of ethics and exploitation. Above all, because the collaboration between insider and outsider takes place in an occupational terrain which is itself inequitably structured, in terms of power, the external researcher still holds many advantages. Moreover the conditions of university careers positively exhort researchers to exploit research data: the requirements of publications and peer review have their own dynamics. So whatever the favourable aspects of a focus on teachers' lives, we must remain deeply watchful.

For if the teacher's practice was a vulnerable focus, the teacher's life is a deeply intimate, highly intrusive, focus. More than ever procedural guidelines are necessary over questions relating to the ownership and publication of the data. These issues themselves must be conceived of in terms of a collaboration in which each party has clear rights, and in this case the teacher's power of veto should be agreed on early and implemented, where necessary, late. The relationship of studies of teachers' lives to the academy sits, I believe, at the centre of one of the major ethical and methodological issues facing this work. Of course, views of the academy cover a wide spectrum from a belief in its role in the 'disinterested pursuit of knowledge' through to the assertion of the Situationist International that 'The intelligentsia is power's hall of mirrors.' In general, I would take a position, for which I see overwhelming empirical evidence, which stresses the *interestedness* rather than disinterestedness of the academy. There is a good deal of empirical evidence that Tripp's contention in this matter may be correct, for he argues that 'when a research method gains currency and academic legitimacy, it tends to be transformed to serve the interests of the academy' (Tripp 1987: 2).

Becker (1970) has commented on the 'hierarchy of credibility regarding those to whom we tend to listen'. This has general relevance to our research on schooling and school systems and specifically to our desire to listen to the teacher's voice, for the academy normally accepts the 'hierarchy of credibility': 'We join officials and the man in the street in an unthinking acceptance of the hierarchy of credibility. We do not realize that there are sides to be taken and that we are taking one of them.' Hence Becker argues that for the academic researcher:

> The hierarchy of credibility is a feature of society whose existence we cannot deny, even if we disagree with its injunction to believe the man at the top. When we acquire sufficient sympathy with subordinates to see things from their perspective, we know that we are flying in the face of what 'everyone knows'. The knowledge gives us pause and causes us to share, however briefly, the doubt of our colleagues.
>
> (Becker 1970: 129)

Research studies then are seldom disinterested and the prime interests at work are dominant interest groups and the academy itself. Acknowledging the primacy of these interests is particularly critical when we conduct studies of the teacher's life and work. The data generated and the reports rendered can, in such circumstances, be misused and abused both by powerful interest groups in politics and bureaucracies and by the academy itself. Schools are sites of social regulation and classification and, as such, surveillance can easily be extended to teachers themselves. Many of the cruder versions of the accountability movement plainly have this as their *modus vivendi*. Studies of the teacher's life and work, then, can be rapidly implicated in such processes unless we patrol who owns the data and who controls the accounts and reports. If Becker is correct in his assertion that 'officials lie', it is also plain that they might appropriate and misuse data about the teacher's life and work. Even more immediately, it is possible that those in the academy who study the teacher's life and work, even if in a collaborative mode, may yet go on to use that data entirely for their own professional purposes.

Becker reminds us that not only does the terrain of research involve differentiated voices, but access to those voices is stratified. It is important to remember that the politicians and bureaucrats who control schools are part of a stratified system where 'those at the top have a more complete picture of what is going on than anyone else'. It would be unfortunate if, in studying teachers' lives, we ignored these contextual parameters which so substantially impinge upon and constantly restrict the teacher's life. It is, therefore, I think, a crucial part of our ethical position as researchers that we do not 'valorize the subjectivity of the powerless' in the name of telling 'their story'. This would be merely to record constrained consciousness – a profoundly conservative posture and one which no doubt explains the popularity of such work during the recent conservative political renaissance. In my view, teachers' life studies should, where possible, provide, not only a *narrative of* action, but also a history or *genealogy of context*. I say this in full knowledge that this opens up substantial dangers of changing the relationship between 'life-story giver', and 'research taker' and of tilting the balance of the relationship further towards the academy. But these dangers must be faced if a genuine collaboration between the life-story giver and the research taker is to be achieved. In a real sense 'it cannot be all give and no take'. In what sense is the 'research taker' in a position to 'give' and thereby provide the basis for a reasonably equitable collaboration? I have argued elsewhere that what we are searching for in developing genuine collaboration in studying teachers' lives is a viable *trading point* between life story giver and research taker. The key to this trading point is, I believe, the differential structural location of the research taker. The academic has the time and the resources to collaborate with teachers in developing 'genealogies of context'. These genealogies can provide teachers as a group with aspects of 'the complete picture' which those who control their lives have (or at least aspire to have).

In arguing for the provision of histories or genealogies of context, I am reminded of V.S. Naipaul's comments. Naipaul has the ultimate sensitivity to the 'stories' that people tell about their lives: for him subjective perceptions are priority data (Naipaul 1987). Buruma (1991) has judged:

> What makes Naipaul one of the world's most civilized writers is his refusal to be engaged by the People, and his insistence on listening to people, individuals, with their own language and their own stories. To this extent he is right when he claims to have no view; he is impatient with abstractions. He is interested in how individual people see

themselves and the world in which they live. He has recorded their histories, their dreams, their stories, their words.

(Buruma 1991: 3)

So far then Naipaul echoes the concern of those educational researchers who have sought to capture teachers' stories and narratives, told in their own words, in their own terms. But I am interested by the more recent shifts in Naipaul's position; he has begun to provide far more historical background, he seems to me to be moving towards providing the stories but also genealogies of context. He is clear that he sees this as empowering those whose stories he once told more passively:

To awaken to history was to cease to live instinctively. It was to begin to see oneself and one's group the way the outside world saw one; and it was to know a kind of rage.

(Buruma 1991: 4)

MacIntyre (1981) has followed a similar line in arguing that man is 'essentially a story-telling animal'. He argues that 'the story of my life is always embedded in the story of those communities from which I derive my identity'.

What I am, therefore, is in key part what I inherit, a specific past that is present to some degree in my present. I find myself part of a history and that is generally to say, whether I like it or not, whether I recognise it or not, one of the bearers of a tradition. It was important when I characterised the concept of a practice to notice that practices always have histories and that at any given moment what a practice is depends on a mode of understanding it which has been transmitted often through many generations. And thus, insofar as the virtues sustain the relationships required for practices, they have to sustain relationships to the past – and to the future – as well as in the present. But the traditions through which particular practices are transmitted and reshaped never exist in isolation from larger social traditions.

(MacIntyre 1981: 206)

He continues:

Within a tradition the pursuit of goods extends through generations, sometimes through many generations. Hence the individual's search for his or her good is generally and characteristically conducted within a context defined by those traditions of which the individual's life is a part, and this is true both of those goods which are internal to practices and of the goods of a single life. Once again the narrative phenomenon

23

of embedding is crucial: the history of a practice in our time is generally and characteristically embedded in and made intelligible in terms of the larger and longer history of the tradition through which the practice in its present form was conveyed to us; the history of each of our own lives is generally and characteristically embedded in and made intelligible in terms of the larger and longer histories of a number of traditions.

(Ibid.: 207)

In many ways Middleton summarizes the aspirations which I share when she says that 'teachers, as well as their students, should analyse the relationship between their individual biographies, historical events, and the constraints imposed on their personal choices by broader power relations, such as those of class, race and gender' (Middleton 1992: 19).

In 'awakening to history' in our studies of teachers' lives, I have felt for some time that life-history work is a most valuable avenue for collaborative, intercontextual work (Goodson, 1988). The distinction between life stories and life histories is an important one to restate. The life story is a personal reconstruction of experience, in this case by the teacher. 'Life-story givers' provide data for the researcher, often in loosely structured interviews. The researcher seeks to elicit the teacher's perceptions and stories but is generally rather passive rather than actively interrogative.

The life history also begins with the life story that the teacher tells, but seeks to build on the information provided. Hence other people's accounts might be elicited, documentary evidence and a range of historical data amassed. The concern is to develop a wide intertextual and intercontextual mode of analysis. This provision of a wider range of data allows a contextual background to be constructed. In this way life stories of teachers build up with a broader social history of teaching but one which is sensitive to their individual lives and experiences.

Acknowledgement

A major part of this text appeared in 1994 in *Teaching and Teacher Education*, 19(1): 29–37, as 'Studying The Teacher's Life and Work'.

References

Ball, S.J. and Goodson, I. (1985) Understanding Teachers: Concepts and Contexts. In S.J. Ball and I.F. Goodson (eds), *Teachers' Lives and Careers*. London and Philadelphia: Falmer Press.

Becker, H.S. (1970) *Sociological Work: Method and Substance*. Chicago: Aldine.

Buruma, I. (1991) Signs of Life. *New York Review of Books*, 14 February, 38(4): 3–4.

Butt, R., Raymond, D., McCue, G. and Yamagishi, L. (1992) Collaborative Auto-biography and the Teacher's Voice. In I.F. Goodson (ed.), *Studying Teachers' Lives*. London: Routledge.

Casey, K. (1992) Why do Progressive Women Activists Leave Teaching? Theory, Methodology and Politics in Life History Research. In I.F. Goodson (ed.), *Studying Teachers' Lives*. London: Routledge.

Gibbons, M., Limoges, C., Nowotny, H., Schwartzman, S., Scott, P. and Trow, M. (1994) *The New Production of Knowledge: The Dynamics of Science and Research in Contemporary Societies*. London, Thousand Oaks, CA and New Delhi: Sage.

Goodson, I.F. (1981) Life History and the Study of Schooling. *Interchange* (Ontario Institute for Studies in Education), 11(4): 62–76.

—— (1988) Teachers, Life Histories and Studies of Curriculum and Schooling. In I.F. Goodson (ed.), *The Making of Curriculum: Collected Essays*. London: Falmer Press.

—— (1990) Studying Curriculum: Towards a Social Constructionist Perspective. *Journal of Curriculum Studies*, 22(4): 299–312.

—— (1991) Sponsoring the Teacher's Voice: Teachers' Lives and Teacher Development. *Cambridge Journal of Education*, 21(1): 35–45.

Goodson, I.F. (ed.) (1992) *Studying Teachers' Lives*. London: Routledge and New York: Teachers College Press.

Harvey, D. (1989) *The Condition of Postmodernity: An Enquiry into the Origins of Cultural Change*. Oxford: Basil Blackwell.

Lortie, D. (1975) *Schoolteacher: A Sociological Study*. Chicago: University of Chicago Press.

MacIntyre, A. (1981) *After Virtue: A Study in Moral Theory*. London: Duckworth.

Middleton, S. (1992) Developing a Radical Pedagogy: Autobiography of a New Zealand Sociologist of Women's Education. In I.F. Goodson (ed.), *Studying Teacher's Lives*. London: Routledge.

Naipaul, V.S. (1987) *The Enigma of Arrival*. London: Viking.

Nelson, M. (1992) Using Oral Histories to Reconstruct the Experiences of Women Teachers in Vermont, 1900–1950. In I.F. Goodson (ed.), *Studying Teachers' Lives*. London: Routledge.

Tripp, D. (1987) Teacher Autobiography and Classroom Practice, Western Australia: Murdoch University (mimeo).

Wolfe, A. (1996) *Marginalized in the Middle*. Chicago: University of Chicago Press.

Woods, P. (1987) Life Histories and Teacher Knowledge. In J. Smyth (ed.), *Educating Teachers: Changing the Nature of Pedagogical Knowledge*. London, New York and Philadelphia: Falmer Press.

2 The Politics of the Secret Garden

Teachers and the School Curriculum in England and Wales

Gary McCulloch

This chapter explores some of the changing political characteristics of the relationship between teachers and the school curriculum in England and Wales over the past fifty years. It focuses upon how teachers' freedom and autonomy has been affected by the curriculum changes in this period and, by looking at what happened in the 1950s and 1960s, questions the 'myth' and 'memory' of teacher freedom in the curriculum often evoked by supporters and by critics of the National Curriculum introduced by the Education Reform Act of 1988. The chapter concludes that although it may appear that teachers in England and Wales have lost their freedom through recent reforms, their work has for a long time been regulated by prescribed syllabuses in the public examinations.

When Sir David Eccles, the then minister of education, referred in March 1960 to the 'secret garden of the curriculum' (*Hansard* 1960), he was coining a phrase that came to symbolize the freedom accorded to school teachers in England and Wales to control what they taught and how they taught it. It is a phrase that increasingly evokes a particular phase or period in educational history, roughly from the 1940s until the 'Great Debate' of the late 1970s, that has been superseded by active state intervention culminating in the 1990s in the National Curriculum. Lawton anticipated (1980a, 1980b) the 'end of the secret garden'. By the late 1980s, Lawn could dismiss the idea of teacher autonomy in curriculum control as 'historically specific to the period 1925–80' (Lawn 1987: 227; see also Chitty and Lawn 1995; Lawn 1996). The National Curriculum introduced under the Education Reform Act of 1988 appears to mark a new phase in the role of teachers in the school curriculum, characterized by centralized control and external accountability.

The present chapter reflects on the limitations and constraints to teachers' supposed freedom that existed even in the 'Golden Age of teacher control (or non-control) of the curriculum' (Lawton 1980a: 22). It also explores some of the changing political characteristics of the relationship between teachers and the school curriculum in England and Wales. During the earlier phase, the ideal of teacher autonomy was frequently belied by reality, but it was repeatedly endorsed among teacher groups and by a range of educational agencies as a central aspiration. In this situation, the integrity of teachers' role in the school curriculum was constantly renegotiated in the face of current and impending threats. By focusing principally on the 1950s and 1960s, with the help of recently released documentary sources, it is possible to highlight the strength of the ideal of teacher autonomy in the curriculum domain, the inherent limitations and contradictions that were involved, and the efforts made to resolve the tensions that resulted.

Moreover, the role of teachers in the curriculum domain has been viewed as a key source of their professionalism in England and Wales over the past fifty years. The incursions of the state and the introduction of the National Curriculum have been widely viewed as marking a major and unprecedented threat to this 'professionalism' (see, e.g. Helsby and McCulloch 1996; McCulloch 1997a). Detailed historical research suggests that threats to teachers' professionalism were present throughout the post-war period, and that while the state was always held in suspicion for the control that it could potentially impose, it was also instrumental in helping to alleviate such threats.

The Ideal of Teacher Freedom

Historians have often emphasized the high degree of freedom enjoyed by teachers in the curriculum domain in the post-war period, often drawing a direct contrast with the contemporary situation of the 1980s and 1990s. The focus of these arguments tends in practice to be on the curriculum of the secondary schools, but a more general case encompassing all teachers is commonly made. Lawton argues, for example (1980a: 19), that after the Education Act of 1944, '*Laissez-faire* rather than rational planning prevailed and continued to be the curriculum philosophy for another twenty years.' According to Lawton, too (ibid.: 21), 'With the removal of the constraints of the Regulations after 1945 schools were free to embark upon any kind of secondary curriculum the teachers chose to offer.' Indeed, he suggests, 'A dangerous vacuum existed: the typical grammar-school curriculum changed very little in the post-war years; secondary-modern-school curricula, free of examination constraints, often lacked structure and purpose.' Thus, Lawton concludes (ibid.: 22), 'little thought was given to the curriculum, either locally or nationally'. In this situation, teachers had a major opportunity to 'take control of the curriculum', but in fact 'failed to take it' (ibid.: 22).

Chitty, in his account of central control of the school curriculum, follows a broadly similar line. He refers (1988: 326) to a 'cosy era of partnership and teacher autonomy' that in spite of apparent conflict in the early 1960s did not come under 'serious threat' until much later, especially following the changed economic circumstances of the mid-1970s. Simon also stresses (1991: 311) that 'the received (and official) view of the 1960s was that the curriculum (or what went on in schools) was the specific responsibility of the *teachers* – not of the local authorities (though their role here was unclear) and certainly not of the state – or the central government'. According to Simon (ibid.: 319), 'any assessment of the 1960s must record this as a period of decisive change in terms of teacher professionalism, control, self-image, and even autonomy'. Above all, in Simon's view, 'teachers were now seen as responsible for the curriculum – for what went on in schools' (ibid.). The 1960s are therefore viewed as the 'heroic period' at least of secondary education in England and Wales, making gains that were later to be 'brought under control and curbed, whatever the cost' (ibid.).

It is clearly true that during these years ideals of teacher freedom in the curriculum domain were uppermost, and that there was generally official approval for teacher control in this area. Attention was concentrated on the teacher as 'a professional who must be directly implicated in the business of curriculum renewal; not as a mere purveyor of other people's bright ideas, but as an innovator himself' (Schools Council 1968: 10). Sir Alec Clegg, chief education officer for the West Riding, was for example a prominent advocate of the teacher as 'a professional making his own diagnoses and prescribing his own treatments', as opposed to being 'a low-grade technician working under someone else's instructions' (ibid.: 25). John F. Kerr, in his inaugural lecture as professor of education at the University of Leicester in 1967, could celebrate the fact that after a long struggle, 'The teachers worked hard to achieve some degree of professional autonomy and by the 1950s it was generally accepted they were free to decide what and how they should teach' (1968: 13). As he noted, 'Although by now local education authorities had statutory responsibility for secular instruction, they had willingly delegated this responsibility to individual teachers and schools' (ibid.). Meanwhile, he added, 'the central government, having set aside much of its responsibility for what went on in the classroom, continued to exercise its authority through control of building programmes and school organization, including examinations' (ibid.: 14).

The ideal of teacher freedom was sometimes questioned and even criticized in official circles, but at least in principle it was generally upheld, often with a helpful detailed explanation of its wider implications. In early 1955, for example, the incoming minister of education, Sir David Eccles, sought to explore the frontiers of his authority. On this occasion, he asked his officials to explain to him the meaning of the maxims offered in the Ministry pamphlet *The New Secondary Education*, which had been published in 1947. He went so far as to wonder whether 'the notion that the

Minister has nothing to do with the curriculum is an illusion', and he concluded:

> It is important when so many new secondary schools are to be built that the Minister should have a view. I do not want to dictate. But it is my duty to guide, and I should have to think very severely if you told me that 'The New Secondary Education' still holds the field. And if it does not, what does?
>
> (Eccles 1955)

Eccles's officials hurried to clarify the situation. It was explained that the pamphlet was now a little 'dated' but it was still being circulated and had not been withdrawn or superseded (Ministry of Education 1955). Religious education was specifically provided for under Section 25(2) of the 1944 Education Act, but, as was emphasized, 'No other subject is prescribed by statute, and the various bodies of Regulations governing the different types of educational establishment can say no more than that "The school shall be kept on a satisfactory level of efficiency"' (ibid.). Section 23 of the Act made the local education authorities responsible for the control of the secular instruction in county and voluntary schools in their area, other than aided secondary schools, and the governors in aided secondary schools, 'save in so far as may be provided otherwise' by the rules of management or articles of government. Therefore:

> It follows that the Minister could not 'insist' on greater emphasis on English. But he can give guidance about the curriculum. Leaving aside the ordinary process of inspecting, and reporting on, individual schools, such guidance is given through the medium of Handbook of Suggestions – the very title is significant – and pamphlets on particular subjects, written by Her Majesty's Inspectors – again the title is significant.
>
> (Ibid.)

Similar cautious testing of the possibilities that were available to the central authorities took place towards the end of the decade, this time with particular reference to the school science curriculum. As in other countries such as the United States, there was a great deal of political concern expressed at this time to ensure a supply of scientific manpower and a wider understanding of scientific and technological change, and this led to pressure being applied to 'modernize' the science curriculum in the schools (see, e.g. McCulloch et al. 1985; Waring 1979). Following the general election of 1959, a minister for science was appointed to stimulate new developments in this field. This minister, the experienced Conservative politician and former minister of education Lord Hailsham, wasted little time in raising key issues about curriculum reform. He argued (1959) in a letter to

Sir David Eccles, who had retained his post as minister of education, that recent reports would tend to 'bring pressure to bear on us to improve still further both the quality and quantity of scientific and technical education'. For example, he suggested, there needed to be some attention given to the possibility of teaching science in primary schools. Moreover, he added:

> Whether primary schools can have a go at science teaching or not, I should have thought it worth a look to see whether the approach to science teaching could not be a little more via simple engines and mechanisms, even at a very early age, and less as now either by way of the birds and bees or by way of what are fundamentally the more academic subjects of elementary physics and chemistry.
>
> (Hailsham 1959)

This initiative was rewarded by a flurry of high-level discussion (Ministry of Education 1960).

Lord Hailsham's next salvo was met with sterner resistance from officials at the Ministry of Education who were increasingly anxious about the potential threat that the minister for science represented for the ideal of teacher freedom. At the beginning of 1961, Hailsham wrote again to Eccles to propose a major new initiative in the curriculum. This would involve developing text books for use in key areas of the curriculum. It would at the same time address what he saw as the 'broader question' of 'whether, and how, modernization of school science curricula can be brought about' (Hailsham 1961). A charitable trust such as the Nuffield Foundation might well be 'better qualified' than the government to 'spark something off' (ibid.), and so he was also happy to encourage the development of what was to be launched, the following year, as the Nuffield Foundation Science Teaching Project.

On this occasion, officials at the Ministry of Education were quick to signal their strong misgivings. Toby Weaver, in particular, insisted: 'I do not believe that strong arm tactics are likely to be in the least effective or that there is any alternative to the patient working out of syllabuses by teachers' (Weaver 1961). This, he explained, was because

> In our system there is no centre of power where differences can be resolved. In practice each science teacher bases his syllabus on a mixture of his own experience, the known views of the professional associations and of H.M. Inspectorate, and the examination syllabus chosen by the school . . . . It is not clear how this process is likely to be improved or accelerated by the intervention of outsiders, however powerful or distinguished.
>
> (Ibid.)

These views were supported by other officials at the Ministry of Education. Dame Mary Smieton, permanent secretary at the Ministry, was prepared to countenance 'outside general enthusiasm on the part of eminent scientists' (Smieton 1961), but she continued to emphasize 'the patient practical work of revising syllabuses and working out new teaching methods which can only be done by those who are close to the task' (ibid.). R.A.R. Tricker, senior inspector for science, was also resolute in his conviction that 'in this country it was not possible to dictate the syllabus from the centre' (Ministry of Education 1961a). It therefore appears that in spite of some temptation to the contrary on the part of ministers, and a deepseated suspicion of central authority that was often shown by representatives of teachers and local education authorities, the state was in general not inclined to assert its own control in the area of the school curriculum during these years.

A greater danger to the ideal of teacher freedom lay elsewhere, in the influence exerted by public examinations and the examination boards. Despite hopes that were often emphasized during the years of the Second World War that examinations would come to play a less important role in the curriculum (see, e.g. McCulloch 1994, esp. Ch. 7), by the 1950s they were increasingly influential, especially in relation to the nature of the secondary school curriculum, but also at other levels. This in turn tended to reduce the freedom of the teachers themselves. The significance of examinations can be seen by tracing their role in the controversy that led to the setting up in 1964 of the Schools Council for the Curriculum and Examinations.

A Crisis of Teacher Professionalism?

The increasing influence of external examinations was strongly emphasized in the early 1960s. It was widely acknowledged at this time that the principles of teacher freedom in the curriculum were being endangered by the influence of examinations, and that urgent action was necessary in order to reassert them. The Ministry of Education supported this view to such an extent that it warned that the professionalism of teachers was itself at risk, especially in the secondary schools.

These concerns came to the fore as the Ministry became increasingly involved in efforts to revise the school curriculum. In 1962, it established a Curriculum Study Group based in the Ministry, a development that was widely criticized as being likely to lead to increased central control over the curriculum (Alexander 1962; Dean 1997). A working party was then set up under Sir John Lockwood to consider a more acceptable arrangement, and a more insidious influence was identified in the form of examinations. The National Union of Teachers, for example, acknowledged the need for new approaches as it accepted that the schools are becoming increasingly the objects of external pressures which are none the less real because they act indirectly through such means as external examinations, the entry requirements of higher education institutions and the professions, and the new technological environment in which the schools have to function.

(Powell-Davies 1963)

Moreover, it added (ibid.), 'We agree that in such a sociological context there is real danger that the autonomy of the school and the freedom of the teacher could become increasingly meaningless.'

The minister of education, Sir Edward Boyle, argued the case for a representative Schools Council in terms that emphasized the existing threat to teacher freedom in the curriculum domain. He explicitly endorsed the principle of teacher freedom and stressed that a new Schools Council would help to uphold it. According to Boyle (1963), it had 'long been public policy in England and Wales to regard the schools curriculum and teaching methods as exclusively the concern of the teachers', so that 'In theory, the teachers are free to decide for themselves what they want to teach, and how they want to teach it.' In practice, however, 'the teacher's freedom in curricular matters has been increasingly curtailed by external examinations, and by other external influences on the curriculum' (ibid.). Indeed, Boyle noted:

Only the nursery and infants' schools escape these pressures. At all other stages of the educational process, public examinations, the entry requirements of professional bodies, selection tests for entry to the grammar schools, and other influences besides, shape curriculum, teaching methods and school organization in degrees varying from almost complete domination to a strong indirect influence.

(Ibid.)

Ministry officials elaborated on this view in their evidence to the working party, as they proposed what they called a 'consortium' to provide a forum for studying common problems (Ministry of Education 1963a). Those who were directly involved in the Ministry's Curriculum Study Group also endorsed the need for curriculum reforms to be '*professionally* controlled neither by the C.S.G. nor the Nuffield Foundation', but 'carried out as a completely independent professional exercise by the teachers concerned' (Curriculum Study Group 1963).

Another long memorandum produced by the Ministry of Education to discuss what it called 'The outlines of the problem' (Ministry of Education 1963b) similarly disavowed any intention of seizing control over the school curriculum, but warned in trenchant tones of the dangers posed by public examinations. It acknowledged that to the 'maximum possible extent', every school should be 'free to adopt a curriculum and teaching methods based on its own needs and evolved by its own staff'. What was at issue, it suggested, was 'the contemporary interpretation of the policy, not the policy itself'. This was because the policy was 'in danger'. It had been interpreted too negatively, and needed to be 'restored to full efficacy' through cooperative action. The Ministry argued (1963b) that current practice recognized 'the right of the schools to take *particular* curricular decisions within a framework of general determinants, or norms, formulated as an expression of the community's interest in the *general* character of the educational process'. However, the line between the 'particular' and the 'general' was in its view moving in the wrong direction, and the scope for particular curricular decisions on the part of the schools was becoming smaller:

> The formulation of norms is tending to pass out of the hands of those to whom the community has entrusted this responsibility, and those responsible for taking particular decisions (namely, the teachers) are not being enabled to play a sufficient part in the processes of formulating the norms which constitute the general framework for their work.
>
> (Ibid.)

In the view of the Ministry, the influence of public examinations was largely responsible for this problem. For example:

> In the case of the grammar schools, the norms which the schools have to observe have invaded the area of the particular to such an extent that there is today little reality in the concept of the school as the basic unit of educational reform, with its curriculum based on its own needs and evolved by its own staff. And this invasion has simply happened: noone has willed it: noone desires it. External examinations have moved in, and now dominate the curriculum more firmly than ever before. To a wholly undesirable extent, the teachers have to teach what someone else has decided to examine.
>
> (Ibid.)

The secondary modern schools and the junior schools were moving in the same direction, it argued, so that it was only the early stages of primary education that remained 'almost wholly free to take the full range of curricular decisions proper to the schools, within norms which press only lightly on their work'. By contrast, the sixth form curriculum in the secondary schools 'has so far passed into the hands of the examining boards as to constitute an effective transfer of responsibility for the establishment of many important norms, as well as a transfer of responsibility for the particular curricular decisions that are proper to the schools'. The Ministry concluded that the examining boards had assumed such control, and examinations had gained such influence, because there was no 'standing machinery' that was adequate to regulate or reverse 'trends that have long been recognised as dangerous'. It was to provide such a means of regulation, through cooperation on the basis of a consortium arrangement, that was necessary to establish the Schools Council.

According to the Ministry, therefore, the accelerating trend towards competitive examinations at all levels of the education system was the root cause of the increasing threat to the ideal of teacher freedom in the curriculum. The popularity of examinations, moreover, had broad social causes rather than being being based on educational principles or even on 'empire building' by the examination boards which, after all, the Ministry conceded, had 'only done their job' (ibid.). It was the nature of social demand that was fundamentally responsible in the form of trends such as 'society's need for more and more better educated citizens and workers, the desire of parents and pupils to respond to this need, and the consequent demand for specific evidence of educational achievement' (ibid.). In other words, it was what Michael Young had satirically described as the 'rise of the meritocracy' (1958) that posed the principal danger to the ideal of teacher freedom in these years.

Conclusions

The Ministry's protestations of innocence, its constant avowals of support for the principle of teacher freedom in the curriculum, need not be taken totally at face value. Teachers and local education authorities were always suspicious of increased central control, and indeed there were some indications of incipient interest in this area, following the lead taken by other countries. In 1961, for example, the Inspectorate's secondary education panel discussed ideas raised at a recent conference held in Sweden on the subject of 'Ability and Educational Opportunity in a Modern Economy'. A 'general discussion' followed on 'the relative merits of a system of laissez faire and of greater central direction' (Ministry of Education 1961b), and it was agreed that all would depend on 'the benevolence and enlightenment of the directing administrators'. Four years later, following a presentation by a Japanese delegation on the prescribed use of textbooks, it was suggested that the 'attitude towards central planning of the curriculum' needed to be considered further:

> We have, on the whole, worked on the principle of freedom for schools to plan their own curricula; but, in fact, public examinations prescribed syllabuses to a considerable extent. There was currently some tendency to doubt the wisdom of entire freedom, and the Schools Council's work was tending to draw curricula together.
>
> (Department of Education and Science 1965)

These were stirrings that, as Chitty and others have suggested, became a decisive theme a decade later in the context of economic and industrial decline.

In the 1950s and 1960s, on the other hand, a more potent and at the same time a more insidious threat existed, in the shape of the competitive pressures surrounding examinations. The expansionism and economic growth that largely characterized these years engendered social and economic influences that effectively contradicted the ideal of teacher freedom. They helped to undermine the distinctive principles of the secondary modern schools, and more generally asserted a role, as Boyle put it, 'varying from almost complete domination to a strong indirect influence' (1963). In the light of these competing pressures, it is important to reassess the characteristics of the 'secret garden' of the school curriculum before the introduction of the National Curriculum, and the nature of the many different initiatives that were developed over these years. The implications of these pressures for teachers in the schools needs also to be appraised in greater depth. The longer-term implications also warrant further investigation. It would appear that despite outward appearances the National Curriculum embodies elements of continuity no less than of change from the kinds of negotiation that took place in preceding years (see also McCulloch 1996). Moreover, the 'myth' and 'memory' of teacher freedom in the curriculum often evoked both by supporters and by critics of the National Curriculum (McCulloch 1997b) may need to be questioned in favour of a more complex and contested reality that was based in the end, not simply in politics, but in the examinations market.

Acknowledgements

I should like to acknowledge the Leverhulme Trust for its support for the research project 'Education and the Working Class: History, Theory, Policy and Practice' (F118AB), on which some of the research for this chapter is based; also the Economic and Social Research Council for its support for the research project 'Teachers' Professional Culture and the Secondary School Curriculum' (R000234738), and my colleagues in this latter project, Gill Helsby, Peter Knight, Murray Saunders, and Terry Warburton. All Ministry of Education and Department of Education and Science papers referred to below are located at the Public Records Office, Kew.

References

Alexander, W. (1962) Week by Week. *Education*, 9 November.
Boyle, E. (1963) Proposed Schools Council for the Curriculum and Examinations. Memo, 13 May (Ministry of Education papers, ED.147/812).

Chitty, C. (1988) Central Control of the School Curriculum, 1944–87. *History of Education*, 17(4): 321–34.

Chitty, C. and Lawn, M. (1995) Introduction: Redefining the Teacher and the Curriculum. *Educational Review*, 47(2): 1–4.

Curriculum Study Group (1963) The Curriculum Study Group. CEWP paper no. 4. (Ministry of Education papers, ED.147/814).

Dean, D.W. (1997) The Rise and Demise of the Curriculum Study Group, 1962–64. *Contemporary British History*, 11(1): 31–58.

Department of Education and Science (1965) Inspectorate secondary education panel (A2), 43rd meeting. 15–16 December, minute 1 (DES papers, ED.158/21).

Eccles, D. (1955) The New Secondary Education, 1947. Note, 3 January (Ministry of Education papers, ED.147/207).

Hailsham, Lord (1959) letter to Sir David Eccles. 22 December (Ministry of Education papers, ED.147/794).

Hailsham, Lord (1961) letter to Sir David Eccles. 10 February (Ministry of Education papers, ED.147/794).

Hansard (1960) House of Commons Debates, 21 March, cols 51–2.

Helsby, G. and McCulloch, G. (1996) Teacher Professionalism and Curriculum Control, in I.F. Goodson and A. Hargreaves (eds), *Teachers' Professional Lives*. London: Falmer Press.

Kerr, J.F. (ed.) (1968) *Changing The Curriculum*. London: University of London Press.

Lawn, M. (1987) The Spur and the Bridle: Changing the Mode of Curriculum Control. *Journal of Curriculum Studies*, 19(5): 227–36.

—— (1996) *Modern Times? Work, Professionalism And Citizenship In Teaching*. London: Falmer Press.

Lawton, D. (1980a) *The Politics Of The School Curriculum*. London: Routledge & Kegan Paul.

—— (1980b) The End of the Secret Garden? A Study in the Politics of the Curriculum. In P. Gordon (ed), *The Study Of Education: A Collection Of Inaugural Lectures*, vol. 2. London: Woburn.

McCulloch, G. (1994) *Educational Reconstruction: The 1944 Education Act And The Twenty-First Century*. London: Woburn.

—— (1996) The Secret Garden of the National Curriculum? Paper presented to British Educational Research Association annual conference, 12–15 September. Lancaster University, UK.

—— (1997a) Teachers and the National Curriculum in England and Wales: Socio-Historical Frameworks. In G. Helsby and G. McCulloch (eds), *Teachers And The National Curriculum*. London: Cassell.

—— (1997b) Teachers, Myth and Memory. Paper presented to PACT network meeting, 19–20 May. Oslo.

McCulloch, G., Jenkins, E. and Layton, D. (1985) *Technological Revolution? The Politics Of School Science And Technology In England And Wales Since 1945*, London: Falmer Press.

Ministry of Education (1955) The New Secondary Education, 1947. Internal note to Minister, n.d. [January] (Ministry of Education papers, ED.147/207).

—— (1960) Scientific and Technical Education. Meeting, 12 January (Ministry of Education papers, ED.147/794).

—— (1961a) Note of Preliminary Meeting on School Science Syllabuses. 27 March (Ministry of Education papers, ED.147/794).

—— (1961b) Inspectorate secondary education panel (A2), 33rd meeting. 5 October, minute 8 (Ministry of Education papers, ED.158/21).

—— (1963a) Towards a Solution. CEWP paper (Ministry of Education papers, ED.147/814).

—— (1963b) The Outlines of the Problem. CEWP paper no. 3 (Ministry of Education papers, ED.147/814).

Powell-Davies, M.G. (1963) letter to D. Morrell. 18 March (Ministry of Education papers, ED.147/812).

Schools Council (1968) *Curriculum Innovation In Practice: A Report By J. Stuart Maclure Of The Third International Curriculum Conference, 1967*. London: Schools Council.

Simon, B. (1991) *Education And The Social Order, 1940–1990* London: Lawrence and Wishart.

Smieton, M. (1961) note to Minister. 24 February (Ministry of Education papers, ED.147/794).

Waring, M. (1979) *Social Pressures And Curriculum Innovation: A Study Of The Nuffield Foundation Science Teaching Project*. London: Methuen.

Weaver, T. (1961) note to Secretary. 20 February (Ministry of Education papers, ED.147/794).

Young, M. (1958) *The Rise Of The Meritocracy*. London: Thames and Hudson.

3 Changing Primary Schools in Hong Kong

Perspectives on Policy and its Impact

Paul Morris, K.K. Chan and Lo Mun Ling

This chapter explores, through the perspectives of policy makers and teachers, the rise and fall of an educational reform, namely the Target Oriented Curriculum (TOC), which was introduced for Hong Kong primary schools in the early 1990s. Three distinct phases were identified. The first was characterized by the conflicting views of the two parties towards the reform. The second phase saw a move to a more flexible and supportive approach to curriculum change by both groups. A vagueness and lack of commitment have distinguished the final phase, as other initiatives have replaced the TOC at the top of the policy agenda. The implications of the study are analysed with reference to the process of policy making and the implementation of change in schools.

The decade prior to the departure of the colonial government in Hong Kong saw the introduction of a wide range of policy initiatives primarily designed to produce a more democratic system of government. In the education arena this period also saw the introduction of a reform initiative in 1990 which attempted to bring about fundamental changes to the nature of the primary school curriculum. The reform was initially termed 'Targets and Target Related Assessment' (TTRA) but in 1993 was renamed the 'Target Oriented Curriculum' (TOC).

The goal of this chapter is to address two interrelated questions arising from the introduction of the TTRA/TOC. First, what were the perspectives on the reform which emerged in the interactions between policy makers (which includes all individuals and groups that developed and promoted the TTRA/TOC policy) and teachers? Second, what was the impact of the reform and what practices did schools introduce to support it? The first question focuses primarily on the period 1990–94 which saw the introduction of, and public response to, the policy. The latter questions focus on the period from 1995 when the TOC was being adopted in some schools.

These questions require us to focus respectively on the differential interpretations of policy initiatives, and on the contexts within which they are operationalized. This avoids the highly problematic assumption which has been implicit within many studies of implementation, that policies are unproblematic and that barriers to change arise primarily within schools and from teachers. It also recognizes that policy making and implementation are overlapping rather than wholly discrete areas of activity. Further, in addressing the two questions we focus on the ways in which schools and teachers perceived and responded to centrally initiated reforms, rather than on the nature of the planned change or the extent to which it was implemented. This approach recognizes that curriculum reforms are recreated in schools and that their effects are often unanticipated.

Our analysis draws on a study we are currently conducting that is designed to examine the impact of the TTRA/TOC in Hong Kong (Morris et al. 1996). TTRA/TOC emerged as a policy initiative in 1990 and after a turbulent reception from teachers was introduced to the Primary One classes of seventy-four mainstream primary schools and two special schools in 1995. A further 449 schools introduced it in 1996. It is planned that it will be adopted in secondary schools in 2001.

Figure 3.1 demonstrates the nature of the changes that the TOC is attempting to promote in the three basic message systems that embody any curriculum, namely its purposes, pedagogy and system of assessment. The arrows indicate how the policy makers portrayed both the prevailing features of the curriculum and the direction of the change the TOC was intended to achieve. In terms of its focus on targets, criterion referencing, and formative assessment, the TOC embodies many of the features associated with outcomes-based education, which has been defined as 'focusing a school's entire programme and instructional efforts around the clearly defined outcomes we want all students to demonstrate when they leave school' (Spady 1994). In terms of pedagogy the reform was premised on a social constructivist (Vygotsky 1978) perspective on learning.

The evaluation team studied the impact of the TOC at three levels or contexts: the policy level, the school/organizational level and the classroom level. Table 3.1 summarizes the questions addressed at each of these levels and the methodologies employed. It can be seen that the study utilizes multiple methods of data collection. Specifically, quantitative data was collected through a questionnaire from the total population of primary schools ($n = 75$) that introduced the TOC in 1995. Subsequently, more in-depth data of both a qualitative and a quantitative nature was obtained from fourteen case study schools that were given the opportunity to comment on the analysis specific to that school. This use of multiple methods and the feedback from the case study schools ensured that our findings were not based on a single source of data and were consistent with the perceptions

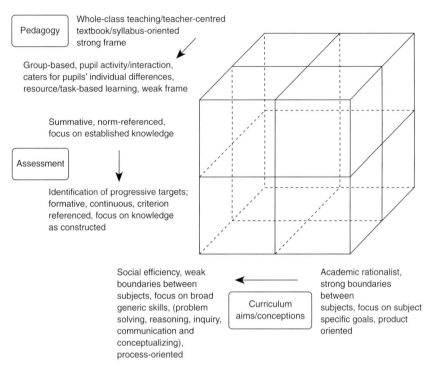

Pedagogy — Whole-class teaching/teacher-centred textbook/syllabus-oriented strong frame

Group-based, pupil activity/interaction, caters for pupils' individual differences, resource/task-based learning, weak frame

Summative, norm-referenced, focus on established knowledge

Assessment

Identification of progressive targets; formative, continuous, criterion referenced, focus on knowledge as constructed

Social efficiency, weak boundaries between subjects, focus on broad generic skills, (problem solving, reasoning, inquiry, communication and conceptualizing), process-oriented

Curriculum aims/conceptions

Academic rationalist, strong boundaries between subjects, focus on subject specific goals, product oriented

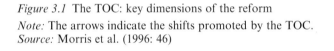

Figure 3.1 The TOC: key dimensions of the reform

Note: The arrows indicate the shifts promoted by the TOC.

Source: Morris et al. (1996: 46)

of the schools. This chapter draws primarily on the first and second levels of analysis.

The radical extent of change envisaged by the TOC and the centralized process of policy making which prevails in Hong Kong (Morris 1996) served to maximize the gap between reformers and teachers. This was reflected in both parties' contrasting perceptions of and concerns about the TOC.

Educational Reform: The Policy Makers' Perspective

Our focus is not on describing the formal doctrine of the TOC, but on how it was promoted and defended in the public arena. The perspective of curriculum policy makers which emerged in their interactions with teachers, principals and parents can be encapsulated in a series of typical statements or directives, which emerged in the process of promoting, justifying and defending the policy. The portrayal below draws on the following sources:

Table 3.1 Key research questions

Levels and purpose of analysis	Questions	Methodologies/sample
1 Systemic/policy level: to examine the genesis, purposes and strategy of developing the TOC.	What were the main features of the innovation? Why was the TOC introduced? Who was involved? What strategies were used?	Documentary analysis and interviews of key persons who contributed to the policy.
2 School/organizational level: to examine the understandings of the TOC by schools and the processes used to support its implementation.	How did schools understand, interpret and operationalize the TOC? What processes did they use to support its implementation? What problems and concerns emerged?	Questionnaire to all 74 mainstream schools that adopted the TOC in 1995. Interviews of school heads, teachers and parents in 14 multi-site case study schools.
3 Subject/classroom level: to determine how teachers operationalize the TOC in their classrooms and how it is implemented in different subjects.	How did teachers implement the TOC? Were there differences between Chinese, English and Mathematics? How did pupils perceive the TOC? What problems and concerns emerged?	Classroom observations and interviews of teachers and pupils in the 14 case study schools. A total of 151 lessons in English, Chinese and Mathematics were observed.

the interviews of policy makers, teachers and school principals; the media coverage of the views of all parties; and the key publicity documents describing the TOC.

Everything You Are Now Doing Is Wrong . . .

Educational reforms are competing for support and resources and as such they are essentially political acts. To demonstrate the need for change, proponents of a reform need to make evident the planned benefits. Changes are often promised that will create a markedly improved educational system. The possibility that the existing system may have some strengths, or that experience demonstrates the value of long-term evolutionary and incremental improvements, is easily forgotten.

In the quest for radical solutions, reformers frequently portray what is currently going on in schools in ways which are highly critical both of the curriculum and of teachers. In the case of the TOC this was done by stressing the limitations of current practice and contrasting it with the radically improved nature of schooling if the reform was fully implemented. In the TOC policy documents, prevailing practice is described as:

- fragmented and overcrowded;
- lacking coherence;
- emphasizing rote memorization and the 'linear mastery of decontextualized skills';
- lacking awareness of the role of language;
- lacking explicit information on 'what learning progress looks like';
- embodying a view that pupils are imbued with a fixed quantity of intelligence;
- emphasizing summative assessment, which focuses on trivial information and over-assessment.

The *Framework* which served as the foundation of the TOC initiative also explains that:

> current educational practices in Hong Kong and elsewhere can be said to be based on the partial conception of learning set out by behaviourist psychologists. Their learning theory was based on studies of animal behaviour from which they generalised their findings to human learning.
> (Clark et al. 1994: 14)

Similarly, in the interviews of policy makers constant use was made of terms such as *rote learning*, *teacher-centred*, *exam-centred* and *passive pupils* to describe both the problematic nature of the existing curriculum and to justify the need for radical reform. In effect what emerged was something akin to what Ball (1994) termed, with reference to the UK government's attitude to teachers, 'a discourse of derision'. But in Hong Kong the critique was directed more at styles of teaching and learning and was thus less of a direct critique of teachers than was the case in the UK.

Whilst this critical portrayal of current practice might have helped gain acceptance of the reform in the policy arena, it had the opposite effect in schools. Many teachers were hurt by the criticisms of their competencies, which suggested that they lacked appropriate professional skills, that what they were doing was problematic, and that they should radically change their behaviours. In effect the initial impact of the reform was both to deskill teachers and to generate a critical response. The strength of the criticism initially was very marked, with politicians standing for election on manifestos primarily critical of the policy, and some school supervisory bodies refusing to adopt it. In the media the TTRA was dubbed 'Teachers Totally Running Away' and its successor the TOC was termed the 'Totally Objectionable Curriculum'.

The criticism was also reinforced by a perception that the policy was a last attempt by the colonial government to influence schools and to impose a curriculum premised on western precepts. The outcome of this critical response was that its introduction was postponed, documents were simplified, the name was changed to the TOC, and more resources and in-service training were provided. The message here is a simple one – do not expect teachers to be wholly accepting of a reform if its introduction has been based on an extensive criticism of their professional competencies.

The Policy Is OK – You Just Don't Understand It!

The response of the policy makers to the public reaction to the TTRA/TOC seemed to involve three interrelated strategies. These were sequential and associated with the extent to which the reform was conceived as a finished and perfected product that was not amenable to revision or adaptation. In the period 1990–93 the TTRA was so viewed but subsequently TOC was viewed as more flexible and open to adaptation.

The first strategy, which is addressed separately below, involved stressing the worthwhile goals of the reform and suggesting that its critics were conservative reactionaries who were defenders of the worst features of the prevailing system.

The second strategy involved explaining to teachers who criticized or queried the reform that their comments were invalid because they did not fully understand the nature and purposes of the policy. This was usually followed by an elaborate restatement of some aspect of the reform and the provision of an array of seminars/lectures designed to dispel misunderstandings. The essential logic was that criticism was a function of misunderstanding and that anyone who fully understood the policy would inevitably support it. In reality the TOC was an extremely complex innovation. It contained a number of internal contradictions and inconsistencies. Even amongst policy makers its nature and purposes were interpreted and promoted in very diverse ways.

The third strategy was used in parallel with the second. It involved stressing that teachers were generally not critical of the goals of the reform but were concerned about some of its operational characteristics. It was inferred, therefore, that teachers were in support of the principles of the reform, but were critical of essentially minor details. This allowed teachers' concerns to be relegated to the realms of the technical and insubstantial, which could be solved by further injections of in-service education and resources.

It's the Vision that Counts – Forget the Details!

The proponents of the TOC focused on the goals of the reform and the inadequacy of the current curriculum. In-service courses stressed its rationale and aims. Teachers meanwhile were asking for operational details – what was the nature of classroom tasks? How did this all link to the existing subject-based curricula? How would pupils be assessed? A focus on goals, as noted above, allows reformers to compete for resources in the policy arena, to gain the moral high ground and to portray critics as poorly informed reactionaries. But in the case of the TOC the tendency to focus on the normative, especially in the early days, was necessitated by the absence of operational details and of practical resources. Thus, whilst teachers were constantly asking questions of a practical nature (Doyle and Ponder 1977), policy makers were unable to respond, essentially because the concerns of teachers had not been either decided or addressed.

Paramount amongst teachers' concerns was the nature of selective assessment and classroom resources. A feature which paralleled this tendency to focus on the vision and goals of reform was a belief amongst proponents of the TOC that a change in beliefs necessarily precedes and leads to a change in behaviour. The resulting failure to focus on operational details contributed to a phenomenon which was evident in some of the case study schools, namely teachers using the language of the reform without making any change to their classroom practices. Whether this is a transitory phase or represents a longer-term accommodation remains to be seen.

It's up to (Professional) Teachers and Schools to Work out the Details!

The critique of prevailing practice and a focus on the normative goals of the TOC were thus the main strands of the strategy employed by the government in its attempts to promote the TOC, especially in the early days. An associated strategy that was employed to justify the lack of attention to the practical issues that concerned teachers was to stress the need for school-based curriculum development and greater teacher professionalism. The essential logic is that policy makers will decide the nature of the curriculum, but teachers and schools should decide how to implement it using strategies which encourage professionalism, participation and empowerment. Thus it was up to schools and teachers to devise appropriate resources and assessment instruments to support the TOC. This allowed policy makers to retain power whilst simultaneously promoting decentralized strategies of reform. It also allowed responsibility for non-implementation to be located in schools (Morris and Chan 1997).

The TOC policy documents make extensive use of the language of school-based approaches to change and the need for teachers to operate as extended professionals. In practice, what was expected of teachers was for them to develop assessment items and tasks suitable for the TOC. Teachers were very aware that they had neither the skills nor the time to perform these duties.

Educational Reform: The Perspective from Schools

The countervailing perspective which emerged in the public debate arose primarily from the concerns of teachers focusing on questions of practicality and ownership, embodied in the key questions elaborated below.

Whose Idea Is It Anyway and What's Your Real Motive?

There is an unsurprising tendency for reforms which have involved practitioners in their development to be more likely to be used than those that have been externally imposed. The TOC was viewed by local teachers as a reform initiated by politicians who were not fully cognizant of the realities of schooling. In this respect the TOC had all the features of a top-down reform imposed on schools. The problems associated with these features were reinforced and exacerbated by the perception that it was developed by an overseas team with no experience in the local context, designed to impose western practices on a Chinese context, attempting to redefine Chinese-language education in terms of the precepts of English as a foreign language, and overall, an attempt to perpetuate the colonial influence beyond 1997.

The way in which the TOC was developed did nothing to counter these claims. As a result of these perceptions, the TOC was greeted with a mixture of disdain and hostility. Its status became highly politicized as the departing colonial government attempted to avoid a lame-duck image and as pressure groups flexed their political muscles. As the criticisms and resistance mounted, the level of government resourcing for the reform increased.

How Does All This Fit In?

As Cuban (1992) has noted, reforms do not emerge within a policy vacuum – they emerge into a context which is replete with earlier reform initiatives. For example, the TOC was preceded by a wave of curriculum and school reform initiatives (the Activity Approach, School-Based Curriculum Tailoring, the School Management Initiative, Mastery Learning) which were promoted by different sections of the government in ways which suggested that they were both ad hoc and discrete.

The TOC was effectively introduced on top of all existing reform initiatives. Its high profile and active promotion by the government suggested that it took precedence over all previous policies, though this was denied by policy makers. There was uncertainty and confusion as teachers attempted to understand the relationship between a plethora of seemingly unrelated reforms. A perception emerged that there was an absence of a clear policy direction, an innovation overload, and that further ad hoc initiatives could be anticipated. Teachers who attended seminars and courses provided by the government to promote the reform regularly reported that they received very different, and often contradictory, messages about the TOC. This confusion was exacerbated by the power struggle which emerged in the bureaucracy as groups whose careers and status were linked to other existing curriculum reforms, e.g. the Activity Approach, Mastery Learning and curriculum integration, attempted to promote and defend their territories against the TOC. This contributed to reinforce the combination of pragmatic scepticism (Hall and Hord 1987) and procrastination which characterized many teachers' attitudes.

Yes – But What Exactly Is It?

A complex change is inevitably more difficult to understand than one which focuses on a single variable. As Rogers and Shoemaker (1971) noted, complex reforms increase the chances that they will be subject to diverse interpretations and that they will be implemented in very different ways.

The TOC attempted to change all three basic message systems of the school curriculum (aims, pedagogy and assessment). It is thus a multi-faceted and complex reform which was interpreted in a variety of ways by both reformers and teachers. Some have associated the TOC with new patterns of assessment reporting, some have linked it to more participatory styles of teaching, and others have focused on its educational aims. The tendency which clearly emerged was for schools to focus on that element of the reform which approximated most closely with their previous priorities. Thus, for example, schools that had adopted the Activity Approach focused more on the pedagogic aspects of the TOC. Those that had previously adopted Mastery Learning focused on the assessment aspects of the TOC and some schools that were in the School Management Initiative stressed the administrative aspects of the reform.

However, the complexity was exacerbated by two further features. First, the nature of the TOC changed over time. Initially its proponents focused on its impact on assessment and latterly on improving the quality of learning. Second, to reduce opposition to the TOC and maximize the rate of adoption, it was defined in ways which became increasingly flexible. Currently a commitment to school improvement is the defining characteristic of a TOC school. Thus, whilst complexity can be viewed as a barrier to reform, it may also sow the seeds of confusion and encourage diverse responses to school improvement.

But How Will It Affect Assessment?

In Hong Kong, formal public examinations have a significant washback (Cheng 1997) or backwash (Biggs 1995) effect on all aspects of the curriculum (Morris 1996), especially styles of teaching and learning. This was recognized in the intentions of the TOC, which was attempting to change positively the nature of teaching and learning through changes to the nature of assessment. The critical issue which concerns teachers is how the TOC will affect the critical examination at the end of Primary Six. At this point pupils are differentiated into five bands on the basis of an academic aptitude test in Chinese and mathematics, and this is used to decide which secondary school they attend (Morris 1997). This is the first point in the school system at which the TOC rhetoric of formative, criterion-referenced and school-based assessment confronts the reality of a selective examination which allocates pupils and significantly affects their future life chances.

Previous experience suggested to teachers that procrastination and inertia were optional strategies, as many earlier curriculum reforms had expounded similar goals but the style of assessment had remained constant. The outcome was that formal assessments often failed to test those competencies which innovations stressed, such as problem solving, communication, critical and creative thinking. Public comments from policy makers also suggested that there were very conflicting views as to whether the Primary Six assessment would need to change. Essentially, implementing changes to assessment, whilst central to the TOC, was treated as a technical issue which would be addressed as the last stage of the reform. The failure to address this point has raised concern as to the extent of the government's commitment to real change.

How Will It Affect Our Workload?

Teachers in Hong Kong primary schools usually teach, on average, six periods a day, with only one free period for marking and lesson preparation. There is also a strong expectation, especially in English and Chinese, that teachers will set and mark large amounts of homework.

A major reason the TOC met with such strong opposition in the beginning was the perception that it would result in a marked increase in teachers' workload. The questionnaire survey of schools adopting the TOC (Morris et al. 1996) showed that over 90 per cent of school heads, TOC co-ordinators and teachers saw as most problematic the heavy workload of individual teachers. Many other initiatives were making demands on teachers' time.

The requirement for new curriculum aims and pedagogy was interpreted to require collaborative efforts in lesson planning, tailoring materials, and collecting and making suitable resources and teaching aids. The changing form of assessment was interpreted as requiring teachers to do more testing and more marking. As the new form of assessment was not clearly understood, to play safe, many schools retained in parallel both kinds of assessment, the traditional term tests and examinations as well as the new Target Oriented Assessments. As a result, teachers found themselves very busy trying to provide the information and satisfy the reporting requirements of both systems. Since formative assessment was not clearly understood by schools, this translated into the administration of many more short tests.

The need for a greater awareness of pupils' individual differences in teaching prompted some teachers to spend more time on remedial work with individual pupils during recess or after school. Teachers, especially TOC co-ordinators, also found themselves busy attending training courses, seminars and workshops on the TOC. Co-ordinators and experienced teachers felt that their workload was very heavy since they also had to train the inexperienced staff. In some schools which were regarded as model schools, teachers often had to entertain a parade of visitors from various outside bodies, and they made an extra effort in preparing the lessons for observation and sometimes even video-recording. The threat of the heavy workload resulted in some teachers leaving their schools to join other non-TOC schools.

1995–97: Adoption in Schools

The distance between the perspectives of reformers and teachers in the early period of the TTRA/TOC history provides a classic illustration of the well-documented limitations of highly centralized strategies of curriculum change. The assumption that new policies would produce change, the failure to address implementation issues, the focus on the ideals of the reform, the attempt to promote radical and complex changes, the piecemeal nature of educational policies, the lack of teacher participation, and the failure to address key features of schooling (especially the nature of assessment) are prototypical features of unsuccessful reform (Fullan and Miles 1995).

The strength of the reaction by teachers did, however, have a significant impact on both the nature of the policy and the overall strategy for promoting change. The government persevered but also made a number of significant adjustments. As noted earlier, the name of the innovation was changed and its implementation delayed. More significantly, resources were produced which were designed for classroom use, as opposed to resources designed to promote the goals of the reform. Key documents were rewritten in a clear and readable style. Teacher training was provided, and this shifted from a centralized mode to a school-based mode of provision. Government personnel began to promote a more consistent message. Most importantly, as opposed to criticizing schools for their failure to change, a more flexible approach emerged which encouraged schools to focus on that aspect of the reform with which they felt most comfortable. This combination of perseverance and flexibility from about 1995 was in marked contrast not only to the earlier period but also to previous reform initiatives which had been more symbolic than real. It became increasingly difficult for schools to ignore the TOC as the government seemed committed to change and, increasingly, was providing support and resources to aid its implementation.

From 1995, seventy-six schools (which is about 15 per cent of all primary schools) responded to this scenario and decided to adopt the TOC. In the following sections of this chapter we draw on the fourteen case study schools that we have studied since 1995 to identify their motives for adoption, the major impact on schools and the strategies used by schools to support change. A caveat needs to be stressed from the outset: our analysis focuses on a sample of those schools that attempted to adopt the TOC, which were not necessarily typical of the wider population of schools.

Motives for Adoption

The prevalence of a top-down and directive style of curriculum development at the macro level was mirrored in schools. This was most evident in the process of deciding whether the school would adopt the TOC. Generally, this decision was made by the school principal with little or no consultation with staff. The motives of school principals for introducing the TOC were multifaceted. However, it was clear that the decision to become a TOC school did not necessarily imply that the principal or teachers shared the vision or goals of the reform. Some principals saw it as a golden opportunity to reform schools that had a history of resisting change, or, from the perspective of the teachers, a history of stability. The prescriptive and top-down features of government policy were used by the principal to explain why the school had to adopt the TOC, in the hope that teachers could appreciate that change and improvement were inevitable and not merely the goal of the individual principal. This happened particularly in schools where the principals were relatively new. In other schools the introduction of the TOC was designed to obtain resources (TOC classes received an extra grant) or to access the teacher training/staff development inputs that were part of the TOC package.

Principals also used the TOC as a means to compete with other schools for prestige and popularity among parents. The government's massive media campaign which promoted the TOC as 'good' learning led some parents to believe that TOC schools were better than non-TOC schools. This happened particularly in schools located in relatively new housing estates where principals were keen to attract the academically more able pupils, whose performance at the end of primary schooling would determine the status of the schools in the community. Some principals claimed that the public image of their schools was enhanced because of their prominent participation in the innovation.

In some schools the decision to adopt the TOC was made by the school's sponsoring body. In the absence of a strong conviction to try to improve the school generally, or to adopt the TOC by the principal and middle managers, little change took place. Further conflicts often arose over a range of issues, including the need for change, promotion opportunities and legitimate responsibilities; there were also personality clashes.

The perceptions of teachers and principals were that the biggest positive impact of the TOC was not on the explicit goals of the TOC (in terms of assessment, pedagogy or the aims of schooling) but on two essentially unplanned areas, namely the strengthening of schools' middle management and the opportunities for teacher collaboration and professional development.

The Strengthening of Middle Management

As recommended, schools appointed TOC co-ordinators to strengthen their middle management. In many schools, as well as appointing an overall TOC co-ordinator, the school principal also appointed a co-ordinator for each TOC subject (Chinese, English and mathematics). The co-ordinators often took on the role of shielding the front-line teachers from the stress and the heavy workload associated with introducing the TOC: this often resulted in the school principal and the co-ordinators attempting to do most of the interpretation of the policy and work to support the TOC. Whilst most principals had read most of the key documents which define the formal doctrine of the TOC, we found that only around 40 per cent of teachers had read the programme of studies for their subject, the assessment guidelines or the exemplar tasks, despite the fact that they were already teaching TOC classes.

However, the function of the TOC co-ordinator was not without constraints. The staffing structure of Hong Kong primary schools, and the status of teachers, is based on seniority and rank. A teacher who is a class teacher has more power over matters related to his or her class than other teachers. Some TOC co-ordinators found that they were handicapped in carrying out their role because of their lower rank when they were not class teachers of the TOC classes. For example, in one case the class teacher forbade group work to be carried out because she felt that class discipline would be out of control. As a result, many policies to support TOC could not be put in place. In other schools senior teachers were appointed as TOC co-ordinators. However, since it is a common practice for senior teachers to teach only higher forms, as TOC co-ordinators they did not feel that they had the legitimacy or experience to provide curricular leadership because they were not teaching Primary One classes. A basic dilemma thus emerged in many schools. Where relatively junior teachers were appointed as TOC co-ordinators they often lacked the seniority to carry out their task effectively. Where senior teachers were appointed as co-ordinators they lacked the recent experience and contact with Primary One and Two classes that was necessary to give them credibility.

The TOC co-ordinators also had to tread a delicate path to avoid invading the territory of other existing middle managers in the school, such as the co-ordinator for the Activity Approach and the deputy principal. Direct support from the school principal proved to be crucial in resolving the potential conflict. The TOC co-ordinators who were found to be operating most effectively were those who had obtained direct legitimacy from the school principal, who gave open support to their work and frequently made adjustments designed to support the reform generally, and the role of the co-ordinator specifically. Examples of such adjustments are provided in what follows.

Despite these constraints and tensions, the role of the TOC co-ordinators allowed them to experience the reform in a variety of contexts, and through a range of interactions (the classroom, other teachers, the principal, parents). Thus, for some co-ordinators, the TOC provided an opportunity for accelerated professional development.

Strategies for Supporting Change

The schools that decided to adopt the TOC were, as noted previously, increasingly provided with resources and teacher training, and were expected to appoint TOC co-ordinators. However, it was up to individual schools how they combined these elements and what adjustments they made to facilitate change. These could be broadly divided into those that focused on changing organizational and administrative arrangements and those that were used to support changes in pedagogy. Examples of the former were:

- timetabling arrangements being changed to allow a teacher to take a TOC class for more than one subject (English, Chinese or mathematics) and to create more double periods;
- bisessional schools (a morning and afternoon school in one building) pooling their teaching resources and staff development activities;
- TOC teachers being put in the same staffroom and given free periods at the same time to encourage collaboration;
- TOC teachers being given lighter teaching loads.

In terms of supporting pedagogic change the main strategies were:

- organizing teachers to observe and comment on each other's work;
- assigning the production of classroom resources at specified levels to different teachers and sharing these with other teachers;

- shielding less experienced teachers from the full impact of the TOC;
- expecting non-TOC teachers to work with the TOC teachers;
- encouraging teachers to get involved with activities outside the school related to the TOC.

The implementation of the TOC, which was perceived as radical, complex and confusing, prompted teachers to communicate with each other as they attempted to understand it and to work out its implications for teaching and learning. In many schools teachers began to meet more regularly in an attempt to understand and operationalize the TOC. This resulted in increased interactions between teachers, including those who taught different subjects. In a number of schools we found that the teachers and principals saw the major impact of the reform as creating a more collaborative school culture, albeit one born of adversity, as teachers attempted to understand the reform and its implications for practice.

Implications and Conclusions

We now summarize the implications of the preceding analysis, focusing first on the implications which arise for policy making and then on schools.

The lessons which emerge from the TOC reform confirm many of those that have been reported in the extensive literature on implementing change in schools (Wise 1977; Sarason and Doris 1979; Eisner 1995; Fullan 1993). The initial period, from 1990 to 1994, demonstrated the dangers of imposing reforms on teachers which are hyper-rational, impractical, complex or radical, and which fail adequately to address implementation issues or to recognize that change is a process. These problems were compounded by the tendency for policy makers to promote change through a critique of teacher competencies, and the failure to address what schools viewed as unresolved issues; especially the nature of high-stakes assessment, the link to prior reform initiatives and uncertainty about the government's long-term commitment.

In the period since around 1995 these constraints to change have not disappeared, but some of them have been ameliorated. A greater degree of flexibility, evidence of commitment and attention to resource and implementation problems reduced the hostility to the reform. This suggests that the 'problem' lay not primarily in the centralized and top-down nature of the reform strategy *per se* but more in its failure to embody those features which emerged after 1995.

The overall pattern which emerged from the ways in which schools attempted to implement the TOC shows that they do not respond to policies as if they were single entities which take precedence over earlier reforms and require a series of rational steps to move from precept to practice. What emerged is a pattern more akin to that described by Elmore (1996) and

Tyack and Cuban (1995), who stress that teachers interpret reforms in terms of their prior experiences and understandings. This involved a process of experimentation and adjustment as schools attempted to identify possibilities for change that were practical and suitable to the realities of their specific contexts. In effect, schools do not respond to reforms in the ahistorical way which policy makers assume, but rather seem to learn in ways consistent with those described by social constructivist portrayals of human learning (Vygotsky 1978). Central to that process is the role of social interaction and collaboration between teachers and the provision of strong support for change by the principal. One of the principal benefits to have emerged for those schools that have attempted to implement the reform was essentially unintended, namely its impact on developing collaborative school cultures and on teachers' professional development.

Recent developments seem to suggest that the TOC may be entering a third phase, characterized by a move to redefine it as a reform that possesses all-encompassing, non-specific and virtual characteristics. Schools have now been 'de-labelled' so that there is no distinction between the adopting and non-adopting schools, and the new language of policy makers stresses that all schooling is imbued with the 'spirit', 'essence' or 'elements' of the TOC. At the same time resources are now being diverted to a new initiative, Information Technology, that has replaced the TOC at the top of the educational policy agenda of the first chief executive of the Hong Kong Special Administrative Region. How this affects schools' perceptions and implementation of the TOC remains to be seen. But, in many respects, this new initiative is being promoted in ways which suggest that policy reformers have learnt little about how to improve schools – history is about to repeat itself as the errors of the TOC initiative are revisited.

References

Ball, S.J. (1994) *Education Reform: A Critical and Post-Structural Approach.* Buckingham: Open University Press.

Biggs, J.B. (1995) Assumptions Underlying New Approaches to Educational Assessment. *Curriculum Forum*, 4(2): 1–22.

Cheng, L. (1997) How Does Washback Influence Teaching? Implications for Hong Kong. *Language and Education*, 11(1): 38–54.

Clark J., Scarino A. and Brownell J. (1994) *Improving the Quality of Learning.* Hong Kong: Hong Kong Bank Language Development Fund/Institute of Language in Education.

Cuban, L. (1992) Curriculum Stability and Change. In P. Jackson (ed.) *Handbook of Research on Curriculum*. New York: Macmillan.

Doyle, W. and Ponder, G.A. (1977) The Practicality Ethic in Teacher Decision Making. *Interchange*, 8(3): 1–12.

Eisner, E.W. (1995) Educational Reform and the Ecology of Schooling. In A.C. Ornstein and L.S. Behar (eds) *Contemporary Issues in Curriculum*. Boston: Allyn & Bacon.

Elmore, R.F. (1996) Commentary: School Reform, Teaching and Learning. *Journal of Education Policy*, 11(4): 499–504.

Fullan, M. (1993) *Change Forces: Probing the Depths of Educational Reform*. London: Falmer Press.

Fullan, M. and Miles, M. (1995) Getting Reform Right. In A.C. Ornstein and L.S. Behar (eds) *Contemporary Issues in Curriculum*. Boston: Allyn & Bacon.

Hall, G.E. and Hord, S.M. (1987) *Change in Schools: Facilitating the Process*. New York: State University of New York Press.

Morris, P. (1996) *The Hong Kong School Curriculum: Development, Issues and Policies*. (2nd revised edition and Chinese translation) Hong Kong: Hong Kong University Press.

—— (1997) School Knowledge, The State and the Market: An Analysis of the Hong Kong Secondary School Curriculum. *Journal of Curriculum Studies*, 29(3): 329–49.

Morris, P. and Chan, K.K. (1997) The Hong Kong School Curriculum and the Political Transition: Politicisation, Contextualisation and Symbolic Action. *Comparative Education*, 33(2): 247–64.

Morris P. Adamson R., Au Mei Lan, Chan Ka Ki, Chan Wai Yin, Ko Po Yuk, Lai Auyeung Winnie, Lo Mun Ling, Morris E., Ng Fung Ping, Ng Yuen Ying, Wong Wai Mei, Wong Pik Ha (1996) *Target Oriented Curriculum Evaluation Project: Interim Report*. Hong Kong: INSTEP, Faculty of Education, The University of Hong Kong. Chinese translation, Education Department, Hong Kong Government Printer (1997).

Rogers, E.M. and Shoemaker, F.F. (1971) *Communication of Innovations: A Cross-cultural Approach*. (2nd edition). New York: Free Press.

Sarason, S. and Doris, J. (1979) *Educational Handicap, Public Policy, and Social History*. New York: Free Press.

Spady W.G. (1994) Choosing Outcomes of Significance. *Educational Leadership*, 51(6): 18–22.

Tyack, D. and Cuban, L. (1995) *Tinkering Toward Utopia: A Century of Public School Reform*. Cambridge, MA: Harvard University Press.

Vygotsky, L.S. (1978) *Minds in Society: The Development of Higher Psychological Processes*. Cambridge, MA: Harvard University Press.

Wise, A. (1977) Why Educational Policies Often Fail: The Hyperrationalization Hypothesis. *Curriculum Studies*, 9(1): 43–57.

4 Educational Researchers

Living with a Lesser Form of Knowledge

David F. Labaree

What kind of knowledge is produced in schools of education and what is the impact of this on the character of their institutional effort and the public perception of this effort? The knowledge focused upon in this chapter is generated by researchers within education schools as distinct from the knowledge about teaching practice that experienced teachers have and that education schools may or may not transmit to prospective teachers. David Labaree claims that educational knowledge is more soft than hard, more applied than pure and has low exchange value but high use value. The consequence is that educational knowledge has a weak authority base of knowledge in education. Implications for educational researchers and schools in communicating with other fields of knowledge at the universities and to a wider audience in the society are discussed.

Schools of Education make easy targets. This is especially true in the United States, where education-school bashing has been a favorite sport for a wide range of participants over a long period of time.[1] There are a number of characteristics of this institution that make it vulnerable to attack. Its origins are seen to be lowly (the nineteenth-century normal school, or teacher training college), as is the social standing of its primary clientele (disproportionately drawn from the ranks of women and the working class), and it prepares students for one of the lesser professions. Its curriculum and academic standards are generally considered weak and its faculty and students less able than their counterparts elsewhere in the university.

All of these elements make the education school easy to pick on and difficult to defend. My aim in this chapter, however, is not to explore these familiar components of the education-school saga but to analyze the role of one particular element that has received less scrutiny than the others. The focus here will be on the kind of knowledge that education schools produce and the impact of this kind of knowledge, for better and worse, on the character of their institutional effort and the public perception of this effort.

In speaking of the knowledge they produce, I mean the body of scholarly work that is generated by researchers within schools of education, as distinct from the knowledge about teaching practice that experienced teachers have and that education schools may or may not transmit to prospective teachers. The issue under study, in short, is research knowledge rather than practitioner knowledge.

My argument is this: The nature of education as a field of study leads to a form of research production that both constrains and enables educational researchers in distinctive ways. On the one hand, the result is (for example) that these researchers find themselves unable to speak authoritatively about their field and feel pressure to imitate unproductive forms of intellectual practice. At the same time, they enjoy a number of advantages over researchers in contrasting fields, including a potential for speaking to a wider lay audience and for participating in a more egalitarian structure of scholarly production.

In what follows I first examine the nature of the knowledge produced by educational researchers and compare it with other forms of knowledge generated within the university. Then I consider the implications of these forms of knowledge production for the ways in which educational and other researchers organize themselves to carry out their work. Next, I review a series of ways in which the nature of research-based educational knowledge and its organizational form produce consequences that are negative for education schools. Finally, I review some of the ways in which these same characteristics produce consequences that are positive for education schools.

The Kinds of Knowledge Produced by Education Schools

Tony Becher has written a richly suggestive book about the nature of the knowledge produced by the different academic disciplines and departments within the British and American university. In this work – with the wonderfully evocative title *Academic Tribes and Territories* (Becher 1989) – he considers the impact of these knowledge differences on both the nature of the intellectual work carried on by academic practitioners and the form of organization employed to sustain this work. He starts with a familiar pair of distinctions – between *hard and soft* knowledge and between *pure and applied* knowledge – and builds his analysis from there. Although he mentions education schools and other professional schools only in passing, his argument provides lovely insights into many of the most familiar and significant characteristics of educational research.

Hard vs. Soft Knowledge

Disciplines seen as producing hard knowledge are those that are most successful in establishing the rhetorical claim that their research findings are verifiable, definitive, and cumulative. The natural sciences are the leading examples in this arena. Practitioners in the natural sciences have developed scientific methodologies, procedures, and verification rules that allow them to produce findings that can be reproduced by others, defended against challenges, and thereby gradually validated to the point where the claims come to be accepted as definitive – seen as an accurate depiction of 'what we know' about a particular component of the natural world. Once this kind of finding is established as functionally definitive, at least temporarily, within a scientific discourse community, then others can build upon it, pushing the pursuit of knowledge in that field to the next level.

Disciplines that produce soft knowledge, by contrast, find themselves working an intellectual terrain that is considerably less clearly defined. The humanities and most of the social sciences are the leading examples of this kind of intellectual endeavor. Research practitioners in these areas pursue forms of inquiry in which it is much more difficult to establish findings that are reproducible and whose validity can be successfully defended against challenges by others. Supporting causal claims is particularly difficult in these fields, so the producers of soft knowledge necessarily focus the bulk of their attention on the problems of description and interpretation: how to portray and make sense of the texts or events under study, in the absence of clear decision rules and validating methodologies. And practitioners in these fields never have the luxury of being able to build upon a solid foundation of previous findings, because these findings are always subject to challenge by researchers who adopt a different interpretive approach. As a result, producers of soft knowledge find themselves constantly rebuilding the foundations of their disciplines, as they continually reinterpret the most fundamental issues in their fields.

I am not arguing that hard knowledge is foundational and soft knowledge is not, only that hard knowledge producers are in a stronger position rhetorically to make the claim that their work is definitive and therefore cumulative. After all, interpretation and intent are irreducible components of all inquiry. The claims of hard science are limited by community norms and purposes, and they are subject to revision and rejection by future researchers whose community norms and purposes are different (Kuhn 1970). As a result, the validity claims of the hard disciplines are still only claims – difficult to contest but still contestable, durable in the short term but vulnerable over time. The advantage of hard over soft knowledge may be short-lived and largely rhetorical, but that does not make it any less substantial for practical purposes in the contest for contemporary credibility.

Two characteristics in particular make it difficult for researchers in soft knowledge fields to establish durable and cumulative causal claims. One is that, unlike workers in hard knowledge fields, they must generally deal with some aspect of human behavior. This means that cause only becomes effect through the medium of willful human action, which introduces a large and unruly error term into any predictive equation. These billiard balls are likely to change direction between the cue ball and the corner pocket. The other is that research projects in behavioral fields have embedded within them the values and the purposes not only of the researchers (as in hard fields) but also of the actors under study. The result is a messy interaction of the researcher and the research subject.

From this perspective, education emerges as the softest of the soft fields of inquiry. Problems of teaching and learning, curriculum and governance, educational organization and educational reform – all of these resist efforts by researchers to establish causal claims about them that are verifiable, definitive, and cumulative in anything like the way that researchers in hard knowledge disciplines can accomplish these things. For one thing, of course, education is the social product of actors – teachers, students, administrators, parents, and policymakers – whose actions both shape this institution and are shaped by it. In addition, educational processes are fundamentally political, reflecting social purposes – such as democratic equality, social efficiency, and individual opportunity – that embed contradictory pressures within education and provide conflicting criteria for evaluating educational success (Labaree 1997a, 1997b). As a result, educational researchers are able at best to make tentative and highly contingent claims that are difficult to sustain in the face of alternative claims by other researchers.

In spite of these difficulties, educational researchers have not been willing to abandon the effort to make their soft knowledge harder. Like knowledge producers in other fields that are grounded in human behavior, they have sought to establish ways of conceptualizing educational processes (such as behaviorism) and methodologies for analyzing these processes (such as statistics) that promise to enhance the claims they can make for the validity and reliability of the resulting educational knowledge. Within limits, this effort has been quite successful. An empirical science of education emerged at the start of the twentieth century and grew into a position of dominance in the field within a few decades, and it is still a strong presence in spite of the recent rise to prominence of an explicitly interpretive approach to educational research (Shulman 1986). The science of education, however, has encountered severe limitations to its claim to produce hard knowledge. It has been much more successful at describing the ways that education works and identifying loose relationships between educational variables than at explaining educational outcomes in light of educational causes. These limitations have confined educational number crunching to the soft side of the knowledge spectrum, since the hardness of the hard sciences is expressed most distinctively in the ability to predict the effects arising from particular causes. But the only causal claims educational research can make are constricted by a mass of qualifying clauses, which show that these claims are only valid within the artificial restrictions of a particular experimental setting or the complex peculiarities of a particular natural context. Why? Because the impact of curriculum on teaching or of teaching on learning is radically indirect, since it relies on the cooperation of teachers and students whose individual goals, urges, and capacities play a large and indeterminate role in shaping the outcome. And at the same time, education as an area of inquiry is more a public policy field than an intellectual discipline, whose central orientation is irreducibly normative – to improve education – and whose research practitioners are less united by a common technical orientation than they are divided by the different educational goals they espouse (Toulmin 1972; Donmoyer 1985).

As a result, despite their best efforts there is little that researchers can do to construct towers of knowledge on the foundations of the work of others. Within a particular research group (defined by shared values and interpretive approaches), it is possible at best to construct temporary huts of knowledge through a short-term effort of intellectual accumulation; but these huts are seen as structurally unsound by researchers who do not share the values and interpretive approaches of those within that group's intellectual compound.

Pure vs. Applied Knowledge

Disciplines that produce pure knowledge are primarily oriented around the construction of theory. Practitioners in these fields work a terrain that is abstracted from particular contexts, focusing on establishing claims of a more universal and generalizable sort than one could make if trapped within a local setting. There is an echo here of Robert Merton's distinction between cosmopolitans and locals, which is grounded in the scope of the cultural group to which people see themselves belonging (Merton 1968). In this sense, pure knowledge researchers are the cosmopolitans of intellectual inquiry, seeking to gain distance from the local scene in order to establish a sense of the larger pattern that is hidden in the clutter of detail within the close-up view. Much of the work in the natural sciences fits in this domain, but the latter also encompasses the most theoretical work that goes on in a wide range of disciplines, from philosophy to sociology and from literary criticism to mathematics.

Disciplines that produce applied knowledge, in contrast, focus primarily on the practical issues that arise from specific contexts. The aim here is not to establish general patterns but to solve particular problems. Success is measured in relatively modest ways, according to whether or not a particular approach works in a particular setting better than alternatives that are available at the time in question. Professional schools in general have an applied orientation to knowledge, and so do a wide array of disciplines – e.g., geology, psychology, and English – when they focus their attention on problem solving more than theory building.

From this perspective, educational knowledge production is overwhelmingly applied in character. For one thing, as noted above, education is not a discipline in the sense that cultural anthropology and physics are, defined by a distinctive theoretical perspective for viewing the world (culture and motion) and by a distinctive research methodology (fieldwork and time-lapse observation). Instead, it is a public policy field focusing on a particular institutional sector. As a result, educational researchers are under pressure to focus their intellectual energies on the most vexing problems that arise within their institutional purview, rather than enjoying the intellectual freedom of pure knowledge researchers who can follow the chain of thought embedded within their own intellectual constructs. And for educational researchers, confinement to the educational arena is combined with necessity of following a normative mandate in exploring this arena. It is not enough to study what is interesting about education; the researcher is under pressure to improve it. Fields like education are sites of public policy, which means they are shaped by public goals for this sector of society and are responsible in part for the powerful consequences of this institution – for good or ill – in the lives of children and the health of society (Toulmin 1972; Donmoyer 1985). Students are not learning what they need to know, race and gender skew educational outcomes, teachers are not being adequately prepared, school resources are not equally distributed – these are the kinds of context-based and time-sensitive problems of practice that dictate the direction taken by researchers in the relentlessly applied field of education.

Exchange Value vs. Use Value

In addition to the hard–soft and pure–applied distinctions, there is another difference, not mentioned by Becher, which divides university researchers from each other based on the way in which knowledge production within the various fields affects the value of the education that a particular department or program provides for its students. On the one hand, a university education can provide students with exchange value, by giving them a credential that can then be exchanged for something that is intrinsically valuable to the students, such as a good job and a nice standard of living. From this perspective, the content of the curriculum they pursue and the actual learning that they accomplish at the university is less important than the reputation of the university (or the program within it) and the perception of its worth among employers and others in the community. On the other hand, a university education can provide students with use value, by giving them a set of skills and an accumulation of knowledge that will prove useful to them in carrying out their varied roles in later life. From this perspective, the content of the knowledge acquired is the most important element of the educational process, quite independent of the university's (or program's) reputation. Consider how this plays out in a high school setting, where the upper curriculum tracks provide abstract academic knowledge that can be exchanged for college admission and eventually a well-paid job (low use value, high exchange value), whereas the lower tracks provide vocational knowledge that can be exchanged for a lower-level job (high use value, low exchange value).[2]

A distinctive characteristic of the knowledge produced by educational researchers and the education offered by education schools is that they have low exchange value and high use value. Education is marked by a variety of stigmas that undermine its ability to provide credentials with high exchange value – for example, an association with women, the lower classes, public employment, and its status as a 'semi-profession,' along with its weak academic standards and modest institutional origins. In addition, the broadly confirmed general perception of both the research and the instructional programs of education schools is that they are weak, which further undercuts their exchange value. In part this is because of the hierarchy within academic knowledge pursuits, which dictates that hard knowledge production outranks soft, and pure knowledge production outranks applied. Education is located firmly at the bottom of both of these rank orders.

Of course, the high use value of the knowledge in a field is not necessarily a threat to the prestige of that field. Medicine is an applied field whose knowledge provides high use value for its graduates, while at the same time occupying an extraordinarily high status within the university. Likewise, a number of hard–pure fields with high social standing, such as mathematics or biochemistry, gain in status when their efforts lead to useful social applications, such as computers and genetic testing. The key seems to be that high exchange value and hard knowledge together immunize a field from the potentially demeaning perception of being 'merely useful.' Medical schools are inextricably linked with the highest paid and most prestigious profession in the American occupational status order, and the demonstrable effectiveness of the hard knowledge they produce reinforces this elevated status. As a result, the exchange value they offer is unassailable. But education schools are bonded to one of the more lowly paid and more ordinary professions (closer to nurses than doctors in the professional hierarchy), and the visible weakness of their soft knowledge base at producing predictable and desirable educational outcomes only reinforces this subordinate position. Cursed with weak exchange value, education schools are doubly cursed by having to justify themselves only on the basis of the use value of the knowledge they produce, even though that knowledge is not very useful.[3] As we will see below, the strong association between education and soft use value has consequences that are both negative and positive for the field.

Organizational Consequences

Becher (1989) argues that the kind of knowledge that provides the central intellectual focus for a discipline or an area within a discipline brings with it its own distinctive form of organization. Hard-pure knowledge production calls for a social organization of intellectual practice that he calls *urban* and *convergent*. The nature of hard knowledge is that, for practical purposes in a particular intellectual context, it can be treated as cumulative. This means that at a given stage in the development of a discipline, everyone is focused on solving the same intellectual problems. The intellectual structure has been raised to a particular level, and all of the thought-workers are clustered at that level. The result is that the work takes on a distinctly urban feel. At the same time, this intellectual convergence makes for a social structure that is quite hierarchical. It takes novices a long time to learn the full body of knowledge in the field from the bottom all the way up to the point where the definitive knowledge ends and the real work of intellectual inquiry begins. This means that senior people occupy a highly authoritative position, since only they can direct the work at the very edge of understanding. It also means that the field needs to develop its own shorthand way of communicating within itself, one that necessarily assumes the reader or listener is informed about all the issues that are already resolved. As a result, writers and speakers in such a field can focus on the interesting material at the top of the structure of knowledge without having to bring the nonexpert up to speed.

By contrast, soft-applied knowledge production calls for a social organization of intellectual practice that Becher calls *rural* and *divergent*. Researchers cannot build towers on the foundations laid by others because these foundations are always being reconstructed. As a result, research work is spread thinly over a wide area, as individuals and groups continually work at rethinking the most basic issues in the field and as they each pursue their own interpretive approaches. The resulting terrain is laid out in a series of rural dwellings and hamlets rather than in the kind of urban high-rises erected by researchers in a field like physics. Novices in this setting find themselves inducted quickly, since the field is wide open and no issues are considered closed off from reconsideration. Senior people have less control over the work of intellectual production, because their own work is so easily subject to challenge. And the field is less turned in on itself, since its boundaries are permeable, its body of knowledge non-esoteric, and its discourse diffused among a variety of divergent research communities.

The organization of knowledge production within education schools fits the pattern of other soft-applied fields by being thoroughly rural and divergent. Intellectual work within this field is spread all over the terrain. Researchers feel free to charge off in all different directions without a great deal of concern about what stage the development of the field has attained at the moment or what directions senior scholars want to set for the field. They constantly re-examine old questions and reconstruct existing theories. What clusters develop – for example, around teacher preparation in one place and subject matter standards in another – are the result of practical needs generated from within the institution of education or from society's concerns about the state of this institution rather than from the internal logic of the research effort itself. And these needs and concerns are so numerous at any given time and so likely to change with changing conditions that they provide only temporary and limited incentives to concentrate resources in the classic urban manner that characterizes the hard-pure realm.

Gary Rhoades (1990) provides an insightful and influential analysis of the organizational peculiarities of American colleges of education, which makes particular sense in light of the preceding discussion about the kind of knowledge that is produced in these institutions. One assertion he makes about them is the following:

> Colleges of education are marked by greater technological ambiguity and more resource dependency on well-organized, vocal constituencies in an environment in flux than are colleges of letters and science. As a result, colleges of education have more diversified organizational structures across colleges and are more unstable both within and across colleges than is the case with letters and sciences colleges.
>
> (Rhoades 1990: 197)

Another assertion is that:

> Colleges of education faculty are more likely than letters and science faculty to expect and accede to managerial control and are also more divided and thus less likely than letters and science faculty to assert faculty influence, forming coalitions to defend and advance the collective interests of the college faculty. Thus, education deans have potentially more impact than letters and science deans.
>
> (Ibid.: 203)

This argument by Rhoades follows naturally from the argument that I have been developing about the role of knowledge in shaping the organization of knowledge production in education. As a soft-applied field, education is characterized by high 'technological ambiguity' (a diffused intellectual focus) and high 'resource dependency' on 'an environment in flux' (that is, a need to respond to practical issues arising from school and society rather than from the theoretical logic of the research effort itself). This means that faculty members in colleges of education do not have natural intellectual communities to draw on for political strength, at least not in the way that psychologists or astronomers, for example, can draw on their national and international disciplinary communities for support. The intellectual labor of education-school faculty members is in service to diffuse demands from the environment rather than to their own colleagues within the field of educational research. The result is that they do not fall into intellectually distinctive social groupings within or across colleges (education schools do not have a standard departmental structure), and therefore they have few social resources for asserting faculty power or for countering the managerial authority of the dean.

Negative Consequences for Education Schools

This analysis of the nature and social organization of knowledge production in education schools has significant implications for the way in which these institutions function and the way they are seen. Consider first some of the negative consequences for education schools and then some of the positive consequences.

Low Status within the University

There is no doubt that education schools are located at the bottom of the academic hierarchy within the American university. An important source of this low status is the nature of the knowledge produced by faculty members in education. One characteristic of educational knowledge that hurts it in the status race is its relentlessly soft and applied character. The pinnacles of the academic status order are reserved for the hardest and purest of intellectual pursuits. It is not difficult to see why this would be so. Hard knowledge disciplines are able to maintain general respect because their claims to validity are so difficult to refute, while the softer disciplines suffer from having to qualify, temporize, and particularize their claims. Whereas the former seem to be standing on a firm empirical platform and speaking with a clear loud voice, the latter wallow around in a swamp of uncertainty and speak in a whisper. There is little doubt which of these will win greater attention and higher esteem. Likewise, pure knowledge fields, by addressing questions of broad theoretical scope, gain a decided status advantage over applied fields, whose scope of address is sharply restricted by time and place.

In addition, educational knowledge suffers from its low exchange value. After all, exchange value is the coin of the realm in the market-based environment of the American university. These universities are unique in their extreme sensitivity to market considerations in comparison to their counterparts elsewhere in the world (Trow 1988). Dependent heavily on tuition and forced to compete for customers in a buyer's market for higher education services, American universities have to give education consumers what they are looking for – credentials that can be exchanged for good jobs and attractive social positions (Brown 1995). In this kind of environment, exchange value counts more than use value. And the root of exchange value is the employers' and public's general perception of the reputation of an institution and of the programs within that institution. This leaves education holding, as usual, the short end of the stick. What education offers is soft use value – usable knowledge of marginal validity – which is not a commodity that can compete effectively with the credentials from the more prestigious realms of the university, which offer hard and pure exchange value.

Weak Authority within Education and Educational Policymaking

It follows from the preceding analysis that the nature of the knowledge produced within education schools also makes it so that the authority of these institutions to speak is relatively weak, even within their own world of schools and educational policy. As Cohen, Garet, and Lindblom have pointed out, the impact of social science research on social policy is indirect at best (Cohen and Garet 1975; Lindblom and Cohen 1979), because of the difficulty it has in representing complex social policy consequences. The more widely researchers throw their net around a complex array of variables, the less valid and reliable their conclusions become; but the more narrowly and rigorously they construct their studies methodologically, the more likely it is that they are leaving out important variables and the more incomprehensible their findings are going to be to policymakers. Educational researchers suffer from this syndrome at least as much as other social scientists. These problems are particularly acute for the empiricists within the field who are trying to create hard knowledge through educational research. The findings of educational studies that have the greatest claim to validity and reliability – e.g., those that zero in on the effects of a particular experimental treatment by tightly controlling for other variables – are also likely to be the most trivial, since real education takes place in extraordinarily complex settings where variables are inextricably intermingled.

Educational researchers have an additional burden, however, which derives from their low academic status, their weak platform, and their whispery voice. The knowledge base of educational researchers leaves them in a position of marginal credibility with the educators and educational policymakers for whom their research findings should be of the greatest utility. As low-status purveyors of educational knowledge that is soft, highly contingent, and largely ungeneralizable, they are not able to speak in tones that are likely to command respect and to shape educational policy. In short, they can easily be ignored. And with the credibility of the institutional experts on education called into question like this, it leaves the field of educational reform and educational policy wide open to the influence of a wide range of others whose voices are granted at least equal standing.

Pressure to Transform Education into a Hard Science

One natural consequence of all this is that educational researchers would seek to transform the nature of their knowledge production from soft to hard and applied to pure. This has been the mission of the American Educational Research Association over the past forty years. All one has to do is examine the burgeoning production of scientific research on education that has arisen from this organization – as evidenced by the explosion in papers presented at its annual meetings and by the compilations of scientific research about teaching and teacher education that have emerged from its membership.[4]

This movement to make educational research harder and purer came to a head with the issuance of the first Holmes Group report in 1986 (*Tomorrow's Teachers*). In this report, the deans of the leading research-oriented education schools in the US proclaimed that the research efforts in their institutions over the preceding decades had produce a true science of teaching – with rock-solid validity and sweeping theoretical scope – which could now serve as the knowledge base for the professionalization of teaching. In a recent article in *Educational Researcher*, former AERA president N.L. Gage restated this faith:

> In the last 20 years . . . meta-analysis has yielded knowledge concerning the impressive magnitude, consistency, and validity across contexts of many generalizations in the behavioral sciences and promising methods for quantifying and analyzing the generalizability of research results. These arguments, findings, and methods justify . . . continuing the effort to build sciences of behavior.
>
> (Gage 1996: 5)

There is a value in the effort to make educational knowledge more quan-tifiable and generalizable, since it pushes researchers not to settle for the softest and most equivocal of findings. It is not very helpful if researchers answer every important question in the field by saying, 'It all depends.' Thus striving to establish and support harder claims is a valuable goal, but there is only so far that we can realistically move in that direction, and that is well short of the condition Gage calls a science of educational behavior. In order to create a solid ground for making hard claims about education, you can try to drain the swamp of human action and political purpose that makes this institution what it is, but the result is a science of something other than education as it is experienced by teachers and students. As I have argued elsewhere, such an effort may have more positive impact on the status of researchers (for whom hard science is the holy grail) than the quality of learning in schools, and it may lead us to reshape education in the image of our own hyper-rationalized and disembodied constructs rather than our visions of the good school (Labaree 1997b, Ch. 6).[5]

Another sign of the effort to move education into something like a hard science is the construction in recent years of large federally funded centers for educational research. These centers mimic the urban-style organization of knowledge production in the hard knowledge fields, which is particularly striking in a field as traditionally rural in research practice as education has been. But these centers arise more from the government's desire to increase the efficiency of its funding and supervision of research (and the university's desire for large infusions of soft money) than from any discovery that educational knowledge has suddenly begun to accumulate into a rising epistemological structure. If anything, the centers are an effort to compensate for the lack of an accumulation of educational knowledge across studies, by organizing large loosely integrated research projects as a proxy for this kind of accumulation. The production coming out of a research center gives the impression of systematic construction, but on close analysis this structure quickly disaggregates into an eclectic array of disparate studies operating under the center's umbrella. In this way, an educational research center is no more urban than the shanty-town on the outskirts of a third world city. Each is a collection of villages rather than a true urban community.

Pressure to Transform Education Schools into Pure Research Institutions

The distinctive nature of educational knowledge has produced another related form of negative impact on education schools by putting pressure on them to change their focus from teacher preparation to a more prestigious mission. Trying to mimic those disciplinary departments on the university campus with the highest academic standing, education schools – especially in the most elite universities – have frequently sought to change themselves into graduate schools of educational studies (Judge 1982).

Geraldine Clifford and James Guthrie (1988) tell the story of this quixotic quest in withering detail in their book, *Ed School*. The idea has been to back away from too close an identification with teaching and with the production of useful knowledge for schools and to focus instead on developing a body of research that is purer than the education school norm, focusing on general theoretical exploration rather than responding to particular educational problems of practice. In addition, this new research direction would yield a higher exchange value, because of its affinities with the decontextualized and theory-driven (rather than environment-driven) explorations of the more prestigious fields in the academy. As Clifford and Guthrie point out, however, these efforts have not been successful. For one thing, the rest of the university has not accorded the desired higher academic standing to the faculty of these graduate schools of educational studies. For another, these efforts have served to wrench researchers away from real educational knowledge production without changing the soft, applied, political, behavioral, and environment-driven character of the field itself.

A Sense that the Field Is Never Getting Anywhere

One last problem that the form of educational knowledge poses for those who seek to produce it is that it often leaves them feeling as though they are perpetually struggling to move ahead but getting nowhere. If Sisyphus were a scholar, his field would be education. At the end of long and distinguished careers, senior educational researchers are likely to find that they are still working on the same questions that confronted them at the beginning. And the new generation of researchers they have trained will be taking up these questions as well, reconstructing the very foundations of the field over which their mentors labored during their entire careers.

This not only poses a problem for the researcher's sense of professional accomplishment and self-esteem: It also leaves the entire field open to ridicule and meddling from those who stand outside. If these people cannot get to first base in their own field of expertise, then they must not be very good, so maybe they ought to step aside and let a talented outsider stand in and swing for the fences. Could these outsiders do worse than the so-called professionals? Since educational researchers are unable to be definitive and to demonstrate that they are making progress, they leave the field wide open to amateur educationists who feel little reason to be reticent about making their own contribution to educational discourse.

Positive Consequences for Education Schools

Having laid out a variety of negative consequences for education schools that arise from the peculiar characteristics of educational knowledge, I now turn to some of the positive outcomes that arise from the same source.

Producing Useful Knowledge Is Not a Bad Thing

The close identification of education with use value and its alienation from exchange value has the potential to work to its long-term advantage socially and politically. After all, the university's practice of selling credentials that are based on appearance and reputation more than substance and real learning is one that is quite vulnerable to public challenge. This practice has all the characteristics of a confidence game, since it rests on an interlocking set of beliefs that are quite shaky. The chain goes something like this: it makes sense for consumers to invest in the credentials of a respected university because the prestigious research carried out there produces capable graduates who then deserve preferential access to jobs. Yet each part of this chain of reasoning depends more on faith than fact, and the whole system can collapse if challenged to prove itself. After all, the value of the credentials has more to do with the prestige of the institution than with the knowledge that students acquire there. In addition, the rising fiscal pressures at all levels of American government puts higher education increasingly in the position of justifying the enormous public investment in terms of verifiable outcomes rather than tradition or belief. This problem is exacerbated by a related issue: the gross social inefficiency of providing a public subsidy for an education system that is grounded more in individual social mobility (helping me get the job I want) than in substantial public benefit (providing us with the capacities we need) (Labaree 1997b).

In this setting, the strong connection between education and usable knowledge can be a valuable asset. For the most part, educational research arises in response to clear current problems within a preeminently important institutional arena. This timeliness, responsiveness, and potential usefulness makes it much easier to justify – in the emerging era of outcomes measurement and cost-effective public investment – than much of the university's more prestigious but less relevant research efforts. Of course, there are several limitations to this pursuit of applied knowledge. One, discussed earlier, is that the findings of educational research are so soft that this applied knowledge is of limited usefulness. Unlike fields that are comfortably buffered by high exchange value, educational research is eager to help improve the practice of education, but its tool kit does not contain the kind of powerful cures that can be found in the medical doctor's black bag. Another is the relentlessly – even proudly – atheoretical quality of much of this research. Theoretical significance (like empirical validation) is something that educational research should aspire to, in spite of the enormous difficulties that this work poses for such efforts. In the absence of theoretical aspiration, educational research often seems rather pinched and pedestrian. But this failing arises more from intellectual laziness than from the characteristics of educational knowledge. The kind of practical knowledge that educational researchers produce can be theoretically provocative even if it is somewhat restricted in theoretical scope, and in this context its potential social usefulness can be both politically advantageous and vocationally gratifying for the producers in ways that are not available to researchers in less applied fields.

Freedom from Consumer Pressures

A related benefit for education that derives from the kind of knowledge it produces is that it is relatively free from the consumer pressures that have shaped the rest of the university. In general, the American university has been compelled to bend to the demand from consumers for programs and credentials that will serve individual ambition in the pursuit of social position. But the close identification of education schools with the vocational preparation of teachers and with the production of research to meet practical educational needs means that these schools are constructed around the accomplishment of social rather than individual ends. Their primary concern is social efficiency rather than individual mobility. This certainly puts constraints on both research and programs, since both must be responsive to the most urgent and current societal concerns. As a result, educational researchers do not enjoy the luxury of pursuing pure inquiry in whatever direction theory might lead them – or pursuing idiosyncratic inquiry in whatever direction personal preference might propel them. But at the same time they are liberated from involvement in a market-dominated instructional process that requires them to provide fickle educational consumers with whatever courses and programs the latter demand. And they have the satisfaction of knowing that they are working on issues that matter, both for the individual actors within education (like teachers and students) and for the larger society.

Freedom from Disciplinary Boundaries

Another advantage that accrues to educational researchers from the nature of the knowledge they produce is that they are free to deal with educational questions from whatever disciplinary perspective or methodological approach they find appropriate. This, as in the previous example, involves several trade-offs. One is that they give up freedom of institutional focus – since educational researchers are compelled to focus on education – in return for considerable freedom in the way they choose to explore this subject. Researchers in the disciplines are often subject to a test of disciplinary correctness that can be quite confining. 'Is this really political science?' (or history or philosophy or biology) they are asked. If not, it does not count in the internal status order as measured by merit pay, promotion in rank, and professional recognition. But educational researchers are free to be as eclectic as they wish in the way they choose to intermingle disciplinary perspectives or methodological orthodoxies. There is an attractive pragmatism within educational research, which prefers to reward approaches that work rather than those that are canonical within a particular theoretical subculture. The downside here is that, at the same time that educational researchers cut loose from unnecessary disciplinary constraints, they also frequently lose some of the methodological rigor that comes from working within a clearly defined disciplinary research tradition. The result is a tolerance for poor research design and sloppy thinking. However, there is nothing in the nature of educational knowledge to prevent researchers in education from creating their own standards of rigor and from policing their own ranks in light of these standards.

Freedom from Hierarchical Constraints

The thoroughly rural and divergent character of educational research makes for a social organization of research effort that is relatively egalitarian. Senior researchers are not in a strong position to control the research process because their authority rests on shaky foundations. The noncumulative character of educational knowledge makes entry into the field easy and leaves newcomers in a position to make contributions that are arguably as valuable as those by the old hands. The same characteristics of educational research that allow policymakers to ignore it and other academics to ridicule it – namely its structural underdevelopment and its vulnerability to challenge – make it a field that is remarkably open and endlessly fascinating in the variety of its voices. There is nothing like confusion to create opportunity. The rural landscape of educational research produces endless possibilities for intellectual homesteaders to stake a claim and start developing their own little piece of the terrain. Of course, large federally funded centers for educational research represent an important counter-trend to this pattern, since they resemble urban enclaves in a largely rural field and inevitably establish a kind of status order within them. But what is different about these centers in education compared with large projects in hard knowledge fields is that they are best understood as collaborations among loosely related independent research projects, pulled together for the effort to obtain funding but not integrated into a strong social or epistemological hierarchy.

Producing Soft Knowledge Is Now the In Thing

In the past decade or two, there has been a strong and highly effective series of attacks on positivism and on the validity of quantitative research.[6] This process has been played out in a wide range of fields, beginning with the philosophy of science and moving eventually into education. All of this is thoroughly familiar to the members of the American Educational Research Association, who have seen the argument played out at great length in the pages of *Educational Researcher* over the past fifteen years. As a result of this epistemological effort, the consensus has shifted toward a position that asserts the essential softness of hard knowledge and the essential uncertainty at the core of the validity claims made by the hard sciences.

This means that soft knowledge fields such as education can now breathe a sigh of relief, since softness is now a generalized condition and not an affliction only affecting educational researchers.

Unfortunately, the newly relaxed philosophical position toward the softness of educational knowledge – combined with its freedom from disciplinary constraints and its openness to newcomers – can (and frequently does) lead to rather cavalier attitudes by educational researchers toward methodological rigor in their work. As confirmation, all one has to do is read a cross section of dissertations in the field or of papers presented at educational conferences. For many educational researchers, apparently, the successful attack on the validity of the hard sciences in recent years has led to the position that softness is not a problem to be dealt with but a virtue to be celebrated. Frequently the result is that qualitative methods are treated less as a cluster of alternative methodologies than as a license to say what one wants without regard to rules of evidence or forms of validation.

I bring up this point about the dangers of soft knowledge (paralleling earlier points about the dangers of applied knowledge and of non-discipline-based research) as a caution to educational researchers against embracing too warmly the necessity imposed on them by the kind of knowledge they produce. For in looking for the silver lining in the cloud of problems surrounding the production of educational knowledge, we should not ignore the significance of the cloud itself. The characteristics of educational knowledge present researchers with both advantages and disadvantages. These elements do not cancel each other out, but instead in combination they define a universe of working possibilities and enduring dilemmas within which educational researchers have to forge their way.

An Ability to Speak to a General Audience

From the perspective of someone in the harder and purer disciplines, educational researchers speak with a voice that is laughably amateurish. Their lack of professionalism is apparent in a discourse that does not have the esoteric language and verbal shorthand of a truly advanced field of study. A paper that is truly interesting in a field such as math or biochemistry – that is, at the leading edge of theoretical development – is one that should be completely incomprehensible to an apprentice in the field, let alone a layperson. By comparison, the discourse within education is transparent in language and widely accessible in meaning. All the complaints about 'educatorese' only serve to prove the point, since they tend to come from those completely outside the educational research community who are looking at its literature. They are not saying they cannot understand what the researchers are saying, only that they themselves could say it better. But none of these critics would think of trying to read the cutting-edge research in math or biochemistry or to complain about math- or biochemist-speak, because these fields are supposed to be esoteric and beyond the reach of the layperson. Education, however, is largely accessible to outsiders and therefore vulnerable to discursive critique from nonexperts.

This situation puts educational researchers in a position to become public intellectuals in a way that is not possible for scholars in fields whose knowledge development makes them incomprehensible to the ordinary citizen. It is easy for outsiders to look into education – to contribute, criticize, and meddle. But at the same time, this makes it easy for educational insiders to reach out directly to members of the public and make a case to them about the problems facing education and the ways we can deal with these problems. In this sense, educational researchers may not have the kind of authority that comes with hard-pure science, but they have a ready rhetorical access to the public that is lacking in more authoritative fields. As a result, the lesser form of knowledge produced by educational researchers may in fact offer them a political and social opportunity that is largely closed to the more prestigious realms of the university.

Acknowledgement

This paper, originally published as Labaree (1998), is copyright © the American Educational Research Association.

Notes

1 Examples include: Bestor (1953), Koerner (1963), Kramer (1991), Goodlad (1990), Clifford and Guthrie (1988), Holmes Group (1995), and Hirsch (1996).
2 For more on the impact of this distinction between exchange value and use value, see Collins (1979) and Berg (1971). I have developed this argument at greater length in Labaree (1997a and 1997b).
3 For a detailed discussion of implications of the low exchange value and high use value of education as a field of knowledge production, see Labaree (1997b, Ch. 9).
4 For example, see AERA (1997), Gage (1963), Travers (1973), Wittrock (1986), Houston (1990), Sikula (1996).
5 Without acknowledging this, the Holmes Group began to back away from its early embrace of the natural science model for educational research in its second report (Holmes Group 1990) and dropped it entirely in its third report (Holmes Group 1995). See Labaree (1995) for a discussion of the sharp changes in argument and rhetoric that characterize these three reports.
6 For example, see Howe (1985).

References

American Educational Research Association (1997) Annual meeting program. Washington, DC: AERA.
Becher, T. (1989) *Academic Tribes and Territories: Intellectual Enquiry and the Culture of Disciplines*. Buckingham, UK: Open University Press.

Berg, I. (1971) *Education and Jobs: The Great Training Robbery*. Boston: Beacon Press.

Bestor, A. (1953) *Educational Wastelands: The Retreat from Learning in our Public Schools*. Urbana, IL: University of Illinois Press.

Brown, D.K. (1995) *Degrees of Control: A Sociology of Educational Expansion and Occupational Credentialism*. New York: Teachers College Press.

Clifford, G.J. and Guthrie, J.W. (1988) *Ed School: A Brief for Professional Education*. Chicago: University of Chicago Press.

Cohen, D.K. and Garet, M.S. (1975) Reforming Educational Policy with Applied Social Research. *Harvard Educational Review*, 45: 17–43.

Collins, R. (1979) *The Credential Society: An Historical Sociology of Education and Stratification*. New York: Academic Press.

Donmoyer, R. (1985) The Rescue from Relativism: Two Failed Attempts and an Alternative Strategy. *Educational Researcher*, 14: 13–20.

Gage, N.L. (1996) Confronting Counsels of Despair for the Behavioral Sciences. *Educational Researcher*, 25(3): 5–15, 22.

Gage, N.L. (ed.) (1963) *Handbook of Research on Teaching*. Chicago: Rand McNally.

Goodlad, J.I. (1990) *Teachers for our Nation's Schools*. San Francisco: Jossey-Bass.

Hirsch, E.D., Jr (1996) *The Schools We Need and Why We Don't Have Them*. New York: Doubleday.

Holmes Group (1986) *Tomorrow's Teachers*. East Lansing, MI: Holmes Group, Michigan State University.

—— (1990) *Tomorrow's Schools*. East Lansing, MI: Holmes Group, Michigan State University.

—— (1995) *Tomorrow's Schools of Education*. East Lansing, MI: Holmes Group, Michigan State University.

Houston, W.R. (ed.) (1990) *Handbook of Research on Teacher Education*. New York: Macmillan.

Howe, K.R. (1985) Two Dogmas of Educational Research. *Educational Researcher*, 14: 10–18.

Judge, H. (1982) *American Graduate Schools of Education: A View from Abroad*. New York: Ford Foundation.

Koerner, J.D. (1963) *The Miseducation of America's Teachers*. Boston: Houghton Mifflin.

Kramer, R. (1991). *Ed School Follies: The Miseducation of America's Teachers*. New York: Free Press.

Kuhn, T.S. (1970) *The Structure of Scientific Revolutions* (2nd edition, enlarged). Chicago: University of Chicago Press.

Labaree, D.F. (1995). A Disabling Vision: Rhetoric and Reality in *Tomorrow's Schools of Education*. *Teachers College Record*, 97: 166–205.

—— (1997a) Public Goods, Private Goods: The American Struggle over Educational Goals. *American Educational Research Journal*, 34: 39–81.

—— (1997b) *How to Succeed in School Without Really Learning: The Credentials Race in American Education*. New Haven: Yale University Press.

—— (1998) Educational Researchers: Living with a Lesser Form of Knowledge. *Educational Researcher*, 27(8): 4–12.

Lindblom, C.E. and Cohen, D.K. (1979) *Usable Knowledge: Social Science and Social Problem Solving*. New Haven: Yale University Press.

Merton, R.K. (1968) Patterns of Influence: Local and Cosmopolitan Influentials. In *Social Theory and Social Structure* (enlarged edition). New York: Free Press.

Rhoades, G. (1990) Change in an Unanchored Enterprise: Colleges of Education. *Review of Higher Education*, 13: 187–214.

Shulman, L.S. (1986) Paradigms and Research Programs in the Study of Teaching: A Contemporary Perspective. In M.C. Wittrock (ed.), *Handbook of Research on Teaching* (3rd edition). New York: Macmillan.

Sikula, J. (ed.) (1996) *Handbook of Research on Teacher Education* (2nd edition). New York: Macmillan.

Toulmin, S. (1972) *Human Understanding*. Princeton: Princeton University Press.

Travers, R.M.W. (ed.) (1973) *Handbook of Research on Teaching* (2nd edition). Chicago: Rand McNally.

Trow, M. (1988) American Higher Education: Past, Present, and Future. *Educational Researcher*, 17: 13–23.

Wittrock, M. (ed.) (1986) *Handbook of Research on Teaching* (3rd edition). New York: Macmillan.

5   Rethinking the Practice of Teacher Professionalism

Judyth Sachs

During the 1980s and 1990s award restructuring and school reform in Australia provided the impetus for public debate regarding teacher professionalism. Two national initiatives aimed at teacher professional development, the Innovative Links *Project between Schools and Universities for Teacher Professional Development and the National Schools Network are examples of initiatives that developed with the project of recasting teacher professionalism. These projects demonstrated how teachers, individually and collectively, have worked towards redefining the agenda and content of debates around teacher professionalism. The chapter presents an argument for the development of a new form of professionalism, which is referred to as activist professionalism. At the core of the argument is the development of the notions, drawn from Anthony Giddens, of active trust and generative politics. These two ideas provide a conceptual and political basis to rethink the activities of teachers and put in place a more active and responsive teacher professional.*

Since the early 1990s a range of school reform and teacher professional development activities have been implemented across Australia in response to wide ranging social and political conditions that have had direct impact on all levels of education. In their wake teachers have had to respond to a variety of challenges at the structural and individual level. Structurally, teachers face the ongoing challenges to:

- be externally accountable to a variety of education stakeholders;
- direct the processes and provision of school education;
- deliver more economical and efficient education provision;
- prepare students to be numerate, literate and able to take civic social responsibility.

Individually, teachers need to be skilled practitioners who are able to solve immediate practical problems, reflect on their practice in order to develop quality learning opportunities for their students and cope with rapid change inside and outside their classrooms.

Rethinking the practice of teacher professionalism can be viewed as a political project which has been seized upon by unions, government and teacher professional associations alike. The project of reclaiming teacher professionalism had its antecedents in industrial and professional activities during the later 1980s and early 1990s. Specifically, award restructuring at the federal level during the early 1990s provided the impetus for school reform and restructuring and the promise for teacher professionalism. These two initiatives created the necessary political conditions both within teaching and outside it to facilitate debate about the nature and scope of teacher professionalism. The watershed for this shift was the Teaching Accord of 1993 which, as the then minister of schools Ross Free pointed out, 'constitutes a very tangible recognition of the fundamental role that teachers must play in the continued development of the profession' (quoted in Preston, 1996: 190). The Accord and its associated initiatives were later to play a significant part in opening up of teacher professionalism for discussion by various education industry stakeholders including academics, teachers and bureaucrats working within education systems as well as professional development agencies and staff working on teacher professional development projects. Indeed, it provided the forum for teacher professionalism to be part of the political agenda and for the profession to be responsible for defining itself. In this chapter, I argue that rethinking the practice of teacher professionalism requires a recasting of professional and industrial issues and relationship between employers, unions and teachers and other education stakeholders. Central to this are five principles that I argue should stand at the core of rethinking the practice of teacher professionalism. I use the examples of two national reform initiatives to indicate how these principles have the potential to contribute to the rethinking of teacher professionalism in practice.

In order to develop this argument it is necessary to contextualize teacher professionalism within the broader framework of award restructuring and school reform as it occurred in Australia during the late 1980s and early 1990s. Both of these initiatives were significant in shaping federal and state policy regarding the teaching profession and how the profession would respond to the broader social and political agenda.

The Context of Rethinking Teacher Professionalism in Australia

During the 1980s issues of teacher professionalism were one of the sites of struggle when Australian industry was restructuring industrial awards.

In education, award restructuring fuelled union activity, mobilized professional groups, and unsettled traditional relations between state government education authorities and between state and federal governments in education. Debate about the relationship between the industrial and professional dimensions of teachers' work, and who represented teachers in those areas, surged into prominence, as did intergovernmental relations and authority (Seddon 1996). However, by 1993 award restructuring had disappeared from the public view. Nevertheless, it left a significant legacy with regard to the development of new types of relationships between the unions, the profession and government, both at the state and federal level. According to Seddon a joint industrial and professional agenda was promoted that affirmed that award restructuring would provide a potent mechanism for reforming the work of teachers and, therefore, the processes of teaching and learning which lie at the heart of education. (ibid.: 3). In 1993 the commonwealth government negotiated a 'Teaching Accord' with the Australian Education Union (AEU) and the Independent Education Union (IEU).[1] The Teaching Accord established priorities and detailed the commitment of the Commonwealth to the involvement of the profession and its financial support for professional development, curriculum assessment and research projects, and seed funding for the National Schools Project and the Australian Teaching Council. According to Sharan Burrow (1996), currently the president of the Australian Education Union, the Accord encouraged school reform, a move towards professional standards, and some greater salary justice and equity through salary scales across the profession. The Accord was contested and conflictual but, on balance, it provided the teaching profession with useful foundations for the future. Burrow argues that in particular, 'award restructuring fuelled the further emergence of the education profession and consolidated its determination to take more control over professional life' (Burrow 1996: 114).

Despite the collapse of the joint union and government initiatives for professional renewal that characterized the early 1990s, several national initiatives survived that had as their focus the revitalization of teacher professionalism. These were the National Schools Network (NSN), an offspring of the National Schools Project (NSP) and the *Innovative Links* Between Schools and Universities Project for Teacher Professional Development.[2] Both these projects seized two contemporary principles of organizational development: networking and a learning organization approach to change and development. Both of them are concerned with raising questions and issues that confront what it means to be a teacher, an academic and a policy activist, and how to deal with the complexities, dilemmas and tensions of contemporary educational life. At the core of both projects is a commitment to improve the work practices and conditions of teachers and students, and in so doing to improve student learning outcomes.

To this point, I have described the political and industrial conditions that gave rise to teacher professionalism being put on the public policy agenda. I now turn to presenting two examples of the issue of rethinking professionalism in practice.

Teacher Professionalism: A Struggle for Meaning

Elsewhere (Sachs 1996, 1997) I have argued that renewing teacher professionalism means moving beyond what Friedson (1994) calls a commonsense idea of professionalism. A commonsense idea of professionalism is developed passively: not so much elaborated, systematized or refined self-consciously as growing out of everyday social usage. Friedson argues that:

> [C]ommonsense usage is expanded to emphasize those characteristics of an occupation that justify special standing and privilege: it becomes a profession's portrayal of profession. Its content is determined largely by the political and ceremonial needs of the profession, and it is used primarily to advance and defend its position.
>
> (Friedson 1994: 170)

Through award restructuring and the various professional development initiatives that emerged during the 1990s in response to federal government support, teacher professionalism in Australia developed beyond Friedson's commonsense view. It became a vehicle for school reform and the political repositioning of the profession, in terms of itself but, more importantly, in the eyes of the community.

One of the hallmarks of being identified externally as a professional is to continue learning throughout a career, deepening knowledge and skill judgement, staying abreast of important developments in the field and experimenting with innovations that promise improvements in practice (Sykes 1990). Here lies one of the paradoxes for teacher professionalism. For as Fullan (1993) notes, as a profession, we are not a learning one. While student learning is a goal, often the continuing learning of teachers is overlooked. While continuous learning and the improvement of our practice should be one of the core values of teacher professionalism, in many instances this is not so.

The type of systemic school reform that has characterized education policy and practices during the 1990s has established new sets of relations among governmental bureaucracies and agencies, unions, professional teaching groups in both primary and secondary areas and research communities. The call for teacher professionalism through award restructuring and school reform became related to a revisioning of occupational identity. Significantly, it gave value to schoolwork that included greater teacher responsibility and flexibility in implementing goal governed approaches of the state (Popkewitz 1996: 30). Under the guise of professionalism, teachers became the vehicles to implement government policy, which had, as its central priorities, increased productivity by being more efficient, effective and economic.

The occupational identity revisioned through education reforms in Australia recast teachers as learners and researchers. This is certainly evident in two recent initiatives aiming at revitalizing teacher professionalism within Australia. These are the NSN and the *Innovative Links* Project referred to earlier. I now turn to elaborate how these two projects have contributed to reclaiming the professional agenda by teachers and other educational industry workers.

Teacher Professionalism in Practice

Sykes (1990: 92) argues that the task for the future is to construct a professional model that accommodates teachings' distinct aspects. The National Schools Network and the *Innovative Links* Project are two contemporary examples of school-based initiatives designed to revision teacher professionalism that can be seen as contributing to the overall vision underlying educational restructuring on a national scale. Both are school-based national projects and break with traditional parochial conceptions of teacher professionalism. Because teachers participate as part of a national network of teachers involved in professional development, teachers become part of the national reform agenda, and are inclusive of a national professional group. Indeed, the national nature of the projects has created a vigorous professional community within schools and across system and state boundaries which has given life to the development of new ideas and practices which move well beyond local needs and interests.

The NSN and the *Innovative Links* Project have both attempted to broaden the base of school restructuring beyond organizational change, to incorporate the view of the need to rethink the practice of teacher professionalism. The aim has been to bring significant changes in teacher practices, which it is argued will improve student learning outcomes. The NSN and the *Innovative Links* Project have provided a legitimate vehicle for the purpose of restructuring becoming one of changing the organization so that good ideas and strategies born in practice can flourish and not be hindered by existing bureaucratic forces (Grimmett 1995).

The NSN and the *Innovative Links* Project have shown the significance of developing a national approach to the renewal of teacher professionalism in several respects. First, they have provided teachers with opportunities to cross over state and system boundaries to access information and best practice which is of professional value. They have facilitated networking of a kind that is different from the cross-local type that is traditional to schools. They have broken teachers out of their local systems, and thus out of the parochialism of that system, enabling them to attach their sense of professional identity to a wider, more open and comparative system orientation. Second, the use of national forums as a strategy for bringing project participants together has helped to facilitate the 'big picture' view of school reform and teacher professionalism, and to support the development of national networks. Third, the presence of the university as part of a reform site known as a roundtable has contributed to the national character of the project. Universities, unlike schools, are federally funded. Teacher education academics identify as members of a national professional group, and see their professional networks as national and international rather than state or local in nature (Yeatman and Sachs 1995). Finally, these projects have contributed in constructive ways to actualizing the possibility of revitalized teaching in revitalized schools (Grimmett 1995).

The National Schools Network

The National Schools Network (NSN) and its precursor the National Schools Project (NSP) were conceived as a tool for system reform, and had the employers, unions and commonwealth government locked into supporting the process through the 'Education Accord' of 1993. As Angus (1996: 145) observes, 'the primary target was not to enable improvement in the over 200 or so pilot schools, but rather to produce systemic changes that would enable the other 9800 schools in Australia to follow suit'. Both the NSP and the NSN were action research projects designed to find out what was stopping schools from implementing their own ideas about improving teaching and learning. Conceptually, both projects operated from the following assumptions. First, the projects rejected the idea that there was one single recipe for school improvement and teacher professionalism. Second, it was recognized that if worthwhile changes were to occur, both the identification of the problem to be addressed by the change and the implementation of the prospective solution had to occur in the school community (Angus 1996). Finally, both projects were framed around the idea of work organization, that is the ways in which teachers' work was structured by organizational parameters, in particular those governed by government awards, industrial agreements, and so on. The NSN at its peak provided support for over 400 Australian schools that were rethinking their work organization and teaching and learning in order to improve learning outcomes for students and staff.

NSN schools have developed projects concerned with asking teachers to examine and question the link between the organization of teachers' work and pedagogy. The NSN continually links teacher professional development with on-going school-based research initiatives. The NSN research framework involves building a research culture among teachers in schools. It promotes and supports collaborative research and collegial reflective practices using critical action research methodologies. Through such an orientation to school practice, teachers in schools are actively concerned with changing various aspects of their own practice. Through these projects, teacher professionalism is being redefined from within the profession rather than from outside.

The Innovative Links *Project*

The *Innovative Links* Project[3] is an example of a nationwide initiative that challenges established conceptions as to what schooling, teacher professionalism and teacher education are about. It complements and builds upon the experience of NSN. This is not by chance. Key academics were members of an NSN academic reference group that asked specific questions about the relationship between research and practice in the work of teachers. Conceptually and organizationally, then, the *Innovative Links* Project was built upon the procedures, learnings and principles of participation established through the NSN (and its predecessor, the NSP). As part of the discussion a new and reciprocal element emerged regarding the relationship between research and practice in the work of university academics in the field of teacher education. It has been designed to move participants beyond their accustomed ways of doing things and their familiar relationships (Yeatman and Sachs 1995).

The *Innovative Links* Project represents formal and explicit partnerships between schools and universities, which are seen as central to the renewal and development of teacher professionalism; this is enabled by the formation of local roundtables comprising five to six schools and academic associates from the affiliated university. As Yeatman and Sachs (1995) observe, for the first time the relationship between teacher education faculties in universities and schools has come onto the school reform/restructuring agenda in Australia. The project focuses the spotlight on the question of how this relationship should be designed and developed so as to facilitate the professional development of both school- and university-based practitioners. The basic premise upon which *Innovative Links* and NSN are formulated is the construction of a learning society. In the context of schooling, teachers can be regarded as providing the leadership and facilitation of processes, whereby students learn the skills and knowledge which enable them to take responsibility for their own learning. Within such a context, student learning is only one of the dimensions. Teacher learning must be incorporated, as must academic learning and systems learning if the idea of a learning society is to be fully realized (Yeatman and Sachs 1995).

Both the NSN and the *Innovative Links* Project have been concerned with revitalizing schools and teacher professionalism through teacher learning. Both projects have emphasized processes of inquiry, a collaborative work context and improving student and teacher work conditions and learning outcomes. The schools associated with both projects have encouraged teachers to understand and engage in the minds of learners, and to devise strategies, individually and collectively, which will improve student learning outcomes.

Teachers working in NSN and *Innovative Links* schools have developed skills and competencies to undertake classroom-based action research into dilemmas of teaching such as investigating problematic aspects of the curriculum, attempting to understand learners' conceptions of subject matter content and examining difficult student behaviour, among many other demanding and confrontational aspects of classroom and school life. The collaboration between the schools and university academics has led to field-based teacher research and to the development of different kinds of relationships (professional and social) between two parties concerned with teacher preparation and development. Importantly, both of these projects have been concerned with developing what Lave and Wenger (1991) refer to as 'communities of practice'. They argue that social practice, what practitioners do and how they talk about what they do is the primary generative phenomenon and learning is one of its characteristics. They locate 'learning not in the acquisition of structure, but in the increased access of learners to participating roles in expert performance' (ibid.: 17). Learning is thus a way of being in a particular social world, not merely knowing about it or describing it. From this perspective, emphasis is placed upon participation in a community of practitioners, rather than merely the acquisition of a set of skills, or practices deemed to satisfy bureaucratic requirements. Through their involvement in the NSN and the *Innovative Links* Project, teachers and academic colleagues move from peripheral involvement to full participation. This process provokes and facilitates a conversation about learning, and how people can learn from projects and each other. This conversation becomes an ongoing aspect of school life.

An indicator of the success of the *Innovative Links* Project is the determination of a number of roundtables to continue their work in spite of the cessation of external funding. In these instances the principles of affiliation and involvement in teacher professional development have become embedded in the structures and processes of both schools and universities. However, it must also be stated that this did not occur in all roundtables.

A Platform for Rethinking the Practice of Teacher Professionalism

The NSN and the *Innovative Links* Project are premised on three core principles: learning, participation and collaboration. To these I would like to add two others: cooperation and activism. Taken together, these values specify what it means to be a socially responsible and active professional for the new millennium. They constitute the fundamentals of a proactive and responsible approach to teacher professionalism. I now turn to elaborate each of these briefly.

Learning

This is the core of rethinking teacher professionalism. As an individual and collective goal teachers should be seen to practise the value of learning, both with their colleagues and with their students. When teachers recast themselves as learners, the social relations of schools and the relations between teachers and teachers, teachers and students and teachers and their communities will be fundamentally reshaped. Learning rather than teaching becomes the core activity of teacher and student life in schools.

Participation

Recasting the social relationship of schooling demands active participation by teachers, students and their communities. Reclaiming teacher professionalism through participation requires that teachers see themselves as active agents in their own professional worlds. This can only happen if they are encouraged to be so, and if structures are developed to tap and develop their agency (Yeatman 1996). A participative approach to teacher professionalism cannot go very far unless it is adopted and agreed upon as a core value and strategy, put in place to be developed and supported by all those involved in the education enterprise.

Collaboration

There are two dimensions to collaboration: internal and external. Internally, Beattie (1995) argues that collaboration, collegiality and conversations provide teachers with a means for professional learning and development within the context of self and community. Coming together as collaborative groups or teams allows for a synergy that would not be possible otherwise. Team-based or collaboratively oriented conversation enables the kind of dialogical process through which people as individuals and as a group change what it is they think and maybe feel about something or someone (Yeatman 1996).

Externally, collaboration involves working with other interested parties outside the school locale. This could include community groups or academics working in universities. These partnerships between interested groups provide opportunities for new kinds of expertise to be developed on the part of both school-based personnel and their university-based colleagues.

Cooperation

Historically, teachers have had limited opportunities to work with their peers in collaborative and cooperative ways. There is little tradition in the teaching profession of teachers learning from each other and developing expertise collectively in written or oral form. As a profession, teachers have developed neither a common language nor a technology for documenting and discussing practice and its outcomes. This is partly due to the pragmatic nature of teaching itself, the conditions under which teachers work, the precedents set by past practice, the intangibility of its consequences and the intensity and immediacy of the work of teaching. Collectively these factors reinforce a professional dialogue in which spoken rather than written language is the more highly valued and practised mode of communication, and which more often than not comprises immediate responses rather than considered reflection on practice. Teaching can be best described as more an oral than written discipline.

Activism

Being active means responding publicly with issues that relate directly or indirectly to education and schooling. It involves participation, collaboration and cooperation from both within and outside the profession. It means standing up for what Fullan (1993) describes as the moral purpose of teaching. It also requires that teachers are involved individually and collectively in change agentry (ibid.). On the role of the individual teacher, it is worth quoting Fullan at length:

> The individual educator is a critical starting point because the leverage for change can be greater through the efforts of individuals, and each educator has some control (more than is exercised) over what he or she does, because it is one's own motives and skills that are in question.
> (Ibid.: 12)

This type of activism is not for the faint-hearted. It requires risk taking and fighting for ideals that enhance education. It also requires passion, determination and energy. Not surprisingly, activism is probably safer as a collective activity rather than an individual one. Nevertheless, individual action has its place.

These five principles for rethinking the practice of teacher professionalism – learning, participation, collaboration, cooperation and activism – together form a platform on which teachers' professionalism can be renewed and developed.

Taken in isolation, any one of these values does not contribute to the overall project of teacher professionalism. Alternatively, when viewed in conjunction with the other values, each value becomes powerful and effective in its overall cultural effect. These values should stand at the core of building a socially and politically responsible profession. Following Goodson and Hargreaves' line of thinking (1996: 20), renewing teacher professionalism to incorporate the above values is a 'struggle which is guided by moral and political visions of the purposes which teacher professionalism should serve within actively caring communities and vigorous social democracies'. It is an activity that is worth intellectual and emotional investment.

Both the NSN and the *Innovative Links* Project represent examples of postmodern professionalism (Goodson and Hargreaves 1996). They provide examples of what is possible when teachers reclaim the professional agenda. These projects, individually and collectively, have been guided by a shared vision of the purposes which teacher professionalism should serve within active social and political communities. In following Goodson and Hargreaves' attributes of teacher professionalism in a complex, postmodern age (1996: 20–1), schools involved with the NSN and the *Innovative Links* Project have had:

- increased opportunity and responsibility to exercise *discretionary judgement* over issues of teaching, curriculum and the care that affects one's students;
- opportunities and expectations to engage with the *moral and social purposes* and value of what teachers teach, along with major curriculum and assessment matters in which these purposes are embedded;
- commitment to working with colleagues in *collaborative* cultures of help and support as ways of using shared expertise to solve ongoing problems of professional practice, rather than engaging in joint work as a motivational device to implement external mandates of others;
- a self-directed search and struggle for continuous learning related to one's own expertise and standards of practice, rather than compliance with the enervating obligations of endless change demanded by others (often under the guise of continuous learning or improvement).

I would like to add another point to this condensed list, namely they have:

- become part of a national social movement in which teachers individually and collectively develop skills, competencies and dispositions of mind that will contribute to the enhancement of teaching and the improvement of student learning outcomes.

These projects by their conception, organization and membership have provided teachers with opportunities to have an active role in defining their own professional needs and how these needs might be achieved.

These projects have recast relationships between a variety of education workers and have contributed significantly to providing models for how teachers can be responsible for their own learning and improving that of students. That these projects transcend state boundaries and confront the conventional wisdom of experience is in no small part due to the vision and commitment of a number of teachers, academics and policy activists working at the state and national level. Their energy and strategic thinking has played a significant part in the project of reclaiming teacher professionalism. However, at the end of the day, it is teachers themselves who have the responsibility of sustaining and reclaiming the professional agenda.

Conclusion

In this chapter I have used the experience from two national teacher professional development projects to demonstrate how award restructuring and school reform can work together to enable teachers to rethink the practice of teacher professionalism. It is clear that teaching and notions of teacher professionalism in the future will require new and different ways of operating and that teachers and academics will need to develop new ways of talking about the work of teaching. New forms of teacher professionalism will emerge in response to changing economic, social and political conditions. Both the *Innovative Links* Project and the National Schools Network have provided models for how teachers, with the support of unions, university academics and education systems, can reclaim the professional ground. These projects have also demonstrated that through strategic partnerships between various education stakeholders the strategy of reclaiming teacher professionalism is a political project that must be worked on at the individual and group level. Furthermore, the projects at school level and national level demonstrate that the development of teacher professionalism is an ongoing struggle that goes beyond the struggle for meaning: it is the struggle for the profession to be in control of its own future. It is the profession itself that provides the moral and intellectual leadership to ensure that student learning is of high quality and that the working conditions of teachers are enhanced.

Acknowledgement

A version of this chapter titled, 'Reclaiming Teacher Professionalism: An Australian Perspective' was presented at the 6th National Conference in Educational Research held in collaboration with the International Network PACT Conference in Oslo, Norway in May 1997. Another version, 'Reclaiming the Agenda of Teacher Professionalism' was published in the *Journal of Education for Teaching*, 23(3) (1997): 263–75.

Notes

1 The AEU is the national union representing teachers working in government schools, while the IEU represents, at the national level, teachers working in independent and Catholic schools.
2 For more detail about these projects, see Sachs (1996), Groundwater-Smith (1996), and Sachs and Groundwater-Smith (1996).
3 In terms of its scope the project has provided the opportunity for fourteen universities, across sixteen campuses, representing all Australian states and one territory, to be involved in a project that has as its core feature the idea of partnerships between practising teachers on a whole-school basis and university-based teacher educators. This involves approximately one-third of universities in Australia in a coherent teacher professional development project. Added to this are some 100 schools which include state, independent and Catholic representatives, and some 80 academic associates.

References

Angus, M. (1996) Award Restructuring in Schools: Educational Idealism Versus Political Pragmatism. In T. Seddon (ed.), *Pay, Professionalism and Politics: Reforming Teachers, Reforming Education.* Melbourne: Australian Council for Educational Research.

Beattie, M. (1995) New Prospects for Teacher Education: Narrative Ways of Knowing Teaching and Teacher Learning. *Education Research*, 37(1): 54–70.

Burrow, S. (1996) Award Restructuring: The Teaching Profession. In T. Seddon (ed.), *Pay, Professionalism and Politics: Reforming Teachers, Reforming Education.* Melbourne: Australian Council for Educational Research.

Friedson, E. (1994) *Professionalism Reborn: Theory, Prophecy and Policy.* Chicago: University of Chicago Press.

Fullan, M. (1993) *Change Forces.* London: Falmer Press.

Goodson, I. and Hargreaves, A. (1996) Teachers' Professional Lives: Aspirations and Actualities. In I. Goodson and A. Hargreaves (eds), *Teachers' Professional Lives.* London: Falmer Press.

Grimmett, P. (1995) Reconceptualizing Teacher Education: Preparing Teachers for Revitalized Schools. In M. Wideen, M. and P. Grimmett (eds), *Changing Times in Teacher Education: Restructuring or Reconceptualization.* London: Falmer Press.

Groundwater-Smith, S. (1996) Putting Teacher Professional Judgment to Work. Keynote address presented at the Practitioner Research and Academic Practices Conferences, 4–6 July. Cambridge Institute of Education.

Lave, J. and Wenger, E. (1991) *Situated Learning: Legitimate Peripheral Participation.* Cambridge: Cambridge University Press.

Popkewitz, T. (1996) Rethinking Decentralization and State/Civil Society Distinctions: The State as a Problematic for Governing. *Journal of Education Policy*, 11(1): 27–51.

Preston, B. (1996) Award Restructuring: A Catalyst in the Evolution of Teacher Professionalism. In T. Seddon (ed.), *Pay, Professionalism and Politics: Reforming Teachers, Reforming Education.* Melbourne: Australian Council for Educational Research.

Sachs, J. (1996). Reinventing Teacher Professionalism though Innovative Links. Paper presented at the Practitioner Research and Academic Practices Conferences, 4–6 July. Cambridge Institute of Education.

—— (1997) Reinventing Teacher Professionalism though Innovative Links. *Educational Action Research*, 5(3): 449–62.

Sachs, J. and Groundwater-Smith, S. (1996) Celebrating Teacher Professional Knowledge: School Reform and Teachers' Professional Judgment. Paper presented at the Re-engineering Education for Change Conference. Unesco and Asia-Pacific Centre of Educational Innovation and Development, Bangkok.

Seddon, T. (ed.) (1996) *Pay, Professionalism and Politics: Reforming Teachers, Reforming Education*. Melbourne: Australian Council for Educational Research.

Sykes, G. (1990) Fostering Teacher Professionalism in Schools. In R. Elmore (ed.), *Restructuring Schools: The Next Generation of Educational Reform*. San Francisco: Jossey-Bass.

Yeatman, A. (1996) Managing the Politics of Uncertainty. Keynote address, Reform Agendas Conference: Making Education Work, University of Sydney.

Yeatman, A. and Sachs, J. (1995) *Making the Links: A Formative Evaluation of the First Year of the Innovative Links between Universities and Schools for Teacher Professional Development*. Perth, WA: Murdoch University.

Part II

The Lives and Work of Teachers

6 Multiple Truths and Contested Realities

The Changing Faces of Teacher Professionalism in England

Gill Helsby

There is nothing simple or static about the concept of teacher profession-alism in England: it is constantly changing and constantly being redefined in different ways by different voices at different times. This chapter draws upon data from a thirty-month study of teachers' professional cultures to explore recent changes in teachers' work and in teacher professionalism. Evidence from interviews with English secondary school teachers suggests a lessening of the extent to which the National Curriculum acts as a constraint upon teacher autonomy and, in some cases at least, an increase in the way in which it acts as a positive prompt to teacher development. At the same time, it is suggested that other factors are now replacing the National Curriculum as the major threat to the exercise of teacher profes-sionalism. Complementary evidence from a small number of senior policy makers and educationalists indicates a degree of movement in thinking at national level towards the necessity and desirability of enhancing teacher professionalism.

There is nothing simple or static about the concept of teacher profession-alism in England: it is constantly changing and constantly being redefined in different ways at different times to serve different interests. Some of the changes are predictable, given the major structural reforms of the educa-tional system that have been taking place in England and in other westernized societies in recent years. Other changes, however, are more unexpected, as a combination of local culture, context and personality inter-acts in varying ways with the structural changes, leading to quite diverse experiences at local level. At the heart of these variations, and a key feature of the education system in England in recent times, is the ongoing con-testation between state control and professional autonomy, particularly with regard to the school curriculum. This chapter will draw upon data from a thirty-month study of the professional cultures of secondary school teachers[1] to explore how recent changes in teachers' work have impacted upon teachers' sense of professionalism.

The English Context

Although such changes are happening in many countries, England provides a particularly interesting context for study because of the sharp contrast between current conditions of work for schoolteachers and those pertaining in the recent past. In the post-war years, there developed an unusually strong tradition of teacher autonomy in the school curriculum (Lawton 1980; Grace 1987). Although, following the Education Act of 1944, decisions about curriculum content and teaching methods were legally the responsibility of the local education authorities (LEAs), in practice they were left to the discretion of headteachers and their staff, subject to the demands of the various examining boards and the generally perfunctory oversight of school governors. So strong was the notion of professional autonomy that a Conservative education minister could complain in March 1960 that the curriculum was a 'secret garden' into which parliament dare not tread (Eccles 1960). Accountability was also based upon a 'professional autonomy' model (Adelman and Alexander 1982), which relied largely upon self-evaluation conducted by teachers and guaranteed by their professional status. The occasional visits to schools by LEA advisors or by Her Majesty's Inspectors were used to gather general intelligence and to support practice rather than to make hard, public judgements of individual teachers.

In stark contrast to this background of state *laissez-faire* and of relative deference to teachers' professional judgements, Conservative education policies since the early 1980s progressively and inexorably sought to diminish the power of educational professionals by vastly increasing central prescription and control whilst at the same time exposing schools to market forces and imposing business management models of governance upon them. In particular, the speedy introduction of the compulsory National Curriculum for all 5- to 16-year-olds in state schools, with prescribed attainment targets and programmes of study, standardized student assessment and output-related systems of accountability, was seen by many as a means of deskilling and deprofessionalizing teachers, who were treated throughout as 'hirelings to be given instructions rather than as professionals to be involved at all stages and at all levels' (Lawton 1993: 66). Indeed, much of the early commentary on the implementation of the National Curriculum was in this vein (e.g. Kogan 1989; Kelly 1990), emphasizing the major structural changes in teachers' working lives and the ways in which a traditionally highly professionalized occupation was being proletarianized though a particularly harsh and aggressive approach to educational reform. The 'golden age' of professional control was being replaced by a production-line approach to education, in which teachers were expected to adopt the role of technicians, following instructions and subject to public scrutiny and external inspection of their compliance and efficiency.

Whilst this interpretation of the situation in England is persuasive, and to a considerable extent grounded in the experiences of many teachers, it nonetheless conveys only a partial account of a more complex reality. On the one hand, the assumed autonomy of teachers in the 1950s and 1960s was only relative, operating more within the confines of their own classrooms than on the broader canvas of school policies, goals and administration (Hoyle 1974). At the same time, the work of secondary school teachers was always overshadowed by the demands of the university-led examination boards and by top-down definitions of what counted as valid knowledge both in the school curriculum and within particular subject areas (Goodson 1994). Finally, relatively few teachers chose to exploit their autonomy by engaging in innovative curriculum development, apparently preferring to continue traditional practices in their teaching.

On the other hand, the notion of teacher proletarianization as a direct result of recent Government policies is itself overly simplistic, since it reduces teachers to automatons and ignores their active role in contesting, resisting or adapting such policies (Ozga and Lawn 1988). In practice, change occurs as a result of the interplay between structure, agency and culture (Acker 1997; Helsby and McCulloch 1997). In this case the structural demands come from the imposition of the National Curriculum and related requirements, 'agency' refers to the part played by teachers in actively translating these government policies into practice and 'culture' denotes the different sets of beliefs, values, norms and patterns of interaction which are inherent in different work groups and which heavily influence the responses of individual teachers. All three aspects are interdependent, and all will influence each other to a greater or lesser extent. Whilst the structural aspects were often more prominent in the early years of National Curriculum implementation, leading many teachers to experience a sense of disempowerment, evidence soon emerged of the limits of central prescription and of the ultimate reliance upon teachers to use their professional experience and 'teacherly knowledge' (Jenkins 1997) to develop policy into practice. Moreover, factors such as strong collegial cultures and growing familiarity with the requirements served to boost teachers' 'professional confidence' in asserting their own judgements upon the situation (Helsby 1995, 1996a).

Thus, there is great variation in teachers' responses to the National Curriculum and in their sense of professionalism, not only between different individuals in different contexts but also over time. Responses of creative primary teachers, for example, range from stress and burnout through resistance to appropriation and even enrichment through innovation (Woods 1994; Woods and Jeffrey 1997). Similar variations occur in secondary

[Technology is] the subject that the government has made the most mess of.

they often felt compelled to comply:

> The schemes of work and [the] timescales mean there's very little chance for us to waver from the National Curriculum.
>
> (History teacher)

One mathematics teacher, who claimed to have 'thrived on change' in the past, found that the excess of imposed change was having a damaging effect:

> I've now reached saturation point, because it's not me that has made the changes, but I've been forced to do things that I don't consider to be the right way of going about it.

Some felt that the overloaded content affected classroom management:

> Teachers are finding things forced upon them so they can't use their professional judgement any more . . . you can't expand on a subject if the kids are responding or move on if they're not.
>
> (History teacher)

This was seen as undermining teacher professionalism:

> [W]e are the experts, the people who've done the geography degrees, who've been trained to teach geography, who are up to date with it, and yet we're told we're wrong.
>
> (Geography teacher)

> The government has bombarded us with so much ill-thought out change, and so we've lost confidence.
>
> (Mathematics teacher)

Despite the many negative comments, the condemnation of the National Curriculum during the initial interviews was not universal, and some teachers felt relatively relaxed about the new requirements. In terms of the curriculum content, some of the mathematics teachers felt that their subject was relatively unchanged ('maths is maths' was a frequent comment) and a minority believed that the National Curriculum offered them a useful framework within which to work. There were one or two positive comments from technology teachers, who believed that the presence of technology as a core subject within the National Curriculum had increased their status, and from teachers working in schools for children with special needs, who felt less isolated because they were following a common curriculum with mainstream schools.

Continuing and Diminishing Constraints

The second round of teacher interviews, which took place approximately a year after the initial ones, revealed that some teachers continued to feel heavily constrained by the amount of curriculum prescription:

> [S]ince implementation of National Curriculum and the constraints that have been placed upon us at [the] side of us, really I find it extremely hard. I'm very disillusioned with what I can do.
>
> (Technology/CDT teacher)

> I find . . . that with the scheme of work from the National Curriculum, it is extremely prescriptive. We've got very little freedom and teacher initiative and inventiveness.
>
> (Geography teacher)

Several continued to comment on the conflict between following National Curriculum prescription and meeting student needs:

> A lot of the National Curriculum is not relevant to them and a lot of what we're expected to teach, they find dull and boring.
>
> (History teacher)

> [W]hat's happening now is that it's tending to be the curriculum that's driving what is taught as opposed to the individual needs of the pupils.
>
> (Mathematics teacher in a special school)

Some described this as a form of deprofessionalization, since it discouraged teacher input:

> [I]t makes me less professional in that it makes me not have to think as much sometimes. I don't have to put as much into it possibly . . . if it is more prescriptive and I'm told what I've got to do.
>
> (Mathematics teacher)

However, compared to the initial interviews, it was clear that many teachers felt a lessening of the constraints of curriculum prescription. Some of this new-found freedom arose because of the reduction in prescribed content that had occurred as a result of the National Curriculum review undertaken by Sir Ron Dearing (Dearing 1993):

[Of the new NC] it's very free, it's very, erm, formless . . . because it's just descriptors, you can meet those in so many more different ways than you could in the old system.

(Mathematics teacher)

Far more frequently, however, the key factor was experience of, and familiarity with, the demands of the National Curriculum:

I think that we now feel more comfortable with the content, slightly more comfortable with the assessment and therefore more, what can I say, not as straitjacketed. That we must do it like this, by the book. We seem to have an overview of it . . . we're happier with the content, not as frightened of it.

(History teacher)

Teachers who had initially kept closely to written schemes of work to ensure that they were meeting the requirements were now developing confidence to digress from these:

The year we actually did [the scheme of work] we were fairly tight, I mean I had it on my desk, just to remind me. Now I haven't had it out of the cabinet for a while this year.

(History teacher)

Some teachers referred to the freedom which they perceived because of the vague wording of the new requirements or the lack of specification in certain areas. Others spoke of their ability to make decisions about resources, activities and topics. Most particularly, many perceived a continuing freedom in terms of pedagogy and classroom management:

[I can make decisions about] the ways in which I teach my subject. We still have our own little ivory tower within our classroom . . . at the end of the day, what I find works for me is what I will do.

(Mathematics teacher)

For some, this freedom of pedagogy was of key importance and went to the heart of their professionalism:

If I was told exactly what to do when I went into my classroom during every lesson, that would impinge on my professionalism . . . but [the National Curriculum] hasn't done that and it hasn't actually changed my feelings of professionalism in any sense whatsoever, which I think has more to do with the way that you actually do the job than with whether I'm ever allowed a decision about whether to teach Pythagoras or not.

> (Mathematics teacher)

Opportunities within the National Curriculum

Whilst the comments recorded so far suggest that teachers were either negative or neutral about the constraining effects of the National Curriculum, a small number of interviewees were much more positive about it and about the ways in which it offered a positive framework for enhancing teacher professionalism. Some welcomed the security of a framework within which they could work:

> I think I understand what the curriculum wants and therefore I feel able to make a positive contribution to what's taught, knowing that, yes, what we've suggested as being taught will actually fulfil the criteria.
>
> (Technology/food teacher)

> I . . . find that, with being told what to do, it can give you a certain degree of security, because you know that you've got this, this and this.
>
> (Geography teacher)

One history teacher believed that the fact of having an agreed body of knowledge and skills to be taught enhanced the role of the teacher in the eyes of students and also helped to counteract the popular stereotype of left-wing teachers preaching Marxism and Leninism. A technology teacher argued that the need to plan and develop schemes of work, to anticipate change and to minimize disruption demanded high-level skills that could be regarded as indicators of professionalism. Another suggested that the certainty that came from an agreed curriculum provided a good basis for development:

> [I]n terms of improving the quality of it . . . if people know what they're doing, that's a good starting point.
>
> (History and geography teacher)

This was certainly the view of some of the thirteen 'key informants' (policy makers and senior educational executives) whom we also interviewed as part of the study. Some felt that there were positive benefits arising from the focus upon teachers' role in the curriculum:

> [I]t's made teachers articulate about what the curriculum is, what it's for and their part in it, and that's bound to have an effect on professionalism.
>
> (Retired senior civil servant, National Curriculum Council)

100

whilst others believed that an established curriculum enabled teachers to give more attention to their pedagogy:

> The coming of the 1988 Education Act provided a curriculum structure that was better than one could get out of textbooks, and for the good teachers it freed them up to develop their pedagogy in relation to a curriculum framework which was given them.
>
> (Senior official at the Teacher Training Agency)

This last point found some echoes amongst the teacher respondents:

> I actually think there's more imagination in teaching now because we specifically don't have a set textbook, so we can sit around our table at lunchtime and say 'Well, I'm teaching Pythagoras and I thought I'd do it by investigation. Does anybody have a good idea of a book we could use?' So, I actually think that maths teachers talk more about maths now than they ever did before.
>
> (Mathematics teacher)

Several of the key informants used the notion of 'reflective practitioner' to describe the proper role of professional teachers:

> A reflective teacher . . . is someone who has a sense of the underlying purposes of what they're doing, so that someone who is professional is not a mere mechanic . . . a reflective teacher is also someone who thinks about the way in which the things that they do meet those purposes, and does so fairly consistently.
>
> (Senior official, School Curriculum and Assessment Authority)

However, this ideal may be thwarted by the current pressures upon teachers' work:

> [Y]ou could argue that, as long as I know what I've got to teach definitely, that could give me the freedom to teach it how, how I think. But I don't really feel that that's what's happening in practice. I think pressures of time, lack of time are becoming more noticeable all the time so . . . I've tended to stick with what they know and what they can cope with, rather than having the time to set up something very innovative and different.
>
> (Mathematics teacher)

This last comment points towards a number of different constraints that may now be posing an even greater threat to teacher professionalism than did the degree of curriculum prescription inherent in the National Curriculum.

Additional Constraints

The constraints that the evidence suggests are now affecting most teachers include:

- the general intensification of working life;
- a marked reduction in the general resourcing of education;
- a growing insularity amongst teachers;
- increased demands for accountability, including the national system of school and teacher inspection;
- a greater emphasis upon national testing accompanied by the publication of league tables of assessment results;
- growing managerialism in schools.

Intensification

Evidence of teachers' increasing workloads is not new, nor is it peculiar to the English context. It is, however, widely recognized that this general 'intensification' of working life (Apple 1986) can have adverse effects upon teachers' professionalism, as increased paperwork, more frequent administrative meetings and other bureaucratic requirements sap teachers' energy and increasingly divert them from the core professional task of teaching:

> I don't actually have the time to put into planning or thinking about my teaching as I used to. I'm doing a lot more teaching sort of on the hoof, which bothers me because I know it isn't as good as I'm capable of doing, but it's the amount of time I have in the day.
>
> (Geography teacher)

Many of our interviewees found this was leading to stress and to a loss of job satisfaction:

> [W]e're increasingly aware that stress is a big problem in teaching . . . people are taking time off if you like through illness, but it's illness that's brought on by the sheer weight of the work that they've got to do.
>
> (History teacher)

> I know what I should be doing but I can't do it because I've not got the time . . . so what I do is I do them because we have to and do them badly and find myself very, very frustrated with that.
>
> (Maths teacher)

Resources

The situation is exacerbated by an increasing lack of adequate resources within schools:

> [W]e're told that we can no longer go on courses, you know, the school's budget has been levelled down all the time, so inevitably you feel undermined and pressurized.
>
> (History teacher)

Many of the teachers interviewed commented on the fact that curricular decisions were increasingly being based upon the availability of resources. At the same time, many felt that classes had become more demanding and harder to motivate.

Insularity

It is generally recognized that teachers' professional development is enhanced through meaningful interchanges with colleagues within the security of collaborative culture (Hargreaves 1992). Working with others not only gives access to new ideas but also increases teachers' confidence in adopting innovative approaches to teaching. It is a prerequisite of the kind of reflective practice advocated by some of our key informants. Evidence from the interviews, however, suggests that not all teachers experience such collaboration, and indeed that it is increasingly constrained by current circumstances:

> [T]here doesn't seem to be a profession any more. We just seem to be so browbeaten, scurrying around, snatching those odd moments to say hello to our colleagues, then we're back into class.
>
> (Geography teacher)

Contact with LEA advisors or with teachers from other schools has decreased significantly, with all the associated dangers of insularity and parochialism (Bullough and Gitlin 1994):

> [Y]ou do miss out on the opportunity to talk to other teachers, particularly teachers from other schools and that . . . has to be recognized as something that is very important. I mean, we exist completely in isolation.
>
> (History teacher)

103

Accountability and inspection

Not only have growing demands for accountability increased teachers' workloads in terms of recording requirements, they were also seen by many as placing important constraints upon professional autonomy:

> You're much more accountable now . . . justifying yourself – you know what you've done, why you've given that child an A or a B or whatever, you know? Where before you could just say, 'Well that's my judgement of them', but now you've got to have evidence.
>
> (Technology/CDT teacher)

In particular the new national system of school and teacher inspection since 1993 by the Office for Standards in Education (OFSTED) was seen as a threat to the notion of teacher professionalism:

> I see OFSTED as an unnecessary evil, because they have created so much harm and damage. . . . This is an intimidating approach and . . . there can be tears on a regular basis when they're around, which is no good because you've got a demoralized workforce to begin with and if it's further eroded then it's not going to give confidence.
>
> (Geography teacher)

Assessment and League Tables

Another factor which was identified as constraining teachers' professional freedom was the system of Standard Assessment Tasks (SATs) which accompanied certain National Curriculum subjects and the publication of 'league tables' of schools' assessment and examination results. It was suggested that this was beginning to influence decisions about curriculum content in the non-compulsory areas:

> [T]here should be personal and social education in the curriculum but I know of some teachers now who are thinking, well that actually doesn't appear in the league tables, if they do more science or more maths, that actually appears in the league tables.
>
> (History and Geography teacher)

Managerialism

Several interviewees commented on the growth of the 'new managerialism' (Clarke et al. 1994) which was changing the traditional culture of many schools. The increasing power of school managers was generally seen as posing a clear threat to the professionalism of classroom teachers:

I think there's also a distinction beginning to emerge within teaching that perhaps people who occupy more senior posts in teaching can actually see themselves as professionals, whereas people who are actually doing the job see themselves very much as being driven by what's required of them, the whole thing is specified for them . . . the sort of professionalism that is coming in to the top end of the teaching profession now is that of manager more than educationalist.

(Geography teacher)

Most of the comments about increased managerial powers were negative, suggesting considerable frustration amongst classroom teachers and ultimately a loss of commitment:

We are held accountable . . . but we are not given the power to make those decisions. We are impotent as far as that's concerned. It's something that we have to push upstairs and the decision is made for us, and quite often it's the wrong decision that's made on our behalf.

(Technology/CDT teacher)

Conclusion

The initial implementation of the National Curriculum in England can be seen as having a broadly negative effect upon teacher professionalism, particularly in so far as its emphasis upon detailed curriculum prescription from the centre overtly challenged the established tradition of teacher autonomy within this domain. However, as has already been indicated, this tradition was a somewhat overplayed and only partial reflection of reality, although it did undoubtedly serve to influence and moderate some of the government reforms (McCulloch 1997). Moreover, it was clear even from the beginning that the impact of the National Curriculum upon secondary school teachers was not uniform: whilst many have felt disempowered, some were able to maintain a more proactive approach to the changes and even to use it as a framework for professional development.

As the Dearing review reduced the amount of prescription within the National Curriculum, and more particularly as teachers became increasingly familiar with its requirements and more confident in manipulating them, a growing proportion began to regard it in a somewhat more positive light. Some saw clear advantages of having a common curriculum across schools, whilst others felt that the National Curriculum structure offered them a degree of security within which they could work to develop their pedagogy. Others emphasized that pedagogy was the principal area within which teachers could exercise their professionalism. This point was made more strongly by some of the key informants:

> I think teachers and others caught up in the argument about curriculum being at the heart of professionalism have fundamentally misunderstood what is at the core of teachers' responsibility. And at the core of teachers' responsibility has always been the delivery, not the content of what is delivered. . . . I don't see the introduction of [the National Curriculum] as de-skilling teachers. I see it as providing a blueprint against which they can develop what is their true professionalism.
>
> (Former senior civil servant of the Education Department)

There may be some truth in this argument. Certainly teachers in France, who have traditionally been subject to strong curriculum prescription from the centre, do not appear to have been automatically deprofessionalized as a result. However, for English teachers to be able to develop their professionalism this way, a number of enabling factors need to be present. These include a degree of professional confidence, adequate time for reflection and planning, and a certain amount of collaboration/collegiality with colleagues (see Helsby 1996b for more detailed discussion of these elements). Unfortunately, the evidence above does not suggest that such enabling factors are likely to be present for most teachers. Professional confidence is too often diminished by top-down forms of accountability and inspection and by increasing managerialism, whilst the intensification of working life and resource constraints place severe limits upon the possibility of finding time for reflection and planning. Finally, collaboration with colleagues is limited by time constraints by the growing insularity of schools and departments and by the competitiveness engendered by published league tables of assessment and examination results in a market-oriented education system.

Underlying all of these are the fundamental contradictions that can be seen in recent government policies. Whilst there have been consistent pledges to improve the quality of education, these have been made against a background of continued reductions in public funding. There has been talk of the importance of developing teachers' skills and professionalism, but there has also been constant and virulent criticism of 'failing teachers' and attempts to impose pedagogic prescription. The Teacher Training Agency, which now has responsibility for overseeing continuing as well as initial teacher education, supports the notion of teacher research and reflective practice, and yet bases professional development upon a reductionist specification of competencies. The contradictions and mixed messages are well captured by one of our teacher interviewees:

> I feel on the one hand teachers are very much encouraged to go out and teach on their own to a class, to make decisions, think on their feet, and then the next minute it's 'You have to conform to all these

new rules and regulations and pieces of paper', and I think there's a bit of a paradox there.

(Maths teacher)

How this paradox will be resolved in the future remains uncertain. Whatever happens, teachers themselves will continue to respond in different ways to their work, and some will undoubtedly feel and behave more professionally than others. What does seem clear is that any attempt to enhance teacher professionalism across the board will require the provision of adequate resources to enable teachers to focus more clearly upon the core tasks of teaching and to facilitate high levels of classroom performance. Moreover, since teaching is an extremely complex activity which demands creativity and non-routine decision making, it will also require a greater degree of trust in the capacity of teachers to act as semi-autonomous professionals, rather than as compliant technicians in need of constant direction, monitoring and inspection. Sadly, the current obsession with public accountability and with careful economic management suggests that good teachers will struggle to maintain their professionalism despite, rather than because of, the occupational and policy context within which they work.

Note

1 Funded by the British Economic and Social Research Council, this study, exploring 'The Professional Culture of Teachers and the Secondary School Curriculum' (R)00234738), ran from January 1994 to June 1996. My colleagues in this project were Peter Knight, Gary McCulloch, Murray Saunders and Terry Warburton.

References

Acker, S. (1997) Primary School Teachers' Work: The Response to Educational Reform. In G. Helsby and G. McCulloch (eds), *Teachers and the National Curriculum*. London: Cassell.

Adelman, C. and Alexander, R. (1982) *The Self-Evaluating Institution: Practice and Principles in the Management of Educational Change*. London: Methuen.

Apple, M.W. (1986) *Teachers and Texts: A Political Economy of Class and Gender Relations in Education*. New York: Routledge.

Bowe, R., Ball, S.J. and Gold, A. (1992) *Reforming Education and Changing Schools*. London: Routledge.

Bullough, R.V. and Gitlin, A.D. (1994) Challenging Teacher Education as Training: Four Propositions. *Journal of Education for Teaching*, 20(1): 67–81.

Campbell, R.J. and Neill, S.R. (1994) *Secondary Teachers at Work*. London: Routledge.

Clark, J., Cochrane, A. and McLaughlin, E. (eds) (1994) *Managing Social Policy*. London: Sage.

Dearing, R. (1993) *The National Curriculum and Its Assessment: Final Report*. London: School Curriculum and Assessment Authority.

Eccles, D. (1960) *House of Commons Debate on the Crowther Report.* Hansard, House of Commons. Vol. 620, cols 51–2.

Goodson, I.F. (1994) *Studying Curriculum: Cases and Methods.* Buckingham: Open University Press.

Grace, G. (1987) Teachers and the State of Britain: A Changing Relationship. In M. Lawn and G. Grace (eds), *Teachers: The Culture and Politics of Work.* London: Falmer Press.

Hargreaves, A. (1992) Cultures of Teaching: A Focus for Change. In A. Hargreaves and M. Fullan (eds), *Understanding Teacher Development.* London: Cassell.

Helsby, G. (1995) Teachers' Construction of Professionalism in England in the 1990s. *Journal of Education for Teaching,* 21(3): 317–32.

—— (1996a) Defining and Developing Professionalism in English Secondary Schools. *Journal of Education for Teaching,* 22(2): 135–48.

—— (1996b) Constraint or Opportunity? Learning to Live with the National Curriculum. Paper presented at the annual conference of the British Educational Research Association 12 December. Lancaster University, UK.

Helsby, G. and McCulloch, G. (1997) Introductory chapter. In G. Helsby and G. McCulloch (eds), *Teachers and the National Curriculum.* London: Cassell.

Hoyle, E. (1974) Professionality, Professionalism and Control in Teaching. *London Educational Review,* 3: 13–19.

Jenkins, E. (1997) Legislating Philosophy and Practice: Teaching and Assessing Scientific Investigation. In G. Helsby and G. McCulloch (eds), *Teachers and the National Curriculum.* London: Cassell.

Kelly, A.V. (1990) *The National Curriculum: A Critical Review.* London: Paul Chapman Publishing.

Kogan, M. (1989) Accountability and Teacher Professionalism. In W. Carr (ed.), *Quality in Teaching.* London: Falmer Press.

Lawton, D. (1980) *The Politics of the School Curriculum.* London: Routledge & Keegan Paul.

—— (1993) Is There Coherence and Purpose in the National Curriculum? In C. Chitty and B. Simon (eds), *Education Answers Back: Critical Responses to Government Policy.* London: Lawrence & Wishart.

McCulloch, G. (1997) Teachers and the National Curriculum in England and Wales: Socio-Historical Frameworks. In G. Helsby and G. McCulloch (eds), *Teachers and the National Curriculum.* London: Cassell.

Ozga, J. and Lawn M. (1988) Interpreting the Labour Process of Teaching. *British Journal of Sociology of Education,* 9: 323–36.

Woods, P. (1994) Adaptation and Self-Determination in English Primary Schools. *Oxford Review of Education,* 20(4): 387–410.

Woods, P. and Jeffrey, B. (1997) Creative Teaching in the Primary National Curriculum. In G. Helsby and G. McCulloch (eds), *Teachers and the National Curriculum.* London: Cassell.

7 Stories of Change and Professional Development

The Costs of Commitment

Christopher Day

The purpose of this chapter is to contribute to knowledge of teacher professionalism and change through an analysis of stories in which fourteen teachers attending a part-time Master's degree course wrote about how their personal and professional lives had been affected by the 1988 Educational Reform Act and subsequent policy initiatives. Teachers' voices are an important and underrepresented part of the macro debate which focuses on whether educational reforms in England and elsewhere are resulting in the 'deprofessionalization' or 'technicization' of teachers' work or whether they result in 'reprofessionalization'. It is not the purpose of this chapter to revisit or analyse the reasons for the various initiatives that have caused the work of teachers in many countries to become increasingly intensified. Nor do I intend to catalogue the changes in their working conditions that have come about through negative media coverage, increased visibility and contractual and professional accountability, involving site-based management, teacher appraisal, external school inspection systems, school development plans and outcomes-orientated curricula. All these changes have been well documented. However, it is necessary, through this, simply to remind ourselves that teachers, like those in other more commercial occupations, now live in uncertain worlds where systemic change is outside their control and where traditions of respect (that teachers have the best interests of students at heart), trust (that teachers have the knowledge and skills to do a good job), autonomy (in which teachers alone are responsible and accountable for educational decision making at classroom and school level) and guaranteed employment for life (regardless of results) are no longer uncontested.

It was the best of times, it was the worst of times, it was the age of wisdom, it was the age of foolishness, it was the epoch of belief, it was the epoch of incredulity, it was the season of Light, it was the season of Darkness, it was the spring of hope, it was the winter of

> despair, we had everything before us, we had nothing before us, we
> were all going direct to Heaven, we were all going direct the other
> way . . .

This quotation from the opening of *A Tale of Two Cities*, written by Charles
Dickens almost 150 years ago, characterizes the world that many teachers in
schools, colleges and universities now inhabit in England and elsewhere. It is
a world that for some is bewildering in its complexity, for others challenging
in the paradoxes that it seems to offer, and for still others depressing in its
effects upon schools, teachers and teaching and learners and learning.
Since politicians began to link the state of the economy with standards in
schools, the walls of the so-called 'secret garden' of teaching, like those of
the city of Jericho so long ago, have come tumbling down. In the years
since then, there is little in education that has remained untouched by
governments in their attempts to raise the quality of educational achievement in order to boost their position in the world competitiveness league.
So far four outcomes are to be seen: more work for teachers, increased
stress levels, fewer attracted into teaching, and a rise in the numbers of
students who are alienated by schools.

The purpose of this chapter is to contribute to knowledge of teacher professionalism and change through an analysis of stories in which fourteen
teachers attending a part-time Master's degree course wrote about how
their personal and professional lives had been affected by the 1988 Educational Reform Act and subsequent policy initiatives. There is no suggestion
that the teachers' stories that form the empirical basis for this chapter are
typical, since this was an opportunity sample. Indeed, given the small proportion of the total population of teachers attending postgraduate degree-
awarding programmes in universities in England, these teachers may not
represent the range of perspectives in the profession as a whole (assuming
that a range exists). However, few stories of teachers from different phases
of education, and with different lengths of service, have yet been documented although, as recipients of imposed change, their voices need to be
heard. The intention is primarily to investigate their perceptions of the contexts in which they live their own development lives, and the interaction
between these. In asking them to write, no 'lead' was provided, other than
for them to tell their stories. The writing was not assessed and was shared
between members of the group as a professional development exercise negotiated within an agreed ethical framework of confidentiality. All names in
this chapter are, therefore, fictitious. My own interest in undertaking this
work stems from an ongoing, career-long concern with teachers' professional development and, within this, a particular interest in bridging perceived theory–practice tensions through the development and dissemination
of grounded data often referred to as 'teacher's voice'. Teachers' voices are
an important and under-represented part of the macro debate which focuses

on whether educational reforms in England and elsewhere are resulting in the 'deprofessionalization' or 'technicization' of teachers' work or whether they result in 'reprofessionalization'. I have quoted extensively partly in an attempt to balance the voices read and heard in this paper, and partly because the richness of the teachers' own texts illustrates their individual and collective stories far more effectively than abstract academic comment.

It is not the purpose of this chapter to revisit or analyse the reasons for the various initiatives that have caused the work of teachers in many countries to become increasingly intensified. Nor do I intend to catalogue the changes in their working conditions that have come about through negative media coverage, increased visibility and contractual and professional accountability, involving site-based management, teacher appraisal, external school inspection systems, school development plans and outcomes-orientated curricula. All these changes have been well documented. However, it is necessary, through this, simply to remind ourselves that teachers, like those in other more commercial occupations, now live in uncertain worlds where systemic change is outside their control and where traditions of respect (that teachers have the best interests of students at heart), trust (that teachers have the knowledge and skills to do a good job), autonomy (in which teachers alone are responsible and accountable for educational decision making at classroom and school level) and guaranteed employment for life (regardless of results) are no longer uncontested.

The theme of the forty-fifth Session of UNESCO's International Conference on Education in 1996 was the role of teachers in a changing world. Its member states cited evidence that structural adjustment (reform) policies in many countries had led to a significant deterioration in the working conditions of teachers.

> The deterioration produced, in its turn, a series of well-known phenomena: demoralization, abandonment of the profession, absenteeism, the search of other occupations and, finally, a negative impact on the quality of education offered.
>
> (Tedesco 1997: 24)

Teaching at its best is a passionate vocation (Fried 1995) and so-called professional practice in classrooms involves immense expenditure of personal emotional energy. Enthusiasm for teaching, learning and pupils is not something that can be sustained without personal commitment – to the pupils who, through force of circumstance or past experience, may not always be highly motivated, whose confidence needs to be encouraged and who need to be challenged and cared for; and to the moral purposes of education to work for the betterment of both the individual and society as a whole. Periods of externally imposed innovation and change often not only challenge existing practices of leadership and teaching in schools but also affect organizational and individual cultures. Less reported are the impacts upon the teacher as *person*. For example, it can be no coincidence that, in England and Wales, the incidence of non-age-related retirements from teaching has increased and the recruitment of new entrants has decreased during the decade following the introduction of a new national curriculum, standardized testing, external punitive inspections (so-called 'naming and shaming' of schools and teachers) and changed conditions of service. Whilst the rhetoric of reform recognizes that problems of teacher morale need to be addressed, there is little in practice that demonstrates an understanding of the essential link between the delivery of sustained high quality teaching and maintenance of personal health and commitment, or the need for continuing professional development of all kinds to take this into account.

Periods of reform may be characterized as 'extrinsic critical incidents' in which macro political changes impinge on and interact with classroom and personal lives. Given that reforms are intended to raise standards of teaching and learning it is important, then, to chart their effect on the teacher as person as well as professional in order to establish what has been called 'genealogy of context' (Goodson 1995: 96).

> It has taken time since the difficulties and pessimism of the 1970's and early 1980's for the perception to be widely shared that the success of educational reforms, no matter how well they are conceived in principle, will only be fortuitous if the teachers who are actually responsible are not made an explicit and pivotal plank of those reforms. An uncommitted and poorly motivated teaching body will have disastrous effects for even the best of intentions for change.
>
> (OECD 1989)

Stories of Change

The teachers were from primary (six) and secondary schools (eight). They were of different ages and levels of experience (from 24 years to 50 + years). All occupied positions of responsibility in their organizations, including a primary (elementary) school subject co-ordinator, a head of year, a head of department, a deputy headteacher and a headteacher (principal), and represented a range of subject interests and specialisms (e.g. music, science, PSE, humanities, PE, SEN). Of the fourteen, six were male and eight female (see Table 7.1).

Their stories were subject to a content analysis during which two broad common categories were identified: (1) *contextual* issues that related to the positive and negative environments in which they worked, and (2) *personal issues* in which teachers wrote about their own development. Whilst the

Table 7.1 Teacher sample

	Schools	Teachers	
		Male	Female
Secondary	8	4	4
Primary	6	2	4

two categories interacted, in the light of some of the critical (and depressing) discourse on the technicization of teaching, it was interesting to note that most of these teachers appeared to be confident in their abilities to engage in development and exercise changes within or despite what for some seemed to be difficult cultural and reform contexts. There is as yet little empirical data on the long-term effects of mandated reform upon the self-confidence and commitment so necessary to good teaching. This small-scale qualitative research indicates that they are affected – positively and negatively – by both their working contexts and their personal values and circumstances. Most had found 'room to manoeuvre', though for some this had been gained at great personal cost. The data will be presented along these two axes as a means of enabling the reader to get a feel of the critical perceptions of the teachers.

The Working Context: Living with Change

All the teachers highlighted in their stories various aspects of the government-initiated changes and their responses to them: the National Curriculum; OFSTED (external, privatized inspection); local management of schools (site-based management); the increase in parental choice so that parents can now choose not to allow their children to attend the school in their own local area; and conditions of service.

The National Curriculum: The Effect of Personal and Institutional Cultures

Although the subject-based National Curriculum in schools in England and Wales is reminiscent of the 'grammar school' curriculum of the early twentieth century, and so its relevance to today's students and tomorrow's workplace is questionable, no teacher was critical of it. However, it was clear that the management of its implementation and kinds of personal and institutional culture into which it was implanted significantly affected the strength of its impact upon teachers and teaching.

Christopher Day

Country of the Young

John, a primary school deputy headteacher who had begun his teaching career aged 25 in 1988, the year of its introduction, felt that now, ten years later, the changes had become almost completely absorbed into the culture. However, he had observed the struggles of older, more experienced colleagues:

> I found the National Curriculum no great hardship when set against my other problems. (What did it matter what Maths you were teaching them when they wouldn't listen anyway?) I took it in my stride and watched my older, more experienced colleagues, trying to unlearn all those years of accumulated wisdom.

Mismanagement of Change

In contrast, Tom, the head of a science department, was still deeply resentful of the unnecessary work to which he and other colleagues had been subjected as a result of 'Version 1' of the National Curriculum, only to have it undone by 'Version 2':

> When the new Orders were published, the department was faced with the huge task of analysing and rewriting schemes of work to fit in. There were 17 so-called attainment targets [ATs]. Each one was decreed by the government as being a 'topic'. Part of the task was to build in an assessment system. . . . In seemingly no time at all the government had taken advice that the format was unworkable. The 17 ATs were reduced to 4. Teachers were livid. They felt that all our work [in preparing for the seventeen ATs] had been to no avail.

Dave, a secondary teacher with similar years of experience, wrote of a particular approach to the implementation of the National Curriculum in which discussions had centred upon considerations of extra workload rather than the effects of the new policy upon the value of education received by the children. He described how the inadequate attention paid to teachers' views had led to feelings of disaffection:

> Most discussions [of issues related to the National Curriculum] were based on considerations of the extra workload . . . rather than on whether the new policies would affect the value of education received by the children. The reaction of the senior managers was to allow the discussion to continue along these self-destructive lines, allowing everyone to have their say and to air their pet grievance and then bring the meeting to a close. Then after a few days the teachers would be

informed of changes of policy which bore no relation to the direction of the discussions in the meetings. The net result was that teachers felt that the meetings were a waste of time, since their ideas were not acted upon. . . . National Curriculum changes were adopted, but within a disgruntled, disaffected group of teachers. . . . Management must take account not only of the substance of innovations but also the feelings or 'culture' involved in the change.

School Leadership: Getting it Right or Losing Commitment

Alison (a primary school home–liaison teacher) and Jenny (a primary school deputy headteacher), both teachers with more than twenty years' experience, described how the leadership support of the headteachers affected teachers. In one school, Jenny wrote:

> The National Curriculum was well received and staff flowered in subject specialisms, went on outside courses and were pleased with the non-contact days. . . . Pressure on teachers from outside influences may have been an infringement on their professionalism.

However, two schools in which Alison was home–school liaison teacher reacted very differently:

> Staff from one school attended courses, fed back information, developed a rolling programme of topics to ensure coverage of the National Curriculum. The other school did nothing.

Balancing Demands with Entitlements: Dilemmas of Judgement

Mary, a secondary school head of special needs, wrote of the serious dilemmas that had been posed, particularly for teachers of pupils with special educational needs:

> The onset of the National Curriculum faced some staff with serious dilemmas about balancing the demands of the curriculum and the issue of entitlement. This was particularly difficult in the case of pupils with special needs. . . . Many staff have felt forced to move away from mixed ability teaching and into a more rigidly 'set' system. . . . The latest policy changes certainly specify clearly what our responsibilities are towards all pupils with special educational need. Unfortunately they stop a long way short of providing real answers as to how some . . . pupils' diverse needs can be actually met in practice.

Financial Delegation

Three teachers wrote critically of the effects of local financial management on schools. In Sue's primary school and Valerie's, Christine's and Matthew's secondary schools, teachers had been made redundant as resources declined.

Matthew wrote of the unexpected consequences for his school which had 'opted out' of the financial control of the local education authority on the expectation of increased finances:

> The expected financial bonanza failed to materialise and colleagues felt the perils of isolation as redundancies were announced without the benefit of an LEA [local education authority] safety net in terms of enhanced early retirements or the possibility of redeployment. The handling of the redundancies had a profound effect on me. . . . The outcome for me and many others was a bitterness and complete mistrust of the managers involved as they failed to appreciate long-serving colleagues as anything other than numbers on the payroll.

Christine, in her sixth year of teaching, wrote:

> My experiences at the school have not always been happy ones. There was one occasion when I felt a significant lack of self-confidence and motivation. In my second year of teaching it was announced that due to [financial] cutbacks there would have to be redundancies. One area [of the curriculum] nominated to lose staff was mine. It was a period of great worry and unpleasantness as unions were involved and interviews took place. My enthusiasm for the job was very low at this stage, but the head and other staff were very supportive. . . . It took a while to regain my interest for school and teaching after that experience.

Parental Choice: Voting with Your Feet

The legislation in England and Wales which allows parents to choose which school to send their children to is founded upon the notion that choice will itself be available and a determinant of quality and that, in the end, good schools will grow and poor schools close down. It is, in other words, underpinned by a market-led, customer-as-purchaser-of-service ideology. Valerie, in the third year of her teaching career, provided evidence of the effects of this in her school:

> A lot of parents vote with their feet and due to a negative image of the area and school, are reluctant to send their children to us. It is

unfortunate, also, that a lot of Asian parents in the area do not send their children to us and appeal to change the allocation because they see the school to be in 'white territory'. This is further compounded by the negative publicity the area receives from the local press, which lowers the self-esteem of our students, many of whom are from poor socio-economic backgrounds.

The New Teaching Contract: A Loss of Good Will

The curriculum reforms of 1988 were accompanied by reforms to teachers' conditions of service. Mary, a secondary school teacher of fifteen years' experience, wrote of a loss of good will which had resulted:

> With the advent of the 1,265 working hours and industrial action, the good will of many previously highly committed teachers was severely damaged and in some cases lost completely. In a school with a previously excellent record of extra curricular activities much good practice was lost and has never really been recovered. This was compounded by the loss of 5 days' holiday for INSET. However valuable and relevant the activities which were planned for these days, many staff came reluctantly to them. . . . In fact there seemed to be little long term planning evident and very little account taken of individual staff development needs.

External Inspection: Cynicism Remains

This perceived demonstration by government of a loss of trust in teachers was compounded by the introduction of a privatized external national school inspection system (OFSTED: the Office for Standards in Education) which issues public judgements upon the quality of schools and provides a graded assessment of teaching for each teacher observed. Several teachers wrote of the consequences, none positively.

A State of Stress

> The whole OFSTED inspection experience . . . left the staff in a state of Post-Inspection Stress and prompted many to question their futures. A number of staff left at the end of the year for a variety of reasons.
>
> (Val)

Getting it Right: An Unconscious Neglect

> [All] the teachers agreed that prior to the inspection [one or two weeks before] they had unconsciously neglected their class lessons in

preparation for OFSTED. This was so that they would get it perfectly right for the inspection week.

(Samantha, a primary teacher of four years' experience)

Nothing We Didn't Already Know

The inspection report said nothing we didn't already know. We knew that the school had come a long way, but still had far to go. . . . The school seemed to be lagging behind many other schools and was playing 'catch up' at a rapid pace.

(Samantha)

Professional Judgement Undermined

Julia, an infant school teacher with almost eight years' experience, wrote of the way in which the actions of a headteacher determined to 'get it right' had undermined and undervalued the teachers' confidence in their abilities:

All aspects of our job came under even closer scrutiny from the head. Her close perusal of OFSTED documents, the Inspectors' criteria and OFSTED school reports is constantly brought to our attention – usually in a negative light. The head has high expectations and clearly wants the school to do well. By interpreting and then implementing certain criteria to the extreme she undermines the professional judgement of teachers. An environment has been created where staff follow certain policies and strategies, not because they believe they are the best policy, but because the head says so.

She pointed to a perceived continuation of restrictions upon the capacity of teachers to use their discretionary judgement to take on-the-spot decisions based upon their view of the best learning interests of their pupils:

The introduction of the National Curriculum has meant that all planning had to be related to [national] Attainment Targets. . . . Teachers became very conscious about what they were allowed to teach . . . they also found that they had to relate their planning to the school policies and schemes . . . teachers now had to plan together. Collaborative planning and teaching was to become the norm. As a result, there has been a greater sharing of expertise and knowledge. Teachers have encouraged each other in their reflective evaluation of teaching skills and strategies. This has ultimately enhanced the quality of teaching and children's learning. . . . A negative effect . . . is that much of the spontaneity that has always been a characteristic of infant teaching has disappeared. The sound judgement and common sense has had to give way to paper bureaucracy. The teacher who realises that an impromptu lesson is necessary to reinforce a specific concept no longer has the freedom to insert something into their weekly plan. This is an example of how accountability has not improved the quality of education, but has actually marginalised and restricted it.

The Personal Context: Learning from Change

Although the changes in their working contexts at national and local levels were the subject of continuing criticism by these teachers, the ways in which they had responded to their perceived adversities constitute an interesting commentary both on their courage and perseverance and on their success in maintaining, asserting or extending their ability to take decisions, albeit within parameters determined more by external forces than had previously been the case. In one case organizational support had been a key factor, but in all others it was the personal–professional qualities that had made the difference. The teachers' substantive self has been described as the core part of their professional lives through which they actively seek to interpret and restructure their work through maintaining self-esteem, job motivation and satisfaction in students' progress (Kelchtermans 1993; Nelson 1993). Such teachers are likely to go beyond the call of duty, are passionate about their calling (Hansen 1995) and, regardless of circumstance, are always looking for room to manoeuvre in order to provide the best learning opportunities for students. They, 'know how they want to teach and are not going to be dictated to. They consequently strongly resist the notion that they are being deprofessionalised' (Woods 1994: 402).

The Supportive Culture of a Learning Organization

Christine had spent the eight years of her teaching career in the same school and attributed her happiness and progress to this:

> My school has a culture which is supportive and encourages staff at all levels of their career to develop professionally. Everyone is given the opportunity to initiate new ideas, courses and activities. It has a dedicated staff and an ambitious and forward-thinking head and governing body who manage change calmly without flustering staff into panic. Motivation and enthusiasm are high, a fact which has been commented upon by parents, visitors, governors and inspectors. There are high expectations of everyone connected with the school from pupils to ancillary staff, to teachers, to management. Due to the support and open culture of the school I feel I have gained in confidence personally and professionally.

Lifelong Learners

Samantha confessed to liking and enjoying change, despite the seemingly adverse conditions.

> As I was still very new to the job, I had loads of energy and was very willing to get involved in things. I wanted the others to be as energetic as I was and pull together. . . . I became one of the founder members of the Parent Staff Association. I began to channel my time and energy into getting parents involved in their children's education and so built up a good rapport with them. I also came into close contact with the local business community and instigated sponsorship to get new book bags for the school. . . . I was willing to try new things and experience as much as possible. . . . I like and enjoy change. Virtually my whole life has been a very steep learning curve.

Change of role

Alison (primary), Valerie (secondary) and John (primary) had all been promoted during the period and so, despite the difficulties and frustrations, had gained positively. Alison had been promoted to acting deputy head of a school for one term, and one of her major roles was to monitor the progress of a newly qualified teacher who had been through a legal dispute (industrial tribunal) with the headteacher:

> On reflection, I learnt more about the management of people in that one term than in the whole of my career. It was a difficult, challenging and often stressful time. As a result I feel that no situation I may encounter in the future could ever prove to be quite so negative.

Valerie had been promoted to head of year but had found it hard to maintain her commitment to teaching in a situation in which she was also developing a staff leadership role:

> Becoming head of year was a critical moment in my career at my present school. . . . I was at a stage in my career where I was ready for professional advancement and also, there was a feeling of commitment on my part to the school and a desire to be involved in the progress of its Action Plan. When I first embarked upon the job, I was very motivated and enthusiastic. I had an opportunity to try out new ideas and methods for carrying out my duties. I was able to give advice with some semblance of authority. I found that I had lots of energy at first to try out my ideas. However, as the term progressed my energy levels decreased. Certain parts of the job were not as satisfying as others.

Change of Location: Change of Culture

Ben, Dave and Tom had all changed secondary schools during the period, and Ron, a primary teacher, had taken 'time out' of teaching. All had benefited as a result of their new experiences.

Making a Difference

> I found my new school to have an entirely different culture. A new headteacher had been in post for less than two years. . . . The school was truly fragmented. The Department was fragmented. There was no Development Plan, no school aims were apparent, or shared with me, and I received no induction or support. . . . There was no consistent teaching, record keeping, assessment practices or sharing. . . . No one in the department had been on a course for years. . . . Departmental meetings, of which no minutes were kept, focused on resources and examinations . . . At the time I was determined to make a difference. I organised departmental meetings to discuss teaching styles; redistribution and control of resources; a reorganised scheme of work reflecting the National Curriculum, consistent assessment. . . . I was used to working in departments where everyone played their part. Here everything proposed was met with no comment. This soon undermined my confidence and caused self-doubt. . . . I persevered. . . . It was as if I represented the threat of change that had been ignored . . . with the arrival of [other] Head of Departments, the school culture began to alter. There was no direction, however, no leadership or whole-school plan or philosophy. There was no cross-fertilization between departments.
>
> (Ben)

Learning Through Experience

Dave wrote of himself as a 'beachcomber' who, when he took a lateral move as head of science to a school in a different part of the community, found himself in bad weather surrounded by alligators:

> I found myself under intense scrutiny from colleagues, senior managers and educationally aware parents. It was raining on my beach. The National Curriculum swept over my beach as a tornado of uncertainty, unwieldy bureaucracy and sophisticated management demands. My canoe sank and I was suddenly surrounded by snapping alligators more ferocious than I could have imagined. . . . I had and was given a bad time. . . . I felt inadequate in the face of demands from colleagues for solutions to the problems presented by the demands of the National

Curriculum, and distressed that an education system I had loyally served could have spawned such a patently unworkable monster. In short, I lost confidence in those responsible for the system.

Dave's response to the alienation caused by an imposed, 'unworkable' curriculum was to learn:

I learnt things about my own leadership, the political agenda and about the qualities of those around me – their huge capacity for loyalty and disloyalty, their own insecurities and tremendous strengths. The most important thing I learnt was the fundamental imperative for integrity to underpin my work. I also learnt that alligators need treating with respect. I have become a strong advocate of teamwork and I have developed an interest in process improvement. This is a significant shift from my old canoe-paddling days. . . . My National Curriculum experiences forced me to evaluate and change my working experiences for the better.'

Tom had learnt how not to manage a department by observing the failure of a colleague who had tried to get his way 'by a mixture of arrogance and insensitivity'. In September 1994, he had taken a lateral move to a job in a different part of the country for personal reasons:

The department needed a complete organisation. . . . I was able to reflect on what was right in [the previous job] and take a fast-track approach . . . the old was unceremoniously discarded and the new (already proven) was installed. . . . We work as a team and while I had the early vision, the rest of the department contributes to the . . . fine-tuning necessary to keep ahead of the game.

Joining Collaborative Inquiry Networks

Opening Windows

Mary and Trish worked in a school that had become part of a series of university-inspired school improvement networks. For both, this had been the most significant learning experience in their careers:

The effects of being involved with this project have been far reaching. On a personal level it has given me much greater confidence to tackle working with colleagues, since although there is a high personal commitment and ownership, no one works without support. It has regenerated my feelings about school since it has opened up many opportunities to try different roles. Despite the amount of hard work and persistence which has been required it has released previously untapped energy levels since the process provides ongoing input. . . . The effect . . . on my teaching is to have heightened my awareness of what I had previously treated as a fairly automatic process. I have had to question why I have done things in a particular way and have been given ideas and strategies to try alternatives. It has created a climate of inquiry and a feeling that solutions can be found through collaboration. The overall effect on my professional life has been to open some windows. I have been prepared to take on greater challenges within school with increased confidence.

(Mary)

Time to Reflect

I was able to form relationships with a group of people which were very different from those in working situations. The network gave us time to reflect upon the issues pertinent to our school. We meet with other schools also as part of this higher education supported project. It keeps people on track, provides time for analysis . . . has been highly influential in bringing about change in our school – a bit like stopping an oil tanker in full flow!! Therefore I have seen a totally new way of working towards shared goals. The short term expense has enabled long term economy and success.

(Trish)

New Directions: Personal Choice, Professional Gain

After nine years teaching in primary schools in England, Ron had decided to teach abroad, 'looking for a challenge', returning twelve years later. He described the way in which the 'congenial atmosphere' in a school in which he was teaching abroad had deteriorated as a result of the poor management of an externally imposed innovation. This, and a 'mid-life transition' desire to return to his roots had caused him to take a complete break from teaching:

I felt I needed a complete change from what I was doing because I had been teaching for 20 years . . . perhaps everybody needs a short break to renew their batteries and give them the impetus to carry on with renewed vigour . . . for me and my teaching career it was the 'rest' that was the best 'change' I had ever had. . . . I felt completely re-vitalised and ready to face any new teaching challenge which could be thrown at me.

Only one of the fourteen teachers seemed to have become permanently disenchanted with the effects of the educational reforms and their management. Matthew, a co-ordinator of personal and social education (PSE), had been fundamentally affected by decisions that had been taken as a consequence of the National Curriculum:

> I took the loss of time for PSE personally as I had been . . . notably zealous in trying to maintain its prestige and influence. I became very disappointed and disillusioned and withdrew from the committees – curriculum, equal opportunities, personnel and staff development – on which I served . . . and local management of schools has changed my perception of management in education and correspondingly altered my career path. . . . I had hoped to become a deputy head but the role in the 1990s seems to be less based on education and leadership than on finance, management and marketing. I am ill at ease with the language of efficiency, accountability and value for money. . . . In all, the effects of educational change over the last eight years have been greatly to diminish my enthusiasm and motivation . . . teachers' loss of autonomy through curriculum prescription and the teacher's contract have led in my view to a numbing and unrewarding daily experience where broader educational issues are submerged under a morass of administrivia, pointless meetings and safe, mundane and routine teaching.

Yet even here, there had been a positive outcome. Matthew's withdrawal from involvement in a number of school activities had been followed by a change in his personal circumstances and had, paradoxically, freed time and energy which he had used to register for postgraduate study. He described this as an opportunity to 'stand back and look critically':

> The birth of a first child caused a profound change and established an enjoyable fixed reality which compensated for the fragmented chaos of school. This, together with the loss of my managerial role and withdrawal from committee involvement enabled me to undertake a post-graduate course which I am enjoying immensely as an opportunity to stand back and look critically, if not at times a little smugly, at the day-to-day dislocation that school seems to have become. . . . The virtual loss of PSE in the school has, I think, affected my self-confidence but I feel that I still have something to offer education and have not yet reached the stage of complete cynicism and burnout. My energy levels remain high . . . and I still have confidence in the future.

(Matthew)

Conclusion: The Costs of Commitment

The data demonstrates that notwithstanding considerations of the changing balance of power, deteriorating conditions of service, ideologically driven economic market imperatives and increased intensification and complexity of their working lives, teachers have retained commitment to the moral purposes of teaching. There was no suggestion from any but one of the fourteen teachers that teaching had become 'just a job', though the temptations to move towards that position had been legion. A number of personal and situational factors (e.g. the quality of school leadership and school culture, their disposition to change) had contributed to this. However, there had also been considerable personal cost.

Reform creates an imperative for those who are to survive successfully to engage in an increased rate of personal adaptation and professional development – the steep learning curve or accelerated uncomfortable learning often associated with imposed change. For these fourteen teachers it is clear that the years since 1988 had been turbulent, stressful, challenging and persistently intensive. For those who began their careers post-1988, the new curriculum itself was relatively unproblematic, though in common with the others they wrote of the 'busyness' and 'stress' of their work, the importance to its success of maintaining their own energy levels and commitment and of having sustained support in this through the quality of leadership in school and the broader educational community. Many of the teachers had been involved in significant personal and professional changes themselves during the period. Not all these changes may be attributed to the reform context. Indeed, the teachers were in different phases of their professional and career development and so might have been expected to respond in different ways to these, to personal contexts and to those created by the external reforms. However, given their enrolment for a Master's degree, it may be assumed reasonably that they were highly motivated. It is all the more worrying, then, that even among this group there were a significant number whose commitment had been tested and who had re-evaluated the personal and professional balance of their work and lives.

Shirley Grundy presents a challenge to the school to play its part in teacher development. She argues that it is 'not sufficient for education systems to "pass the buck" for educational improvement to teachers and construe the school as simply the location of teachers' work', and that 'just as professional autonomy needs to be reconceptualised in terms of the professional community of the school, so also we need to understand that responsibility for the quality of education is also a matter for the school, not just for the individual teacher' (Grundy 1994: 25). Yet many teachers work within 'non or miseducative environments' (Cole 1997: 13). Ardra Cole, a Canadian academic investigating impediments to reflective practice (a necessary part of teacher development) through analysis of the current conditions in schools, argues that 'the conditions under which teachers work have generated feelings and psychological states that militate against reflective practice and professional growth' (ibid.: 7). By 'conditions under which teachers work' she is referring to 'external structures imposed by schools and school systems, the profession, government and the public at large'. By 'psychological states', she refers to perceptions that interfere with 'optimum productivity and practice' (ibid.: 13).

Jersild's (1995) work in exploring the effects of anxiety, fear, loneliness, helplessness, meaning and meaninglessness and hostility in relation to understanding self is particularly relevant here. He argues that these emotions are prevalent in teachers' lives in schools and classrooms and must, therefore, be addressed as part of teachers' professional education. Cole asserts that 'until these issues are addressed teachers will not be able freely and meaningfully to engage in the kind of reflective practice and professional development that brings meaning to their own lives and the lives of their students' (Cole 1997: 14). Writing in the context of recent systemic reforms in the province of Ontario, Canada, in which 'perhaps the most persistent and poignant [example] of teacher helplessness is within the context of formalised professional development' (ibid.: 16), Cole describes most initiatives as being still, for the most part, conceptualised, designed and delivered for teachers, not *by* them (ibid.: 17).

For those involved in promoting change, then, the lessons are clear:

1 *Respect* those who are implementing it by listening to them and demonstrating an understanding that extra time, energy and support are needed.
2 *Ensure* that those who are implementing change are well led.
3 *Recognize* that change is a complex process which involves the head and the heart, the personal and the professional.
4 *Provide* sustained critical support for teachers' autonomy through an external inspection system which is collaborative rather than confrontational.

For those who write about the political, economic and social policy conditions of schooling, the lessons are:

1 *Beware* of making judgements about teacher technicization which underestimate or do not take account of the power of local, institutional and personal professional contexts. The teachers in this study had clearly adapted and, during the transition from initiation to internalization of change, had reasserted their autonomy.
2 *Undertake* more studies which integrate the theoretical debate with practitioner perspectives.

What seemed to have happened during the period of change which had been the focus of these teachers' stories was that control over various aspects of their working lives had been ruthlessly relocated through legislation, but that almost all had found room to manoeuvre and thus to reassert autonomy, albeit within newly defined parameters. They had been proactive in taking action which protected their 'substantive selves' (Nias 1989) and their core moral purposes had survived. Far from being 'technicized' these teachers' resolve had, if anything, been strengthened by the negative experiences of externally imposed change. Initial compliance to external control had been a temporary, if painful, phenomenon for most. Self-motivated ambition to do the best for the school, pupils and their own development had prevailed. They had continued to behave as professionals, 'displaying . . . degress of dedication and commitment . . . accepting the open-ended nature of the task involved . . . [with the] . . . maximum effort to "do the best you possibly can" and a constant quest for improved performance' (Helsby et al. 1997: 9–10).

Others have noted the apparently contradictory consequences of imposed change upon teachers Ball (1994, 1996). In work with primary schools, Peter Woods (1994) and Troman (1996) found that teachers have regained control of decisions about their teaching by first complying and then strategically redefining the work so that it remained underpinned by their own values and identity *as professionals with moral purposes*. Helsby, too, found that secondary school teachers have been able to find spaces in which to 'manipulate the requirements in accordance with their own professional judgements' (Helsby 1996).

These findings do not suggest a denial of the great personal and professional costs to teachers of the manner with which reforms have been implemented. Nor do they support an argument that the reforms themselves have been worthwhile. That their management has been poor is manifested by the many older professionals who have been alienated or unable to cope. Together, however, they do challenge those who argue that teachers' work is becoming proleterianized and that teachers have 'misrecognized' the increasing intensification of teaching as a sign of increased professionalism (Apple 1989). Either/or notions of professionalization and proletarianization as consequences of reform are too simplistic. Whilst they may occur simultaneously (Hargreaves and Goodson 1996) it seems likely that they represent options rather than imperatives, and that they may be represented better as forces. The continuing dynamic tension between them is part of establishing, maintaining and developing the role of the person and the professional in the purposes and acts of teaching. Much more empirical work needs to be carried out on what it means to be a professional over a career span. This small-scale inquiry reveals the need for analyses of change to take into account complex strands of history, situation, personhood, professionality and disposition to change which contribute to defining what being a professional means and the costs of sustaining professionalism over a career.

References

Apple, M. (1989) Critical Introduction: Ideology and the State in Educational Policy. In R. Dale (ed.), *The State and Educational Policy*. Buckingham: Open University Press.

Ball, S.J. (1994) *Education Reform: A Critical and Post-Structural Approach*. Buckingham: Open University Press.

—— (1996) Good School/Bad School. Paper presented at British Educational Research Association Annual Conference. September, Lancaster, UK.

Cole, A. (1997) Impediments to Reflective Practice: Toward a New Agenda for Research on Teaching. *Teachers and Teaching: Theory and Practice*, 3(1): 7–27.

Fried, R. (1995) *The Passionate Teacher*. Boston: Beacon Press.

Goodson, I.F. (1995) The Story So Far: Personal Knowledge and the Political. In J. Hatch and R. Wisniewski (eds), *Life History and Narrative*. London: Falmer Press.

Grundy, S. (1994) Action Research at the School Level: Possibilities and Problems. *Educational Action Research Journal*, 2(1): 23–38.

Hansen, D.T. (1995) *The Call to Teach*. New York: Teachers College Press.

Hargreaves, A. and Goodson, I. (1996) Teachers' Professional Lives: Aspirations and Actualities. In I.F. Goodson and A. Hargreaves (eds), *Teachers' Professional Lives*. London: Falmer Press.

Helsby, G. (1996) Defining and Developing Professionalism in English Secondary Schools. *Journal of Education for Teaching*, 22(2): 135–148.

Helsby, G., Knight, P., McCulloch, G., Saunders, M. and Warburton, T. (1997) Professionalism in Crisis. A Report to Participants on the Professional Cultures of Teaching Project, January. Lancaster University, UK.

Jersild, A.T. (1995) *When Teachers Face Themselves*. New York: Teachers College Press.

Kelchtermans, G. (1993) Teachers and their Career Story: A Biographical Perspective. In C. Day, J. Calderhead and P. Denicolo (eds), *Research on Teacher Thinking: Understanding Professional Development*. London: Falmer Press.

Nelson, M.H. (1993) Teachers' Stories: An Analysis of the Themes. In C. Day, J. Calderhead and P. Denicolo (eds), *Research on Teacher Thinking: Understanding Professional Development*. London: Falmer Press.

Nias, J. (1989) *Primary Teachers Talking: A Study of Teaching as Work*. London: Routledge.

OECD (1989) The Conditions of Teaching: General Report. Restricted Draft, Paris. Quoted in Sikes P.J. (1992) Imposed Change and the Experienced Teacher. In M. Fullan and A. Hargreaves (eds), *Teacher Development and Educational Change*. London: Falmer Press.

Tedesco, J.C. (1997) Enhancing the Role of Teachers. In C. Day, D. van Veen and S. Wong-Kooi (eds), *Teachers and Teaching: International Perspectives on School Reform and Teacher Education*. Leuven and Apeldoorn: Garant.

Troman, G. (1996) The Rise of The New Professionals? The Restructuring of Primary Teachers' Work and Professionalism. *British Journal of Sociology of Education*, 17(4): 473–87.

Woods, P. (1994) Adaptation and Self-Determination in English Primary Schools. *Oxford Review of Education*, 20(4): 387–410.

8 The New Work Order and Australian Schools

Shirley Grundy and Stewart Bonser

The phenomenon of school restructuring has been as much a feature of Australian school education systems as it has been elsewhere. This chapter explores some of the characteristics of what Gee et al. (1996) have called the 'new work order' in relation to school restructuring in Australian schools. To Gee et al. the 'new work order' is one in which work organization and work practices encapsulate values of common and agreed goals that are shared and worked towards by a workforce that is empowered to control its own work practices. Thus shared decision making, participatory management and teamwork are features of the 'restructured' work environment. Drawing upon a research project investigating the phenomenon of school restructuring in Australia, the chapter examines the extent to which this 'new work order' is evident in Australian school organization and practice. This national study sought to identify the extent to which certain work practices, particularly participatory decision making practices, are evident in a range of randomly selected school sites. The chapter does not, however, assume that evidence of 'the new work order' in Australian schools should be uniformly applauded. Rather, it identifies some of the complexities and contradictions inherent in the discourse of school restructuring in Australia.

The term 'the new work order' is used by Gee et al. (1996) to characterize work during this time of perpetual 'change'. The 'new work order', the authors argue, is the form of work associated with 'fast capitalism'. Four features of the discourse of 'fast capitalism' are highlighted. These are:

- increased dependence upon science and technology in processes of production, distribution, consumption and change.
- a pronounced trend away from material production and toward information-processing activities.

- devolved and decentralised work organization with flattened management and decision-making structures.
- globalization and increased competitiveness of markets.

(Ibid.: 36–41)

While each of these has relevance to the restructuring of work practices in general and to the restructuring of educational practices in particular, it is the third feature that is specifically addressed in this paper. The authors expand upon this aspect as follows:

> [T]he new capitalism reflects dramatic changes from the old capitalism in the ways in which production and other economic processes are organised. This . . . is the feature most heavily stressed in the fast capitalist storyline. Hierarchy is reduced among employees; borders are eased between businesses (producers and suppliers) and business units. Decentralization, networking, flexibility, cooperation, collaboration, customization, getting close to the customer, and small, flexible and local organisation – these indeed are major motifs of the fast capitalist literature.

(Ibid.: 39)

Gee et al. provide case study examples of the application of these 'new work order' features from within a US context. These 'new work order' features are also evident in a study of exemplary business practices within Western Australia (Harris and Volet 1997). In both studies the principles of collaborative, team-based organization and implementation are identified as central.

It should be noted, however, that the seemingly democratic language of the 'new work order' masks a number of the contradictory elements in this discourse. As Rizvi and Lingard (1996) note:

> The vocabulary that accompanies [these organisational changes] is suggestive of a commitment to democracy. Words like 'collaboration', 'participation', 'devolution' and 'empowerment' are used to indicate a partnership between the managers and the workers. . . . Workers are no longer viewed as motivated simply by monetary rewards but also by their proactive commitment to organisational goals. . . . [H]owever, the language of the new work order is inherently contradictory because, while it preaches organisational democracy and empowerment, it does not really permit workers to question some of the fundamental assumptions underlying the new business of capitalism.

(Ibid.: viii, ix)

Over the last decade the language of fast capitalist business organization has been applied to schools, which have been exhorted to comply with this 'new work order' (see Davies 1996; Donero 1996; Hough and Paine 1997, as examples of this advocacy literature). Shulman (1989), has remarked upon the way in which the culture of the new capitalism has been applied to schools, particularly in relation to the reduction of hierarchy:

> Schools are asked to become like our best corporations, employing modern methods of management to decentralise authority, to make important decisions. . . . Leadership is not monopolised by administrators, but is shared with teachers.
>
> (Ibid.; cited in Hargreaves 1994: 187)

Restructuring, not only of the organization and management of the school, but also of teachers' work practices, has been evident in Australian schooling systems, as it has been elsewhere (Beare 1995; Gamage et al. 1996; Sharpe 1996; Grundy and Bonser 1997a, 1997b). Key 'restructuring' policy documents that consistently espouse the application of 'new work order' features to the schooling sector have been produced by all Australian state schooling systems. The following examples illustrate this point.

In the Western Australian Education Department's indicators of school performance there is a defined preference for collaborative work practices. For example, a school in which leadership is 'undeveloped' is one where: 'Staff work independently in isolation.' A school in which leadership is 'establishing' is one where 'Team-work is evident in the school, with staff involved in management roles' and a school that is 'achieving' in the area of leadership is one where 'A collaborative approach exists in the school, with staff involved in leadership and management roles' (Education Department of Western Australia 1997: 17).

The Queensland model of school-based management, titled *Leading Schools* (Education Queensland 1997), expresses a commitment to decentralization and a customer focus in the delivery of educational services. The model:

> provides opportunities for schools and their communities to take control over the direction of the school; to ensure the delivery of quality educational service to students; and to respond to community needs.
>
> (Ibid.: 4)

Whilst the 'new work order' is conceptually present in systemic policy documents this does not necessarily mean that the practices of Australian schools have been reconstructed to reflect these features. Indeed, it is the complexity and contradictory nature of the 'underlife' of policy translation that is of interest and is explored here. Ball (1994:19) reminds us of the

need to research the 'underlife' of the relationship between teacher, context and policy. This underlife is one in which the relationship between policy, context and teachers' work is seen as non-linear. That is, context and work are not simply determined by and adjusted to policy.

In this chapter we report the results of a study designed to investigate the application of 'new work order' principles to and by those working in Australian schools. The research question that we specifically addressed was: 'How is the restructuring discourse of new capitalism which is embedded in the policy documents of Australian schooling systems manifesting itself in the organization, management and work practices of school practitioners?' While the larger study encompassed policy analysis, a survey, interviews and case studies, it is the results of the questionnaire survey that provide the data for the analysis reported here.

Methodology

The questionnaire survey was designed to gain insights into the perceptions of school staff across Australia on a range of issues relating to school restructuring.

Of the total of 234 respondents the frequency of distribution across school types was 60 percent primary school and 40 percent secondary school personnel. Respondents by role included 98 Teachers, 68 Key Teachers/Heads of Department, 56 Principals/Assistant Principals and 12 'other' school staff. The data analysis reported here excluded the category of 'other'. The overall rate of return, when calculated as a percentage of the minimum expectation, was 90 percent ['n' received/'n' expected].

Data from the questionnaire were collated quantitatively (using the SPSS computer program) through percentage of responses for all respondents across the response categories of:

- not at all;
- to some extent;
- to a considerable extent;
- to a great extent;

and by the three role types of:

- Teacher;
- Key Teacher (including Heads of Department and Advanced Skills Teachers);
- Principal (including Assistant or Deputy Principals).

Although the motif of 'the new work order' is employed as a theoretical construct for this chapter, and while it is demonstrated that the aspects of

this ideology are present in the policy documents of Australian school systems, a broader set of categories, which relate more specifically to the items addressed on the questionnaire, is used to discuss the results of the study.

Issues relating to reduced hierarchy, decentralization and small, flexible local organization are discussed under the heading 'Devolution and School Development Planning'. Issues relating to cooperation and collaboration are taken up under the heading 'Decision Making, Organizational and Work Practices'. Issues relating to the easing of borders, networking, and flexibility are taken up under the heading: 'Easing of Borders: The School, the System and the Community'.

Devolution and School Development Planning (SDP)

One of the manifestations of decentralization and flexible local organization and management within schooling in Australia is to be found in the School Development Plan (also called the School Improvement Plan, School Charter, Partnership Plan, Strategic Plan). This is the process by which the school sets priorities and prepares plans and strategies for addressing the priorities and for monitoring their achievements.

Through a range of questions relating to School Development Planning the investigation noted, amongst other things, whether local school staff had the opportunity to participate in planning and management.

Participation in School Development Planning

The initial question asked: 'To what extent can you contribute to the development of school policy and purpose?' The majority of respondents perceived they could contribute to the development of school policy and purpose 'to a considerable/great' extent. The nature of this overall response indicates that School Development Planning is well established as a mechanism that devolves to schools the capacity to influence school policy and purpose.

A complementary question explored the perceptions of school staff regarding responsibility for school planning. School staff were asked: 'To what extent do you feel responsible for school planning?' Respondents felt they had a lesser responsibility for school planning. The levels of participation in developing school policy and purpose were perceived to be greater than the responsibility they felt towards school planning.

These and other data indicate that the aspects of the 'new work order' identified with decentralization and small local organization are generally in place within Australian schools. Data from other items showed that setting school priorities and purposes which respond to the dual demands

of students and systemic policies appear to be in place 'to a considerable/ great extent', although participatory financial planning and management seems to be more of an emerging feature rather than an established feature across the surveyed schools.

Devolving To and Within Schools

If we distinguish between devolving participation in developing policies and purposes *to* schools and *within* schools, a different picture emerges. When these data were analysed according to responses from Teachers, Key Teachers and 'Principals' statistically significant differences in the response patterns emerged for a number of items.

Analysis by Role

Analysis of these data by role type indicated that all Principal respondents and approximately two-thirds of the Teacher/Key Teacher cohort perceived they could contribute to the development of school policy and purpose 'to a considerable/great extent'.

Whereas 95 percent of Principals believed they could contribute to the development of school policy and purpose 'to a great extent' only 32 percent of Key Teachers and 26 percent of Teachers perceived that to be the case. Moreover, a significantly larger proportion of Key Teachers than general Teachers perceived that they could contribute to the development of school policy and purpose 'to a considerable/great extent'.

A Culture of Hierarchical Decision Making

The distinction made above is important in that it suggests a separation of power within schools where development of school policy is involved. These data show significantly more Key Teachers than classroom Teachers and more Principals than either Key Teachers or classroom Teachers as being optimistic about their opportunities to contribute to policy, as well as expecting that they *will be* involved in the development of such policy. The notion that promotional status contributes to the maintenance of a hierarchical structure in the decision-making processes within schools is supported by these and by subsequent data.

The significant differences in responses across these groups appear indicative of devolvement *to* rather than *within* schools. This hierarchical response pattern was also reflected in responses to the question 'To what extent do you feel responsible for school planning?'

Differences in responses to this item were even more marked between Teachers and Principals. The cohort of Principals perceived a significantly greater responsibility for school planning than did Teachers. Although opportunities to contribute to the development of school policy and purpose were perceived by Teachers to be available to varying extents they did not feel responsible for influencing school planning to the same extent as other school staff. When these data are analysed across the role groupings of Principal, Key Teacher and Teacher, it is the Teacher cohort that perceives itself as being less responsible for influencing school planning.

This evidence suggests that participation in school planning may still be considered as largely optional for Teachers. That is, while Teachers by and large have the opportunity to contribute to the development of school policy and purpose, they do not feel particularly responsible for influencing school planning, whereas Principals reported feeling highly responsible.

In relation to the desire for increased control of financial resources, similar response differences between role categories were also apparent. When participants were asked the question 'To what extent would it be desirable to have more control of the financial resources available?' the Principal cohort responded in a significantly different way from other role groups. Almost 25 percent of Principals indicated they would like a great deal more control over financial resources, but around 35 percent indicated that they desired more control 'not at all'.

The responses to this question and others suggests that, while there is some desire for greater devolution and control of financial resources at the school level, there was no great clamour for increased control. Respondents did not exhibit a high degree of confidence that the school would benefit from a further devolution of centrally controlled funds.

Reduced Hierarchy?

It was noted previously that 'reduced hierarchy' is a feature of the 'new work order'. While this study produced evidence of the other aspects of restructured capitalist management practices such as devolution and local organization, the analysis of responses by group does not support an assertion of reduced hierarchy. On the contrary, whilst there is evidence of devolution *to* schools, there is not the same degree of evidence of devolution *within* schools. Principal responses indicated that this group is able to contribute more to school policy and purposes, feels a greater level of responsibility for school planning and desires greater degrees of control of the financial resources of the school.

The patterns of response in these data may be taken as being indicative of a culture of managerial devolution of responsibility for planning rather than a broadly democratic involvement by staff. The influence of role demarcation upon the responsibility for school planning could be seen as limiting for the development of collaborative and consultative practices.

Decision Making, Organizational and Work Practices

It is arguable that deciding 'what the work will be' (in terms of setting priorities and planning) is only one dimension of the 'new work order'. Maybe of more significance is the way in which 'the work gets done'. It is, therefore, to the decision-making processes and the organizational and work practices of schools that this discussion now turns.

Collaboration and Teamwork

Gee et al. (1996) identify networking, cooperation and collaboration as features of the 'new work order'. Within schools, teachers have traditionally prized their autonomy, but more recently, in line with the orthodoxies of the 'new work order', there has been strong advocacy of the need for school staff to become more collaborative and to engage in team-based practices.

In considering the desires and expectations of school staff in relation to these issues, the following questions were asked: 'To what extent should the decision-making process in the school be consultative?' and 'To what extent should the decision-making process in the school reflect collaborative approaches to decision making?'

Responses to these questions provided evidence of a strong professional commitment to collegiality. Over 90 percent of respondents advocated that decision making should be consultative and reflect collaborative approaches. In contrast to the data reported earlier, in which response patterns between Principals and Teachers were differential, it is of interest to note that response patterns for Teachers and Principals were in this case similar.

The dimensions of collaboration and teamwork were explored through a variety of questions, including, 'To what extent:

- is there group participation in school decision making?
- are you able to collaborate with other teachers in decision making?
- do you perceive that your decisions about teaching and learning involve colleagues?
- are you able to engage in teamwork?
- do you perceive that teamwork is being used to share ideas in the development of student learning?'

Although the majority of respondents perceived that these work practices were occurring to a 'considerable/great' extent it is also clear that the aspiration towards consultative and collaborative decision making as yet outstrips the experience. This is illustrated in Figure 8.1, which presents a graphic comparison of responses for several of these key questions.

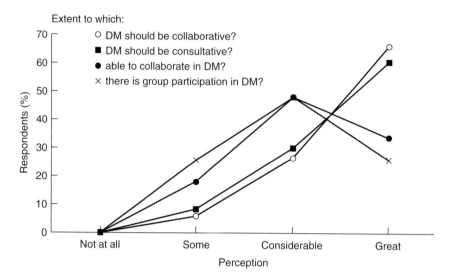

Figure 8.1 Collaboration and teamwork in decision making

Further analysis of these data indicates a difference in response patterns between the respondent groups, with the Principals' cohort returning significantly more optimistic responses than Teachers with regard to participation in decision making, decisions involving colleagues and the ability to engage in teamwork.

Individual Work Practices

While a strong commitment to collegiality and collaborative work practices was evident in the responses, a continuing assertion of the rights for teachers to make decisions in isolation from colleagues was also expressed. The following items addressed this issue:

'To what extent should a teacher working in isolation from colleagues have the discretion to make decisions about:

- learning outcomes?
- how the learning program is managed and presented to the students?
- the application of technological resources?'

Responses across all of these questions reflected a continuing commitment by teachers and school administrative personnel to individual discretionary decision making.

Almost half the respondents believed that teachers should have discretion to make individual decisions about learning outcomes. Respondents were even stronger in their advocacy of individual discretion in relation to making decisions in isolation about the management and presentation of the learning program. Sixty-five percent of all respondents felt 'to a considerable/great extent' that a teacher working in isolation from col-leagues *should* have the discretion to make decisions about how the learning program is managed and presented to the students, including discretionary decision making in the application of technological resources.

Teachers expressed stronger views in favour of individual autonomy than did Principals. In each case (whether it be making decisions about learning outcomes, or about the management and presentation of the learning program, or the application of technological resources) the majority of Teachers believed that this discretion should lie to a 'considerable/great' extent with the individual Teacher in isolation from colleagues. In each case, the majority of Principals believed that isolated decision making should occur only 'to some extent'.

It appears, therefore, that on the one hand there is a continuing assertion of individual autonomy and on the other an acknowledgment of collabora-tive decision making and collaborative work practices.

Figure 8.2 provides a contrasting depiction of the overall response data for those items where participants were asked 'To what extent should the decision-making process in the school:

- be consultative?
- reflect collaborative approaches to decision making?'

and

'To what extent should a teacher working in isolation from colleagues have the discretion to make decisions about:

- learning outcomes?
- how the learning program is managed and presented to the students?'

There are two possibly contradictory discourses at work here. The dis-course of 'individual autonomy' is placed alongside that of 'collegiality', although it should be noted that there is a stronger preference expressed for consultative and collaborative decision making than for individual, isolated decision making.

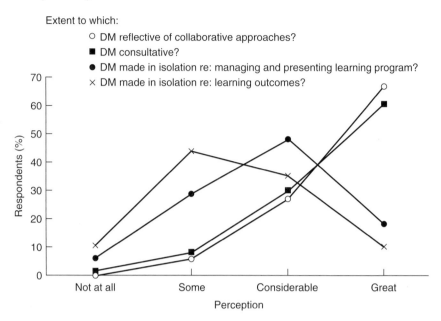

Extent to which:
○ DM reflective of collaborative approaches?
■ DM consultative?
● DM made in isolation re: managing and presenting learning program?
× DM made in isolation re: learning outcomes?

Figure 8.2 Individual autonomy in decision making

Easing of Borders: The School, The System and the Community

One of the features of Gee et al.'s 'storyline of fast capitalism' (1996: 39) is the easing of borders 'between businesses (producers and suppliers) and business units'. In education one would expect such easing of borders to manifest itself in flexible interactions between the centralized educational bureaucracy and the school, and between the school and its community. The notion of 'flexible borders' between schools and their environments (be they the political, administrative or social environments) has long been part of the storyline of educational administration through the application of the metaphor of 'open systems' to schools (Hough and Paine 1997; Lakomski and Evers 1995).

Although this research project did not specifically set out to investigate schools as open systems, a number of items provide data about the extent to which schools might be interpreted as organizations with flexible borders.

Questionnaire respondents regarded the border between the centralized system and themselves as being permeable in terms of the influence of central guidelines upon school priorities. While there may be inputs from central authorities regarding the setting of priorities, those from other sectors of the education establishment (including personnel from other levels of the system and academics) and from the community were not seen as affecting decisions about the actual work of teaching and learning. Participants were asked, 'To what extent do decisions about teaching and learning involve:

- colleagues?
- regional office personnel?
- consultants?
- personnel from central office?
- the general community?
- academics?'

Overall respondents felt that there was very little involvement in decisions about teaching and learning by anyone outside the school. Colleagues are clearly perceived as having much greater influence upon decisions about teaching and learning made by school staff than any of the other groups. The general community is perceived to be involved more than any other outside group and this most probably occurs through parents and citizens organizations, school councils and general parental interaction with teachers in relation to their children. Consultants are perceived as more likely to be involved in the decisions made by school staff than are regional office personnel, central office personnel or university academics. The picture that emerges here is of the 'self-contained' school. If these data are taken as an index of school autonomy, then schools look highly autonomous. However, these data do not provide a strong indicator of the school as an 'open system' with flexible borders in relation to the influence of others upon the learning program.

Not only do these data question the idea of schools as 'open systems', they also raise questions about whether schools are utilizing as many opportunities as they might to further their development. Fullan (1993) describes a study by Baker et al. (1993) of forty-eight school districts in Illinois which suggested that 'internal development and external involvement must go together'. In the cited study 'thirteen of the forty-eight districts were classified as engaged in systematic improvement on a sustained basis'. The researchers noted:

It is no accident that all thirteen successful districts were found to be users of external support from regional educational service centres and several other sources. By contrast in all eight cases that had no external support, there was no evidence of school improvement. Time and again we find that seeking external support and training is a sign of vitality. It is the organizations that act self-sufficient, that are going nowhere.

(Fullan, 1993: 86)

In contrast, these data from a sample of Australian schools indicate very little use of 'regional educational service centres' or, for that matter, any other support groups. If the seeking of outside assistance is taken as an index of improvement, it does not appear to have strong applicability within these schools.

Another area in which it could be expected that flexible borders might be noticeable is in the area of reporting and dissemination of information about the outcomes of the school's core business, that is, student learning. A series of questions was asked about the reporting of information regarding student learning outcomes, 'To what extent is information about student performance reported as learning outcomes to:

- parents?
- the school governing body?
- the local community?
- the director general (CEO; Secretary of Education, etc.)?
- the minister in parliament?'

Schools have traditionally reported on student achievement to parents. It is, therefore, no surprise that respondents perceived this to be occurring to a 'considerable/great' extent. Reporting to other stakeholders, however, was perceived to be occurring only 'to some extent', if at all. The picture that emerges is one of schools being strongly inwardly accountable (to themselves and their parents). Upward accountability (to systems) is not strong but neither is outward accountability to the community (Corbett 1996, has described upward, downward, outward and inward accountability in public sector organizations). These data again challenge the concept of schools as 'open systems' in terms of their accountability.

The responses to yet another set of items further question whether the feature of 'flexible boundaries' can be identified as applying to these schools. Participants were asked, 'To what extent do you think the purposes of your school are understood by:

- the students?
- the parents?
- the community?
- the staff?'

Participants perceived that 'staff' understood the purposes of the school to a significantly greater extent than did the community, students and parents.

None of the items discussed above (whether it be in relation to involvement of others in decisions about teaching and learning, reporting student learning outcomes or understanding the purposes of the school) provides evidence of strong links between school staff and other stakeholders. These data, in turn, do not add weight to a perception of 'flexible boundaries' between the various sectors and interest groups within the 'business' of schooling, calling into question the common designation of schools as 'open systems'. Rather, the picture that emerges is of a semi-autonomous educational unit, confident in its understandings of purpose, practice and product, drawing strength and inspiration from amongst its own ranks (i.e. the staff) in relation to its core business of teaching and learning.

Conclusion

Using the form of questioning incorporated into the survey, it is appropriate to ask, 'To what extent is the so-called "new work order" identifiable in this sample of Australian schools?' The general answer to this question appears to be 'to some extent'.

The above analysis indicates that some features of this work order are established in schools. This applies particularly to decentralized, local organization and to collaborative, cooperative work practices. School Development Planning, in which members of a school staff participate in identifying appropriate priorities and deciding upon strategies to achieve their goals, appears well established and generally well understood.

Perhaps the most striking feature of this 'new work order' that was identified through this research was the commitment to cooperative, collaborative and participative decision making in schools. While there was still present a commitment to individual, professional autonomy in the responses to the questionnaire, the stronger commitment was to collaborative work practices and participative decision making.

To say that these aspects of the 'new work order' are identifiable in Australian schools through this study, is not, however, necessarily to applaud such developments. The rhetoric of School Development Planning can be understood in two ways. On the one hand, power to plan might be devolved hierarchically to those with management responsibilities in the school. Involvement of members of the school in planning will then be a structural or managerial matter. That is, involvement will be determined by administrative principles such as efficiency (i.e. getting the best job done for the least expenditure of resources), structural capacity (i.e. having knowledge or information relevant to the planning task) or role (i.e. responsibility for the task being built into job description or expectations).

On the other hand, power to plan might be devolved democratically to the members of the school community. Involvement of members of the school community in planning might be a matter of democratic rights. That is, involvement in school planning might be seen as a matter of having control of one's work, being able to contribute diverse views and perspectives and to draw upon the knowledge of those most closely familiar

Shirley Grundy and Stewart Bonser

with the needs and expectations of the community whom the school serves. Hargreaves (1994: 192–6) calls these two forms of participatory practice in schools 'contrived collegiality' and 'collaborative cultures'. Contrived collegiality is 'administratively regulated . . . compulsory . . . implementation-oriented . . . [and] predictable', while collaborative cultures are 'spontaneous . . . voluntary . . . development-oriented . . . unpredictable'.

While our study indicated a uniform desire for collegial, collaborative decision making, the differences between the responses of Teachers and Principals in their reports of the extent of participation raises a question about both the extent and the quality of the participation.

Some other aspects of the so-called 'new work order' were not reflected in these data, however. This applied specifically to 'reduced hierarchy', 'flexible borders' and 'customer focus'. Yet it needs to be asked to what extent these are possible within a system that appears to decentralize, but then put in place line management structures and accountability procedures that further entrench hierarchy and override local autonomy and accountability. An important question arises concerning whether these business principles can be applied to and by schools in public sector systems of education.

More important, however, is the question of whether it is desirable to apply this discourse to schools. Gee et al.'s (1996) analysis of the 'new work order' within industry serves to highlight the complexity and contradictions of the application of the discourse of participatory commitment and devolved decision making within business. The application of these principles to public education is equally, if not more, problematic.

While there are opportunities for improved practice and for furthering human wellbeing through the application of some of these principles, it is also the case that there are dangers lurking in the wholesale application of the 'new work order' to education. It is, perhaps, fortunate after all that these features are being ambiguously taken up by those working within our schools.

Acknowledgements

This research was funded by a grant from the Australian Research Council. Full details of the results of the survey reported in this paper are available in Grundy and Bonser (1997c).

References

Baker, P., Curtis, D. and Berensen, W. (1993) Collaborative Opportunities to Build Better Schools. Illinois, Illinois Association for Supervision and Curriculum Development. In M. Fullan (ed.), *Change Forces. Probing the Depths of Educational Reform.* London: Falmer Press.

Ball, S. (1994) *Education Reform: A Critical and Post-structural Approach.* Buckingham: Open University Press.

Beare, H. (1995) New Patterns for Managing Schools and School Systems. In C. Evers and G. Lakomski (eds), *Educational Administration: An Australian Perspective.* Sydney: Allen & Unwin.

Corbett, D. (1996) *Australian Public Sector Management* (2nd edition). Sydney: Allen & Unwin.

Davies, B. (1996) Re-engineering School Leadership. *International Journal of Educational Management*, 10(2): 11–16.

Donero, G. (1996) School Restructuring American Style: Flattening the Decision-Making Pyramid. *International Journal of Educational Management*, 10(2): 43–7.

Education Department of Western Australia (1997) *School Performance: A Framework for Improving and Reporting.* Perth: Education Department of Western Australia.

Education Queensland (1997) *Leading Schools: Partnerships for Excellence. The Pilot Program 1997.* Brisbane: Education Queensland.

Fullan, M. (1993) *Change Forces: Probing the Depths of Educational Reform.* London: Falmer Press.

Gamage, D., Sipple, P. and Partridge, P. (1996) Research on School-Based Management in Victoria. *Journal of Educational Administration*, 34(1): 24–40.

Gee, J., Hull, G. and Lankshear, C. (1996) *The New Work Order: Behind the Language of the New Capitalism.* Sydney: Allen & Unwin.

Grundy, S. and Bonser, S. (1997a) National Initiatives and Primary Schooling. In L. Logan and J. Sachs (eds), *Meeting the Challenges of Primary Schooling.* Sydney: Routledge.

—— (1997b) In Whose Interests? Competing Discourses in the Policy and Practice of School Restructuring. *Australian Journal of Education*, 41(2): 150–68.

— (1997c) Restructuring Australia's Schools: Changes to Organisational, Management and Pedagogical Practices. Technical report. Murdoch University, Perth, Western Australia.

Hargreaves, A. (1994) *Changing Teachers, Changing Times: Teachers' Work and Culture in the Postmodern Age.* London: Cassell.

Harris, L. and Volet, S. (1997) *Developing a Learning Culture in the Workplace.* Perth, Western Australia: Murdoch University.

Hough, M. and Paine, J. (1997) *Creating Quality Learning Communities.* Melbourne: Macmillan.

Lakomski, G. and Evers, C. (1995) Theory in Educational Administration. In C. Evers, and J. Chapman (eds), *Educational Administration: An Australian Perspective.* Sydney: Allen & Unwin.

Rizvi, F. and Lingard, B. (1996) Foreword. In J. Gee, G. Hull and C. Lankshear, *The New Work Order: Behind the Language of the New Capitalism.* Sydney: Allen & Unwin.

Sharpe, F. (1996) Towards a Research Paradigm on Devolution. *Journal of Educational Administration*, 34(1): 4–23.

Shulman, L. (1989) Teaching Alone, Learning Together: Needed Agendas for the New Reforms. A paper prepared for the conference on Restructuring Schooling for Quality Education. Trinity University, San Antonio, TX.

9   Working-Time Blues

How Norwegian Teachers Experience Restructuring in Education

Kirsti Klette

Teachers' work has been the subject of restructuring over the past decades. In Norway, recent changes in education in terms of deregulation and steering by means of goals have placed new professional demands on teachers. These changes have implications for teachers' work. Results of preliminary analysis of teachers' perceptions and experience of a new policy on work-time agreement suggest that rather than being a change instrument to enhance teacher professionalism, the policy has in fact become an instrument of control which could transform Norwegian teachers into mere obedient and loyal civil servants.

Teachers' work has been the subject of major restructuring efforts over the past decades. Several scholars like Ball (1990), Lawn (1991), Hargreaves (1994) and Klette (1996) have shown how the working life of teachers has undergone profound and dramatic changes. Curriculum demands are broadening and the impact and pressure of reform are intensifying. Teachers are being urged to widen their role as professionals and take more responsibility beyond the classroom door as curriculum planners and leaders, as mentors for new teachers, and as collaborative planners and decision makers with colleagues.

The focus of this study is the recent change in the work-time schedule and work-time agreement for teachers in Norway. This is a preliminary analysis and will need further interpretations and a more thorough theoretical framework. It is an initial attempt to see how these data could be interpreted, understood and used in search of a broader understanding of teachers' work. For instance, should these findings be seen as just another story of teachers' resistance to educational change? Or could they be seen as part of teachers' professional and competent evaluation of their own working conditions? Furthermore, will these data illustrate the ongoing discussion about powerlessness and proletarianization in teaching?

Throughout the 1980s, in Norway, as in other European and western countries, the traditional welfare state model came under greater scrutiny and was subject to enough pressure to cause a pendulum shift in educational policy. There was a swing from a highly centralized model to a decentralized one in terms of regulation, economic planning, steering and decision making. The pendulum shift in policy took several forms. For example, in 1984, a new decentralized and locally based school improvement model was introduced in Norway. This was followed in 1986 by a new income system for local authorities, implying bulk funding and leaving fiscal responsibilities and priorities to the municipal level. In 1987, a new national curriculum that emphasized local knowledge and competence was introduced.

Educational restructuring continued in the early 1990s with a new curriculum reform in response to the criticism of the highly decentralized and locally oriented system of the 1980s. A new model based on steering by goals was implemented in 1991. In 1994, the upper secondary school curriculum integrated vocational and academic training. In 1997, ten-year compulsory comprehensive schooling, starting from age 6 instead of 7, was put in place. Moreover, specific and detailed knowledge areas were identified, with detailed specifications of what pupils were supposed to learn at each and every level. Last but not least, a new working-time regulation between the state and the teachers was negotiated in 1993, ushering in new professional demands on teachers. This new policy is the focus of this study.

The purpose of this study is to explore how these forms of restructuring in teaching affect teachers' work. Specifically, how do the new working conditions like 'imposed collaboration' and new rules of school attendance affect teachers' professional school life? How will these changes affect teachers' work?

Vehicles of Professionalization

One of the main vehicles of school improvement pursued by the government was setting aside time for teacher-collaborative work. This move towards collaboration in work settings was supported by both the state and the educational research community. Indeed, past educational studies demonstrated the benefits in, and the need of, collaboration in teachers' work (see Stenhouse 1975; Lieberman 1988; Little 1992; Hopkins 1994). Not only was it seen as a means for a better and more flexible use of resources, but collaborative planning and the building of professional communities was also viewed as an important part of the teacher-professionalization process. It has been suggested that collaboration is a vital part in the development of professional competence, and since professional competence is at the heart of the professionalization process, many restructuring efforts carried this theme. Lindblad (1993) and Carlgren (1994) extend the argument by asserting that professional competence can play an important part in developing schools into a more decentralized and deregulated educational system.

Despite these convincing reasons, other studies, such as those of Densmore (1987) point out that pushing school improvement through the theme of professionalism could be problematic. In her study, she notes how teachers themselves voluntarily enhanced their working responsibilities because they misrecognized them as symbols of increased professionalism, when perhaps they might have been an instrument that legitimized and reinforced proletarianization through intensification of teachers' work (ibid.). Whilst professionalization might be a compelling ideology of change, educational historians such as Labaree (1992) also point out that teacher professionalization could have been more a part of the agenda of teacher training institutions and educational research communities than of teachers themselves. Hargreaves (1994) and Lindblad (1995) had warned against 'imposed professionalism', or what I have characterized elsewhere as 'arranged professionalism' (Klette 1994, 1997). The focus of analysis in this study is related to how teachers see and experience these new forms of 'imposed professionalism'.

Imposed Professionalism: Proletarianization or Mobilization?

The question of whether teachers can be defined as professionals, semi-professionals or white collar workers has been a subject of numerous studies.[1] Traditionally, the conditions that distinguish a profession from other occupations are: a specialized knowledge base and shared standards of practice (technical culture); commitment to meeting client needs (a service ethic); strong identity with the profession (professional commitment); and collegial as opposed to bureaucratic control over practice and profession (professional autonomy) (Etzioni 1969; Larson 1977; Talbert and McLaughlin 1993). These features of professionalism are derived from aspects of the working performance and serve as an example of a trait theory approach within the literature of professionalism (see Ginsburg 1987).

But professionalism could also describe a certain group's struggle for professional status over a certain historical period. As such, professionalization is described as a historical process rather than in terms of the qualities or nature of work (Johnson 1972; Torgersen 1972; Larson 1977; Fauske 1986).[2] Ozga and Lawn (1988) argue along the same line:

> Our argument would be that the term 'professionalism' in its use by teachers and central and local state changes, and includes variations of

meaning and contains elements remarkably similar to the aims and actions of other workers.

(Ibid.: 82)

The Danish educator Finn Horn (1993) points to a similar distinction, focusing on the internally defined criteria of professionalism versus those that are externally defined. He analyses the ongoing discussion in Denmark and shows how professionalism can be interpreted in different ways. On one hand, the pursuit of professionalism could be a vehicle for gaining status or restoring teachers' loss of authority, but on the other hand it could also be a reaction to neo-liberal and neo-conservative pressure and the campaign to undermine teachers' theoretical knowledge.

The concepts of externally defined versus internally defined criteria of teacher professionalism might be useful as a theoretical framework for interpreting the new work-time agreement for Norwegian teachers. The agreement can serve as an example of imposed and externally defined criteria of professionalism. Using this as a framework of investigation, several questions could be asked. What is the relationship between imposed professionalism and experienced professionalism? How is this related to an internally defined criteria of professionalism? Could, for instance, externally defined criteria of professionalism be transformed into internally defined professionalism or would this *de facto* imply just another aspect of pro-letarianization and intensification of teachers' work? Will changes in teachers' work-time illustrate what Densmore (1987) and other scholars have characterized as a way of legitimating the intensification and prole-tarianization of teachers' work? Or could externally defined professionalism be used as part of the mobilization of teachers to gain control over their own professional standards? Would mobilization then serve as an alterna-tive to proletarianization in the current debate on teachers' professionalism?

The Study

The research project was initiated by the Norwegian Teachers' Union, the biggest teacher union in Norway.[3] The aim of the project was to gain infor-mation about how members viewed, experienced and made use of the new work-time agreement. The study aimed to gain information:

- on organizational structures and the amounts of time used for the different parts of the work-time agreement;
- and different viewpoints regarding teachers' experiences of the 190 hours agreement;
- on how different types of schools and municipalities made use of and organized the work-time agreement;

- on the differences between groups of teachers in terms of their opinions and experiences.

A random selection of teachers in primary and lower secondary schools and of members of the Norwegian Teachers' Union were surveyed. In all about 5,000 teachers were sent a questionnaire. There was a 49 per cent response, representing 2,400 teachers.

Results of the Study

Organizational Forms and Experiences

In large schools the new work-time agreement was mainly used for two purposes: arranging joint staff meetings and the organization of meetings in smaller, more specific groups. Most teachers reported several types of meetings for professional debate and discussion within the whole staff. These mainly took the form of information meetings (90 per cent positive response), staff meetings (90 per cent positive response) and joint staff or consultation meetings (93 per cent positive response). A fairly large proportion of the 190 hours agreement was tied to whole-staff meetings. A joint staff or consultation meeting was combined with information meetings to form one category labelled 'joint staff meetings'. Information meetings were meetings which dealt with the dissemination of information, relaying messages and the like. Joint staff or consultation meetings dealt with pedagogical, planning and general school improvement issues. Most meetings were conducted after the end of school teaching time. Taken together, a pattern of use of time emerged: see Table 9.1.

Translated into hours used for meetings, primary schools used 2 hours and 38 minutes per week while the secondary schools used 2 hours and 15 minutes per week for joint staff meetings. In sum, the average time used by schools was 2 hours and 27 minutes.

Table 9.1 Distribution of total time used for joint staff meetings per week

Minutes	%
0–60	8
61–90	15
91–120	23
121–180	34
181–240	14
241+	6

Evaluation of Joint Staff Meetings

Apart from mapping different types of meetings, teachers were also asked to evaluate the value of these meetings on the scale of 1 (unsatisfactory) to 4 (very satisfactory). The replies varied according to the type of meeting.

Information meetings rated highest on the evaluation scale. Seventy per cent of respondents rated meetings satisfactory (3) or very satisfactory (4). Staff meetings were rated the lowest; 42 per cent of the teachers gave staff meetings a rating of unsatisfactory (1) and fairly unsatisfactory (2).

Focus of Joint Staff Meetings

To obtain a picture of the focus of joint staff meetings, teachers were asked to what degree certain discussions occurred and to give their view of how valuable these discussions were to teachers' work. Predetermined categories such as discussions about tuition, students, the need for cooperation, and accumulated tasks were rated on a scale of 1 to 4: see Table 9.2.

Responses showed that discussion of issues related to students was largely the focus of most joint staff meetings and was also perceived as valuable use of meeting time. Only 42 per cent of teachers perceived these meetings as useful for addressing their needs for cooperation, and only 38 per cent saw the value of joint staff meetings in completing accumulated tasks.

With regard to the question directed at teachers' views on the effect of the 190 hours agreement on the running of the school, the response was equally divided between its positive and not so positive effect. Fifty-six per cent of the respondents perceived the agreement to have had a small/fairly small degree of positive effect, while 44 per cent thought that the framework had had a large/fairly large degree of positive effect on daily school life.

Small Differentiated Group Meetings

Teachers reported a wide range of meetings in differentiated groups. The most usual were team-work meetings, class-staff meetings, subject-matter meetings, project/school meetings and meetings with external specialists.

Table 9.2 Degree of focus of joint staff meetings

Focus of discussion	Small (1) to fairly small (2) degree (%)	Large (3) to fairly large (4) degree (%)
Tuition	62	38
Students	55	45
Need for cooperation	58	42
Accumulated tasks	62	38

Seventy-four per cent of the respondents acknowledged that team-work forums had been established at their school. Class-staff meetings were also well established, although they occurred more in lower secondary schools than in primary schools. Fifty-one per cent of teachers reported class-staff meetings as an established type of meeting at their school. Project/school improvement meetings were more usual, both in primary (67 per cent) and lower secondary schools (62 per cent).

Duration of Differentiated Meetings

Teachers reported that on average, they spent 70 minutes per week on team-work meetings. Response from primary and secondary school teachers showed that they used an average of 39 minutes per week for class-staff meetings. Subject-matter meetings occurred more in lower secondary schools than in primary schools. On average, secondary schools spent 34 minutes per week, while primary schools spent an average of 44 minutes. Project/school improvement meetings were prevalent in both primary and secondary schools. Primary teachers reported spending an average of 62 minutes per week on these meetings, while secondary school teachers spent 32 minutes per week.

Taking all the differentiated meetings together, primary teachers spent an average of 2 hours and 38 minutes on their meetings, while lower secondary school teachers spent 2 hours and 26 minutes.

Focus of Differentiated Meetings

The same predetermined categories of focus of meetings used in joint staff meetings were utilized to determine teachers' experience and view of time spent in differentiated meetings. Results of the study suggest that teachers were more satisfied with meetings in differentiated groups than with joint staff meetings.

Eighty per cent of respondents stated that differentiated meetings were to a large/fairly large degree concerned with tuition. Discussion of issues pertaining to students was viewed even more positively (88 per cent). Answers were split equally between those stating that meetings were concerned with the need for cooperation to a small/fairly small degree and those stating that it was to a large/fairly large degree, while time used for accumulated tasks was perceived to be valuable to a large/fairly large degree by 45 per cent of our respondents. Likewise, answers to the questions about the effect of the 190 hours agreement disclosed that 43 per cent of teachers thought that it had had a positive effect. These responses more closely corresponded with the results of the evaluation of joint staff meetings.

Experiences with the Work-Time Agreement

The organization and practice of the work-time agreement was charted through several questions focused on how the change affected teachers' working environment and time schedule, the degree of adult cooperation they experienced and their professional development. Data presented here are related to responses regarding the last two categories.

A large percentage of teachers agreed that the work-time agreement had led to a greater degree of cooperation amongst the adults in the school. Seventy-seven per cent answered affirmatively, while only 23 per cent stated that it had not led to increased cooperation. Of the affirmative responses, 69 per cent were males and 81 per cent were females.

The perception of its impact on professional development was markedly different. Here 61 per cent answered that practice of the agreement had not led to professional development. There was also some differences of opinion between male and female respondents. Fifty-seven per cent of the female teachers gave a negative evaluation, as compared to 69 per cent of the males. This is interesting because, generally, women had been less negative in their responses.

The agreement's impact on personal professional development was even more negative: 66 per cent stated that it had not led to individual development. Although male and female respondents had different opinions, the women were generally slightly less negative than the men.

Over half (54 per cent) gave a positive response to the question about whether the agreement had led to the attainment of the school's principal aims, while 46 per cent said that the agreement had not led to increased target attainment.

Finally, we asked teachers to evaluate the relationship between the three components of the working agreement: tuition, organized collaborative work and time for homework and preparation. Here, 75 per cent of the teachers described the percentage of time devoted to these three components of the agreement as unsatisfactory/fairly satisfactory, while 25 per cent described it as satisfactory/very satisfactory. When asked what they would like to change, 18 per cent wanted to change the weekly hours spent on tuition, 7 per cent wanted to change the amount of time spent on organized collaborative work, while 74 per cent wished to give priority to homework and preparation work plus time for updating/professional development.

Summary of Findings

Preliminary analysis of the data seems to suggest that the work-time agreement was mainly used for two purposes: joint staff meetings and meetings in smaller/more differentiated groups. Joint staff meetings were mostly concerned with pedagogical, planning and staff or information questions. Meetings in differentiated groups covered a wide range of themes, such as team-work meetings, class-staff meetings or subject-matter meetings. Quite a lot of time made available for organized collaborative work through the work-time agreement was tied up in joint staff meetings. On average teachers spent 2 hours and 27 minutes per week on these: primary teachers spent 2 hours and 37 minutes per week while lower secondary teachers spent 2 hours and 15 minutes. Time spent on meetings in differentiated groups was almost the same as for joint meetings. Teachers spent an average of 2 hours and 33 minutes per week on meetings in differentiated groups: primary teachers spent 2 hours and 38 minutes, while their lower secondary counterparts spent 2 hours 26 minutes.

Apart from mapping different types of meetings at the schools, we also asked teachers to estimate the value of these meetings. Results suggest that teachers were fairly dissatisfied with joint staff meetings. For instance, 42 per cent of teachers rated staff meetings as unsatisfactory or fairly unsatisfactory. Likewise, 40 per cent rated joint/consultation meetings unsatisfactory or fairly unsatisfactory. In contrast, meetings in differentiated groups were rated more favourably. The value of team-work meetings, class-staff meetings and subject-matter meetings were rated highly by respondents. Respectively 77 per cent, 81 per cent, and 66 per cent stated that these meetings were satisfactory/very satisfactory.

Discussion

This evaluation of the meetings, together with the questions concerning general aspects of the work-time agreement, suggests that, to a certain degree, it has had a positive impact for adult collaboration or cooperation in schools. It is important to note, however, that adult cooperation did not lead to professional development, either at an institutional or an individual level. Furthermore, teachers stated that the high degree of imposed collaborative work had not been valuable in terms of the efficient performance of accumulated tasks.

One of the most striking features of this investigation was the lack of context differences. Several studies have shown how teacher cooperation, professional development and job satisfaction were linked to context factors (Handal 1991; Talbert and McLaughlin 1993; Lindblad 1995). Yet, in our study, context – type of school, size, location (urban or rural), age and sex – did not make a difference. However, female respondents tended to be a little less negative in their evaluation of both joint staff meetings and differentiated meetings than their male counterparts.

Teacher Resistance to Change

Data in this study suggest a fairly dissatisfied and demobilized teaching group. It might be worthwhile to view these findings from several viewpoints. In some ways, the results could be viewed as teacher resistance to the new work-time agreement. Teachers' views and evaluation of their experiences gave us a picture of how they see their own working conditions. Although they were not against the new work-time agreement itself, they did not feel comfortable with the way it was practised. This last point may have a double-edged consequence for how teachers view the new agreement and act towards it. Historically, time available for collaborative work has been one of the issues for disputes between the state and the teachers in Norway. Since the early 1970s, teachers have complained about the shortage of collaborative time in schools. It is ironic therefore that the new work-time agreement enforced by the state, which should increase collaborative time, has been greeted with passivity and apathy by teachers.

Imposed Professionalism or Proletarianization?

Changes in working conditions in terms of decreased control, autonomy and flexibility are at the heart of defining the proletarianization theme. In teaching, restrictions in preparation time and time for exercising professional judgement, together with flexibility in working performance, have been deeply influenced and restricted by recent changes in working conditions. It could be argued that the new work-time agreement for Norwegian teachers serves as an example of the de-skilling and proletarianization of teachers' work.

One of the disconcerting findings in this study is the extensive discontent with the practice of the existing working-time agreement. This, combined with the perception of powerlessness and apathy among teachers, could be interpreted as reason enough for teachers' apparent resistance and passivity towards the new policy. Larson (1977), who did an analysis of professionalism in highly industrial societies, points to time control as a central part of decreasing educated labour. Referring to Robert Blauner, she states that:

> [T]he lack of control over the immediate work situation – in particular the rhythm and pace of work – is a fundamental determinant of their [worker's] sense of powerlessness.
>
> (Larson 1977: 235)

Time control has an important symbolic value within educated labour. Professionals have ordinarily been protected from 'the tyranny of the clock'; they have been the masters of their own time. The right to schedule their own working time has been one of the main privileges of their professional status. Formally acknowledged for their competence and skill, professionals won the right to exercise and schedule their own timetables based on the client's needs, their own skilful judgement and the time available. In teaching, this is only partially true. A large amount of teachers' work is highly influenced by the 'tyranny of the clock'. The ringing of the school bell every forty-five minutes to indicate new lessons, new subjects, new classes and new responsibilities, is the most obvious and best-known signature of restricted time control for teachers. Even coffee breaks and lunch time are slotted within a schedule in the teaching profession. It is, however, important to note that within this tradition of controlled time, teachers were free to determine how, where and when to undertake their homework and preparatory work. The new work-time agreement influences radically and dramatically the historically constituted 'privileges' in teaching and therefore contributes to making teaching more like other types of employed labour.

Professionalism as Ideology

Several researchers have shown how the teaching occupation has undergone deep changes throughout the last years. Many of these changes were brought forward in the name of professionalism. As a result, the concept of professionalism takes on an ideological function which masks and obscures the realities of the changing conditions of teaching. Larson (1977) for example, persuasively argues that the significance of professionalism lies in its ideological content, not in its description of actual work conditions. In the introduction to her insightful work on professionalism, she proclaims:

> The persistence of professionalism as a social category of social practice suggests that the model constituted by the first movements of professionalism has become an ideology – not only an image which consciously inspires collective or individual efforts, but a mystification which unconsciously obscures real social structures and relations.
>
> (Larson 1977: xviii)

Densmore (1987) states that the notion of professionalism legitimates teachers to voluntarily draw upon extra responsibilities and workload to give them 'a sense of professional pride and responsibility. Professionalism is best interpreted as an ideological response to degraded and decreased work conditions in teaching' (ibid.: 139). Densmore goes on to argue that 'viewing themselves as workers may help teachers to recognize both the sources of troubles schools face and potential means of effective action' (ibid.: 132).

Conclusion

At the beginning of this chapter, I drew attention to the distinction between externally defined criteria of professionalism and internally defined criteria. It could be argued that the practice of the new working-time agreement in Norwegian schools illustrates how externally defined criteria of professionalism shape and eventually overpower the development of internally defined criteria in teaching. Although teachers may be going through the motions of implementing the policy in schools, they do so because they have been rendered powerless by change which is couched in the rhetoric of professional responsibility and competence. In this sense, the ideology of professionalism ignores the existence of the structural conditions in teaching. In doing so, it serves as a hindrance for well-informed and skilful practice and contributes to the transformation of Norwegian teachers into mere obedient and loyal civil servants.

Notes

1 See for example the studies of Etzioni (1969), Johnson (1972), Lortie (1975), Langford (1987), and Ginsburg (1987).
2 In this sense, professionalism is related to a strong market position (based on professional skill), a considerable degree of autonomy in the workplace (especially in comparison with the industrialized proletariat) and high status. Sarfatti Larson asserts that standardization of knowledge and market control are essential features of professionalism in highly developed capitalist societies (1977: 40–1).
3 Norway has three teacher unions, two of them, the Norwegian Teachers' Union and the Laererforbundet older and much larger and more influential than the third. The Norwegian Teachers' Union mainly recruits its members from primary schools and, to a certain degree, lower secondary schools, while the second-largest, the Laererforbundet, mainly recruits from primary schools.

References

Ball, S. (1990) *Politics and Policy Making in Education: Explorations in Policy Sociology.* London: Routledge.

Carlgren, I. (1994) Curriculum as a Social Compromise or Accident. In D. Kallos and S. Lindblad (eds), *New Policy Contexts for Education.* Umeå University, Seden, Educational Report no. 42.

Densmore, K. (1987) Professionalism, Proleterianization and Teachers' Work. In T. Popkewitz (ed.), *Critical Studies in Teacher Education.* London: Falmer Press.

Etzioni, A. (1969) *The Semi Professions and Their Organizations: Teachers, Nurses, Social Workers.* New York: Free Press.

Fauske, H. (1986) *Nar tid ikke er penger. . .?* Fagbevegelsens Forskningssenter (Working Unions Research Centre) Report no. 062: FAFO.

Ginsburg, M.B. (1987) Reproduction, Contradiction and Conceptions of Professionalism: The Case of Pre-Service Teachers. In T. Popkewitz (ed.), *Critical Studies in Teacher Education.* London: Falmer Press.

Ginsburg, M.B., Meyenn, R.J. and Miller, H.D.R. (1980) Teachers' Conceptions of Professionalization and Trade Unionism. in P. Woods (ed.), *Teacher Strategies: Exploration in the Sociology of the School*. London: Croom Helm.

Handal, G. (1991) Collective Time – Collective Practice? *Journal of Curriculum*, 2(3): 317–33.

Hargreaves, A. (1994) *Changing Teachers, Changing Times: Teachers' Work and Culture in the Postmodern Age*. London: Cassell.

Hopkins, D. (1994) *School Improvement in an Era of Change*. London: Cassell.

Horn, F. (1993) Professionalismens utfordring. In J. Cederstrom, L. Moos, L. Rahbek Schon and J. Rasmuisen (eds), *Laererprofessionalisme*. Copenhagen: Unge Paedagoger.

Johnson, T.J. (1972) *Profession and Power*. New York: Macmillan.

Klette, K. (1994) *Skolekultur go endringsstrategier. Utviklingsarbeidet ved Fjell skole: en naerstudie*. Avhandling til dr. polit graden. University of Oslo: Pedagogisk forskningsinstitutt.

—— (1996) *Report on the New Working Time Agreement for Norwegian Teachers*. Norwegian Teachers' Union.

—— (1997) Teacher Individuality, Teacher Collaboration and Repertoire Building: Some Principal Dilemmas. *Teachers and Teaching: Theory and Practice*, 3(2): 243–57.

Labaree, D.F. (1992) Power, Knowledge and the Rationalization of Teaching: A Genealogy of the Movement to Professionalize Teaching. *Harvard Educational Review*, 62: 123–54.

Langford, G. (1987) *Teaching as a Profession*. Manchester: Manchester University Press.

Larson, M.S. (1977) *The Rise of Professionalism. A Sociological Analysis*. Berkeley, CA: University of California Press.

Lawn, M. (1991) Social Constructions of Quality in Teaching. In G. Grace and M. Lawn (eds), *Teacher Supply and Teacher Quality: Issues for the 1990s*. Clevedon: Multilingual Matters.

Lieberman, A. (1988) *Building a Professional Culture in Schools*. New York: Teachers College Press.

Lindblad, S. (1993) On Teachers' Invisible Experience and Professional Accountability. Paper presented at the PACT meeting, 25–27 September. London, Ontario.

—— (1995) On Teachers' Experience of Restructuring of Education in Sweden. Paper presented at the PACT meeting, April. London, UK.

Little, J.W. (1992) Opening the Black Box of Professional Community. In A. Lieberman (ed.), *The Changing Contexts of Teaching*. Chicago: University of Chicago Press.

Lortie, D. (1975) *Schoolteacher: A Sociological Study*. Chicago: University of Chicago Press.

Ozga, J. and Lawn, M. (1988) *Teachers, Professionalism and Class: A Study of Organized Teachers*. London: Falmer Press.

Stenhouse, L. (1975) *An Introduction to Curriculum Research and Development*. London: Heinemann.

Talbert, J. and McLaughlin, M. (1993) Teacher Professionalism in Local School Contexts. Paper presented at the PACT meeting, September. London, Ontario.

Torgersen, U. (1972) *Profesjonssosiologi*. Oslo: Universitetsforlaget.

10 Student Teachers' Struggle in Becoming Professionals

Hopes and Dilemmas in Teacher Education

Trond E. Hauge

Learning to teach is a personal, complex and context-specific task. This is a lesson drawn from a study of three student teachers in a university-based teacher education programme in Norway. The chapter reveals that learning to teach is personal because of the dependency on students' personal learning histories, their preconceptions and beliefs about learning and teaching. It is complex because of the variety of competencies that have to be learned in different settings, and it is context specific because of its dependency of situations offered the student teachers during their teacher education. The optimistic lesson from the study seems to be that teacher education contributes to student teachers' professional development in various ways. However, the problem is that the learning outcome is very open and dependent on the quality of learning situations offered to student teachers at the university and in schools where they practise teaching. The supervisory conditions in schools play an important part in this context.

Student teachers are confronted with a series of challenges in their education. They are expected to abandon a long-standing student role and move into a responsible and accountable teacher role. They are asked to focus on other people's learning in an educational setting which is to a large extent created by themselves. They are in charge of class management and are expected to behave as leaders in the classroom. Student teachers are also expected to be able to transmit meaningfully their own subject knowledge to pupils. At the same time, they are expected to reflect critically on their own teaching and professional development. Do we really understand the complexity of this task in initial teacher education?

James Calderhead and Susan B. Shorrock's (1997) follow-up study of a group of twenty student teachers in initial teacher education describes excellently what teacher education research has repeatedly affirmed about student teachers' learning to teach: learning to teach is a complex task, which is frequently content-, context- and person-specific. Calderhead and

Shorrock conclude that understanding the complexity of the learning process and how it can be facilitated is more important than agreeing on an ideal end-state of competencies, as is often described in policy documents and curriculum guidelines in teacher education.

This chapter, which is based on a study focusing on the questions raised in Calderhead and Shorrock's study moves three student teachers and their learning histories in teacher education to the front of the analysis. These students, referred to here by pseudonyms, were sampled from a group of twenty students followed up intensively through teacher education. Their motives for becoming teachers, and their attitudes to and thinking about teacher education, are described. Their learning and development as teachers in the classroom are analysed in an attempt to understand their individual learning and what teacher education has to offer them in this process. Finally, some questions of how professional learning may be promoted in teacher education are discussed, together with a particular focus on conditions significant for students' learning.

Background of the Study

The student teachers are Erik, Tone and Anne. They belong to a group of 150 students who went through a half-year teacher education programme at the University of Oslo in 1993. This programme had for many years been obligatory for all university students who want to be certified as school teachers.[1] Students could apply to enter the programme at the end of their academic studies. It was composed of three main courses: pedagogy, pedagogical subject knowledge and practice training in school. The students' practice training was organized as supervised individual practice for a period of eight weeks, scheduled in between two periods of theory courses at the university. The first theory period lasted for about four or five weeks, the second one for about three weeks after the practice period. About one out of five supervisors in schools had no formal education as supervisors. The majority of the supervisors were hired for only one semester at a time.

The student group as a whole was followed up by questionnaires at the beginning and the end of their education. Twenty students were sampled for an intensive follow-up study during that period: they were interviewed twice and observed twice while teaching during their eight weeks of practice training in schools. In analysing the histories of Erik, Tone and Anne we thus draw upon a large data set based on observations, questionnaires and interviews with the three students. Information about the students' backgrounds, their attitudes to and motivation for teacher education, beliefs about teaching and learning in school, classroom management, teaching and leadership styles in the classroom and assessments of teacher education were collected. Earlier descriptions of the research project are given by

Hauge (1995a, 1995b, 1997a). Erik, Tone and Anne seem to be representative of what students in general experienced during the teacher education programme.

Stories about Struggling and Knowing

Erik

Erik was the oldest of the students. In 1993 he was 49 and had been working as an aircraft engineer for twenty-three years. He was unemployed and willing to re-educate himself. His degree included mathematics and natural sciences. He entered teacher education with an expressed low confidence in his own subject knowledge, but signalled a strong motivation for teacher education. He wanted to work as a teacher, and he expected that the education would help him to develop his own abilities as a teacher. He was especially concerned with how he could transfer his subject knowledge to students in school.

Erik said that friends and relatives had influenced his perceptions of being a teacher quite significantly. His self-understanding carried much weight. Previous experience from work with children and young people in general was of minor importance in this respect. He expressed a positive attitude to teaching and working with students in schools.

When describing his leadership abilities, Erik said he was not a typical leader, but he strongly believed he would manage to master the job of teacher as soon as he had learned the right tricks. He characterized himself as a humorous person and said he was fairly good at combining authority with a careful attitude to children. 'I am not a good organizer, but I am sure I can manage problems coming up in my classes – and I can be quite decisive.' Such opinions captured some of Erik's beliefs about teaching. He looked forward to writing on the blackboard as a means of explaining new concepts and solving subject-matter problems for the students. Erik's preference concerning his own way of teaching seemed to be that of the directive teacher, but this style was mixed with open listening and co-operative attitudes towards his students. He underlined that there had to be a pleasant atmosphere in the classroom.

What were Erik's thoughts about learning? 'When students have learned something – then they can remember it, understand and explain it. Or – they can do something they never have done before. Attitude changes are also a part of it', he said. 'To check out if students understand what we are doing, well – let's have a test, or we can ask them to do some assignments when you walk around in the class and supervise their work', he explained further. When Erik was asked to explain what he meant by meaningful learning, he responded: 'By this I mean something useful for the students, even though they don't realise it at the moment.' He was also invited to explain his view on pupils' responsibility for their own learning in school and what this meant for his way of teaching. He said: 'I am not so very happy about that way of teaching in eighth or ninth grade in lower secondary school. I believe students at that age must be told in detail what they have to do. I don't believe these students are able to learn on their own.'

When Erik was observed teaching natural sciences in the eighth grade, he showed a directive teaching style. He was concerned about explaining to the students what they had to do, and he demonstrated good skills in questioning and answering. He was less concerned about co-operative work and group work. His relations with students in the class were fairly good, and the students seemed to have confidence in him, something that grew even stronger during his training period. In the first observed lesson he demonstrated that he still needed to develop skills in managing a good learning situation for the class as a whole. In the second observation he was controlling the class in a firm but pleasant manner. There was a clear progression in teaching skills during the training period.

When he looked back at his own practice training in school, Erik reported that he had learned a lot, e.g. to plan a lesson, how to behave in the classroom, to organize, to be conscious of matters of content, to be aware of the students' needs and to vary teaching methods. 'Sometimes I had a feeling of not doing the right things. . . . However, the supervisor was too kind to me – she should have criticised me much more', he said.

Erik's ability to reflect upon teaching improved during his practice training. In the last interview he was more concerned with the students' learning than he had been in the first interview. He also said that the students were more responsible than he had believed at first and that he was in the process of modifying his opinions about teaching and learning. 'I have less strong opinions after having gone through this teacher education.'

Like the other student teachers, Erik was not eager to express his opinions about the theory courses in the education programme. The experiences from practice training in school seemed to be the most important aspect at that time.

Tone

Tone was 29 years old and had had a strong and broad education in social economics, and one year's study in law. She had some teaching experience as a substitute teacher in primary and lower secondary schools and two years' experience as a kindergarten assistant. At our first meeting she said that she wanted to work as a teacher after completing her BA, a decision she had made before she entered university. Tone was well motivated towards teacher education and judged her own knowledge in economics as fairly good for teaching. She expected that teacher education would help her develop her own abilities as a teacher. The strongest influence on her conceptions of being a teacher was her earlier experience with children: friends, relatives and university studies played a minor role.

When confronted with a sample of pre-described teaching problems in school, Tone showed a balanced view of teaching: she paid attention to the needs of the students, and wanted to talk and discuss the problems with her students and to be a responsible leader for social processes in the class.

There was consistency between Tone's reflections about teaching and her own way of teaching. We observed her work in one class in upper secondary school, twice giving lessons in economics, where she clearly demonstrated a firm but caring way of teaching, and a good balance between a teacher-centred and a pupil-centred approach. She demonstrated good skills in questioning and answering, delegated responsibility for doing assignments without losing control of the class and was a good listener to the students. The atmosphere was pleasant during the lessons. Tone was concerned about varying her teaching and she tried to adapt her teaching to the students' prior knowledge:

> For me it is important to understand how students are thinking . . . I need to know where my students are. . . . The dialogue between me and my students is very important, both to perceive difficult problems and to find out what the difficulties consist of. . . . I am often conscious of the mood in the class. . . . It is also important for me to admit my faults.

These quotations taken from the first interview express in a nutshell her conceptions about teaching.

Tone's conceptions of learning seem to reflect a distinction between what Marton (1986) and Entwistle and Ramsden (1983) call 'surface learning' and 'deep learning':

> When I was a student in upper secondary school . . . I was a typical bright school girl, I could read and recall . . . but I never had a feeling of understanding, in depth. I got a taste of many things. But that's not necessarily wrong, because you can work on it later on. The first seed – that has something to do with learning. Understanding is something deeper.

Learning represents various things for Tone; it is a broad concept connecting conscious and unconscious aspects of learning.

Reflecting upon her own practice teaching in school, Tone was disappointed about the way she was supervised. Her supervisor did not function very well and she was left too much on her own. However, being an open-minded person she got feedback from the students about her teaching, something which compensated for some of the weaknesses of the supervision, she said. When she reflected on her own conceptions of teaching and learning in the second interview, she did not develop these any further, compared to the first interview. She still believed in a dialogue with students and letting them take responsibility for their own learning. Her practice teaching had confirmed in a positive way her approach to teaching.

At the end of her teacher education Tone was not quite sure whether or not she would apply for a job in school. She wanted to think about it a bit more. Her experience of teaching and the supervision she had received seemed to have influenced her decision.

Anne

Anne was 28 years old and held an MA in sociology, social economics and political science. She had had some months of experience as a substitute teacher in lower secondary school and two years' work experience as an insurance consultant, an assistant at a health institution and a secretary in a travel agency. Her practice teaching consisted of teaching social science and economics in an upper secondary school in her home city in the south of Norway. According to the first interview, she was well motivated towards teacher education, had good confidence in her own subject knowledge and wanted to be a teacher.

Like the other two student teachers, Anne expected that the education would help her to become a good teacher. She was quite concerned about instructional matters, how students in school learned the subject she was teaching and how she could transmit her own knowledge to her students. She was not very much concerned about the functioning of the school as a whole. Anne liked to work with children and young people and looked forward to teaching because of all the opportunities it offered for contact with other people. Experience with children and young people, and her self-understanding, were the strongest influencing factors on her perceptions of the role of teacher. Friends, relatives and her own school experiences did not matter very much in this respect.

What were Anne's conceptions of learning? This is how she described it:

> Well . . . thinking back on situations when I learned in school . . . that's when you suddenly understood. . . . The first step is not to be afraid to talk in the class. That's a great victory. . . . And to be able to express your thoughts. . . . Learning has occurred when you can use your own words . . . and your own examples and experiences.

She elaborated these thoughts further, saying:

[Meaningful learning, that's connected] to the understanding of what you are working on, to have a new understanding . . . and students must like the work, be happy with it. A meaningful learning situation, that's when you give the students an understanding that they are significant persons . . . and you are helping them to improve their self-confidence . . . [and there must be] a pleasant working atmosphere.

Anne showed an open attitude to students in school when she was confronted with a sample of pre-constructed teaching situations in the first interview. She wanted to talk to her students and to discuss relevant solutions with them before they made a co-operative decision, but she was quite aware of the role conflict that could arise between being a friend to the students and being a leader of the class at the same time. Her friendly profile seemed to be transferred to her own teaching, where she preferred to create interactive and co-operative learning situations in the class. She had a non-directive teaching style, without any class-management problems. Students seemed to be engaged and motivated in her lessons.

However, in one of her classes she ran into difficulties with her supervisor, because of conflicting teaching styles. The supervisor behaved in an unprofessional manner, and Anne decided to adapt her style to avoid the problems. This experience had a negative effect upon the way she assessed her own teaching abilities. In one of her other practice classes the conditions of supervision were more comfortable, although still without the real professional support she needed. She characterized the supervision she had received in the following way:

The supervisor made me insecure – nothing was good enough. There was always something wrong. She never pointed out the good things for me. . . . Sometimes she corrected me during my teaching, and gave me and the students directions for work.

From the observer's point of view Anne 'survived' these problems, mostly because of her own ability to reflect constructively on them. But she was disappointed. The following statement gives a flavour of her reflections: 'Teachers in school are much more concerned about teaching than learning. They believe these two concepts are identical'. The disappointment may also be a reason for the change of attitude towards being a teacher during the programme. At the end Anne no longer knew whether or not she wanted to be a teacher.

The practice training period in school influenced Anne's opinions about teaching and learning, but not dramatically. In the last interview she claimed that her student-centred teaching style had to be modified. She wanted to be more directive, especially when taking over a new class. The style of teaching always depends on the class situation, she said. Anne was quite critical of many things in school, including the way teachers treated their students. But she was also critical regarding her own skills and abilities. She looked forward to being more structured in teaching and more confident handling her own subject-matter knowledge.

Learning to Teach: A Personal, Complex and Context-Specific Task

These case studies are only 3 out of 150 stories that could have been told about this group of students. When the findings are compared with the extensive investigation of the group as a whole, they reveal some common characteristics of the students passing through this teacher education programme.

The three students approached the classroom setting and the work of teaching quite personally, using their prior experiences and conceptions of teaching as a platform for individual experimenting. Their life histories seemed to influence their behaviour. However, the students were open minded with regard to their own skills and abilities as teachers, and they expected to learn.

Opinions of learning and teaching changed to some extent for the students during their education, primarily owing to their experience as student teachers in school. Erik was the one who most expressed explicit changes. For him the easy way of teaching by using tricks lost its importance. All three of them seemed to develop more balanced views on learning and teaching. However, their stories do not give clear directions with regard to this type of learning: the students had to struggle on an individual basis, sometimes driven by unforeseen contextual problems and with unsupportive supervisors.

Changes in opinions are reflected in the students' teaching behaviour: Erik believed in a directive teaching style when he entered teacher education, while the two female students were inclined to use dialogue as the main strategy for knowledge transferral. Erik modified his style during practice training and became more responsive and a better listener to his students. Anne adjusted her dialogue-oriented style and took on a somewhat more directive teaching style in the classroom, in one of her classes in particular. Tone seemed to be confident in her role performance, which was based on a balance between a teacher-centred and a student-centred way of teaching.

The present case studies have a clear message regarding the supervision conditions in schools for the students. The supervisors' attitudes and their support or lack of support for the students played a significant role in their learning processes. Tone was left too much alone by her supervisor, while Anne ran into a conflict with a supervisor who did not appreciate her teaching style. About 20 per cent of the entire group of students experienced some kind of conflict or communication problem with their supervisors in schools (Hauge 1997a). We can only speculate what might have happened to Erik if he had had to practise in Anne's supervisory setting, or if Tone or Anne had had to teach in a class that rejected their co-operative and dialogue-oriented teaching style. The study affirms that the contextual conditions for practice training in schools, particularly the supervisory setting, are strongly significant for student teachers' learning and development during their education.

When confronted with questions regarding the importance of the theory courses in the programme, the case study students were quite vague and evasive. They found it difficult to assess the impact of these courses on their own conceptions about learning and teaching or on their teaching performances. Their minds were primarily occupied with what had happened to them during their practice training in schools. However, the reluctance to express thoughts in this matter should also be considered as part of the interview situation itself, in which the students had to talk to one of their teacher educators at the university. In contrast to this situation, observations in schools were undertaken by an independent observer. By and large the students' views in this respect confirm what seems to be a common conclusion in the international teacher education research literature, that practice training plays a major role for students in the process of becoming a teacher.

The Way Ahead

The present study adds to research on teacher education in the 1990s, underlining the fact that learning to teach is a multi-dimensional task, and one which is highly personal and context oriented. The study reveals that the student teachers' individual learning histories and teaching preferences, as these were constituted before teacher education started, were reflected in both their attitudes and teaching behaviour. At the same time, the study points towards interactions between personal dimensions in the students and contextual dimensions in school as significant to the students' learning. The supervisory setting plays a significant role in this process.

Despite this complexity, recent studies in the field support the actual study in the sense that well-designed teacher education programmes do have an effect on student teachers' teaching behaviour and beliefs about teaching and being a teacher (cf. Calderhead and Shorrock 1997; Kwo 1996; Kettle and Sellars 1996; Korthagen and Wubbels 1995; Jones and Vesilind 1995; Winitsky and Hauchak 1995; McDiarmids 1993; Calderhead and Robson 1991; Grossman 1990). This may be the most optimistic message from the study and should be considered when specific reforms and improvements in teacher education are planned.

The kind of research being done in the current study is based on an understanding of the reflective teacher, extensively discussed in international teacher education literature (Day 1999; Richardson 1997; Korthagen and Lagerwerf 1996; Grimmett and Erickson 1988). These are attitudes that were also espoused in the old national curriculum guidelines for teacher education at Norwegian universities in 1993, which were later revised in 1998. The latest version has a more specific and elaborated understanding of the reflective teacher than the first. The 1998 guidelines should be looked upon as important vehicles for the kind of teacher education practices that are focused upon in the present study. However, when looking at the guidelines of 1993 and the implemented version for the actual group of students, the study has revealed well-known problems connected to the classic gap between intentions and practices in teacher education. Growth in skill performance or reflection did not happened as expected: to a large extent these processes were determined by contextual factors in schools and what the students themselves brought with them from their own learning history. We may criticize the 1993 teacher education programme for not being aware of these powerful conditions of learning to become a teacher, which for two of the case study teachers ran directly counter both to what they wanted to learn and to the aim of the programme. The 1993 half-year programme did not seem as useful for solving key conflicts of learning as the students had expected. Weak internal cohesion in the programme and weak control of supervisors' qualifications were the main reasons behind this problem.

The old theory–practice dilemma in teacher education is revealed once again by the present study. At first glance, practice training in school seems to be the winner in the game. However, the study underlines how vulnerable this practice may be for students, when contextual factors in classrooms and the supervisory settings are considered. The revised teacher education programme of 1998 seems to express an understanding of this problem, underlining that teacher education has to be more practice-based and cohesive in its work with student teachers. This has to be done without neglecting the importance of theoretical perspectives as significant bases for the understanding of being a teacher. The English way of solving the dilemma, making use of extensive school-based training programmes, seems not to be an acceptable solution in the Norwegian setting.

The revised, 1998, teacher education programme at Oslo University needs to be supported by extensive research on topics important for its success. Ideas for such an activity are already given internationally through research on theory–practice dilemmas in teacher education, which provide insight into specific aspects of learning to be a teacher. Research reported by Hargreaves and Evans (1997), Calderhead and Shorrock (1997), McLaughlin and Oberman (1996), Russell and Korthagen (1995), Grimmett and Neufeld (1994) are important in this matter. Hopes of overcoming the dilemmas of teacher education are taken a step further now that new models of learning are being investigated and analysed, for example by using action research models (cf. Richardson 1994, 1997; Elliott 1993; Tabachnick and Zeichner 1991). Norwegian teacher education has been opening up to case study methods over the last years and should be much more concerned about how these methods may stimulate students' experiential learning, not only when they are training in schools, but also when they are studying on the university campus (cf. reviews of Merseth 1996; McAninch 1993; Shulman 1992). Finally, the improvement of the context of practice training in school is one the most important factors for moving teacher education to the forefront of professional education. Making alliances and partnerships between schools, local governments and the university seems to be necessary in this respect (cf. Yinger 1997; Griffiths and Owen 1995; Goodlad 1994).

Norwegian teacher education is still in the position of receiving support and trust from the national government and is looked upon as a key factor in the implemention of national educational policy in schools (Ministry of Education 1996; 1990–91). To remain in this positive climate it is important for Norway to move on in teacher education research, with the aim of compiling a body of knowledge that makes a significant contribution to our understanding of the complexity of learning to be a teacher and how teacher education may stimulate student teachers' growth and development in various professional skill and reflection domains.

Note

1 This programme was extended to a full-year programme at the end of 1993. The present study was done on the last group of students following the half-year programme.

References

Calderhead, J. and Robson, M. (1991) Images of Teaching: Student Teachers' Early Conceptions of Classroom Practice. *Teaching and Teacher Education*, 7: 1–8.

Calderhead, J. and Shorrock, S.B. (1997) *Understanding Teacher Education*. London: Falmer Press.

Day, C. (1999) *Developing Teachers: The Challenges of Lifelong Learning*. London: Falmer Press.

Elliott, J. (1993) *Reconstructing Teacher Education*. London: Falmer Press.

Entwistle, N.J. and Ramsden, P. (1983) *Understanding Student Learning*. London: Croom Helm.

Goodlad, J.I. (1994) *Educational Renewal: Better Teachers, Better Schools*. San Francisco: Jossey-Bass.

Griffiths, V. and Owen, P. (eds) (1995) *Schools in Partnership*. London: Paul Chapman.

Grimmett, P. and Erickson, G.L. (eds) (1988) *Reflection in Teacher Education*. New York: Teachers College Press.

Grimmett, P.P. and Neufeld, J. (1994) *Teacher Development and the Struggle for Authenticity*. New York: Teachers College Press.

Grossman, P.L. (1990) *The Making of a Teacher, Teacher Knowledge and Teacher Education*. New York: Teachers College Press.

Hargreaves, A. and Evans, R. (1997) *Beyond Educational Reform: Bringing Teachers Back In*. Open University Press.

Hauge, T.E (1995a) Lærerstudent og læringsutbytte (Student teacher and learning outcomes). In Imsen, G., Skaalvik, E. and Telhaug, A.O. (eds), *Frontlinjer i pedagogisk forskning* (Front lines in educational research). Rapport fra Nasjonal fagkonferanse i pedagogikk Røros oktober 1993. University of Trondheim: Norsk Senter for barnesforskning.

—— (1995b) Perceptions of Teaching and Learning and the Story of Teaching Practice: Effects and Dilemmas in a Preservice Teacher Education Program for Secondary Teachers. Paper presented at the seventh biennial conference of the International Study Association on Teacher Thinking, July. Brock University, St Catharines, Ontario, Canada.

—— (1997a) Student teachers and their Leadership and Management Preferences in the Classroom. Paper presented at the eighth biennial conference of the International Study Association on Teacher Thinking, October. Kiel, Germany.

—— (1997b) Research on Teachers and Teacher Education in Norway. Reflections on the Understanding of Teacher Professionalism. Paper presented at the sixth Norwegian National Conference in Educational Research, 20–22 May. University of Oslo.

Jones, M. G. and Vesilind, E. (1995) Preservice Teachers' Cognitive Framework for Class Management. *Teaching and Teacher Education*, 11(4): 313–30.

Kettle, B. and Sellars, N. (1996) The Development of Student Teachers' Practical Theory of Teaching. *Teaching and Teacher Education*, 12(1): 1–24.

Korthagen, F.A.J. and Wubbels, T. (1995) Characteristics of Reflective Practitioners: Towards an Operationalization of the Concept of Reflection. *Teachers and Teaching: Theory and Practice*, 1(1): 51–72.

Korthagen, F. and Lagerwerf, B. (1996) Reframing the Relationship between Teacher Thinking and Teacher Behaviour: Levels of Learning about Teaching. *Teachers and Teaching: Theory and Practice*, 2(2): 161–90.

Kwo, O.W.Y. (1996) Reflective Classroom Practice: Case Studies of Student Teachers at Work. *Teachers and Teaching: Theory and Practice*, 2(2): 273–98.

Marton, F. (1986) Describing and Improving Learning. In R.R. Schmeck (ed.), *Styles and Strategies of Learning*. New York: Plenum.

McAninch, A.R. (1993) *Teacher Thinking and the Case Method*. New York: Teachers College Press.

McDiarmid, G.W. (1993) Changes in Beliefs about Learners among Participants in Eleven Teacher Education Programs. In J. Calderhead and P. Gates (eds), *Conceptualizing Reflection in Teacher Development*. London: Falmer Press.

McLaughlin, M.W. and Oberman, I. (1996) *Teacher Learning. New Policies, New Practices.* New York: Teachers College Press.

Merseth, K.K. (1996) Cases and Case Methods in Teacher Education. In J. Sikula (ed.), *Handbook of Research on Teacher Education* (2nd edition). London: Prentice Hall International.

Ministry of Education (1990–91) *Om organizering og styring i utdanningssektoren* (Organizing and governing in the education system). White Paper no. 37. Oslo.

—— (1996) *Lærerutdanning: Mellom krav og ideal* (Teacher education: Between demands and ideals). Public report no. 22. Oslo.

Richardson, V. (1994) *Teacher Change and the Staff Development Process.* New York: Teachers College Press.

—— (1997) *Constructivist Teacher Education.* London: Falmer Press.

Russell, T. and Korthagen, F. (1995) *Teachers who Teach Teachers: Reflections on Teacher Education.* London: Falmer Press.

Shulman, J. (ed.) (1992) *Case Methods in Teacher Education.* New York: Teachers College Press.

Tabachnick, B.R. and Zeichner, K. (eds) (1991) *Issues and Practices in Inquiry-Oriented Teacher Education.* London: Falmer Press.

Winitsky, N. and Hauchak, D. (1995) Learning to Teach: Knowledge Development in Classroom Management. *Teaching and Teacher Education*, 11(3): 215–27.

Yinger, R.J. (1997) Professional Development Standards as a New Context for Professional Development in the USA. Paper presented at the eighth biennial conference of the International Study Association on Teacher Thinking, October. Kiel, Germany.

Part III

Dilemmas of School Leadership

11 Rethinking the Work of Teachers and School Leaders in an Age of Change

Ibrahim Bajunid

This chapter explores the meaning of being a teacher through the ages, across various cultures. Against the background of the educational wisdom of human civilizations, a critical analysis of the Malay indigenous perspective on teaching, and the place of the guru in traditional Malay society, is presented. The notion of professionalism within a spiritual perspective on educational development and evolutionary change in society is examined. The unique characteristics of teachers' work and professional ethics are elicited from inter-professional work demands and work ethics. Noting 'megatrends', the chapter predicts the challenges to the work of teachers. A reflective definition of the meaning of educational leadership within changing contexts is offered, outlining its unique ideals. Finally, the chapter suggests that teachers and school leaders have a unique opportunity to contribute to society's thinking and action on significant ethical and social development issues.

> The ink of the scholar is more holy than the blood of the martyr.
> He who travels in search of knowledge, to him God shows the way to paradise.
>
> Prophet Muhammad (Peace be Upon Him)

In every age and in every context teachers and school leaders always try to find subjective and objective meanings for what they do, specifically, in relation to who they are and to their professionalism. This quest for meaning has to do with the nature of their enterprise, with change and with society. Observing this phenomenon several decades ago, an educator observed what was valid then and is valid now:

> We are fumbling around in education because we know so little about the future and do not bother to know enough about the past. Education is not only one of the greatest human enterprises in immediate

planning, with parents, teachers, 'educators,' school administrators, and college presidents as its leaders. It is also a long-enduring process of cultural self-evolution. This process expresses itself through the minds of men who are interested in, and capable of, looking deeper into the nature, the needs and the aspirations of human beings than are most people. As long as the daily planning, doing, and structuring in education are constantly nourished by the wellsprings of the total cultural evolution, education and civilization are in a state of health; when the contact is cut they are sick and a crisis occurs. We live now in such a crisis. The degree of futile busy-ness constantly increases in proportion to the loss of a feeling for cultural depth and continuity.

(Ulich 1971: v)

In Ulich's conception of the work of teachers, emphasis is given to the process of cultural self-evolution and looking deeper into human nature, needs and aspirations. To maintain stability there is need for cultural depth and continuity. While three thousand years of educational wisdom provide the kaleidoscopic panorama of educational ideas from all the major human civilizations, as we enter the next millennium, over and above traditional cultural literacy, scientific and technological literacy has become the culture of the transitional present and the promised future. The cyberspace culture, for instance, with the introduction of the Internet, heralds a new and dramatic phase in human civilization, affecting education. The challenge is responded to in many ways by different societies (Gates 1995).

The Meaning of Being a Teacher Through the Ages

Through the ages the great leaders of mankind have been considered as the exemplars par excellence. In addition to the prophets, every civilization has had its own great teachers. Teachers have provided lessons which resonated universally and became relevant across cultures. Ideas of the great teachers were recorded in all kinds of documents within a particular cultural tradition, and most of their works were translated into other languages and somehow became assimilated into the intellectual traditions of the recipient culture. Ulich (1971), for instance, compiled *Three Thousand Years of Educational Wisdom* from such documents, providing a very brief acquaintance with some of the great thinkers and teachers of mankind. Novak (1995) has also provided a glimpse of the world's wisdom from the great sacred texts of the world's religions. Likewise, Adler (1981) has provided a lexicon of western intellectual thought focusing on great ideas.

If teachers are knowledge leaders, what aspects of the initial teacher education curriculum or of the in-service continuing education curriculum incorporate the wisdom from mankind's gurus? The powerful content of their thought provides guidance for teachers in the further development of their own understanding, without necessarily becoming a discipline. Understanding and application of their teachings will contribute to teachers' capacity to confront the challenges of our era from the perspective of mankind's wisdom. This insight is particularly convincing if we accept Thomas Moore's axiom that 'all the wisdom we need is already available to us in abundance'. Al-Ghazzaliyy's study on Islamic epistemology makes distinctions between *ilham* (inspiration), *'aql* (reason), *miz* (rational discernment) and *ittirad al-adat* (consistency of habits). In discussing the sources of knowledge, al-Ghazzaliyy asserts that rational discernment is the source of knowledge and *tamyiz* (discernment) is ranked higher than the senses and lower than reason (Abu-Sway 1996). If teaching is a profession, with a relatively universal corpus of professional knowledge, what is the status of the contributions of the significant thinkers and gurus in the intellectual and professional growth of teachers and educational leaders? Interesting contributions are recorded: for instance, the sayings of Mencius (born 372 BC), encapsulating wisdom in a chaotic era (Tsai Chih Chung 1991). In a different vein, Rusk (1965) contributes importantly by summarizing the doctrines of the great educators.

The Teacher in Malay Indigenous Society

In Malay society, the teacher – whether the religious teacher or the teacher of secular subjects – has an esteemed position. The Malay Annals and other documents of Malay literature have recorded the high status of the teacher in society. In the traditional Malay psyche and in cultural practice there is a prevalent cultural norm that operates when parents send their children to be under the care of the teacher, whether in a *pondok* (private) school or a government school. Typically, in the past, parents would speak to the teacher along the following lines: 'Please educate my child and make him/her a person. Treat my child like your own. Do what you will with my child, punish when necessary in any way that does not involve blinding the child or breaking his bones.' Today, few parents would allow corporal punishment in schools by teachers. It is interesting to note that during the era when teaching as a profession hardly existed, teachers had high status in society. Today, with the professionalization of teaching, the status of teachers is lower than that of other professions, specifically, doctors, lawyers or engineers.

There are many explanations of this state of affairs, some of the most important being the length of training and the level of education, the distinction between the novice and expert professional, the economic remuneration and the overall recognition accorded by society to those in particular professions, symbolically and in real terms. In the past, besides the aristocratic governing feudal class and the few business elites, teachers were the intellectuals in Malay society. Even under the secular educational system established by the British, the 'Master' was a person well respected in society. The teachers were, in fact, the leaders in the independence movement at a time when the majority of the populace was illiterate (Roff 1967). With the universal provision of primary and secondary education, the majority of Malaysians are now literate. Today, with the democratization of tertiary education and with a larger base of educated citizenry, teachers do not monopolize the knowledge industry anymore. With regard to both present and future conditions for the production of knowledge workers with opportunities for learning throughout their lifespan, there is a critical need for teachers to rethink the meaning and relevance of their profession. As Malay society experiences the alteration of the status accorded to those in the teaching profession, other societies are experiencing similar changes. To reclaim their status as a dynamic and contributing profession, teachers and teacher leaders in all domains in Malaysian society are rethinking their roles.

One common agreement among teachers and teacher leaders in Malaysian society in their efforts at reassessment is that teachers must once again strive to reclaim leadership as the intellectuals in their society, and must take leadership roles at various levels in their communities. To do this effectively, they must be life-long learners with a knowledge-based culture of excellence and mastery of the core technology of education, specifically in educational foundations, the curriculum, pedagogy and evaluation studies. And they must be knowledge workers and knowledge managers, turning their organizations into learning organizations in reality, not merely in rhetoric. To reclaim this leadership position, there is a need to create positive myths, symbols and rituals, all of which will constitute a self-fulfilling prophecy for the profession.

In Islamic civilization, Prophet Muhammad is regarded as the encourager and patron of education (Choudhury 1993). The Prophet preached the value of knowledge, as recorded in the following affirmations:

> Acquire knowledge, because he who acquires it in the way of the Lord performs an act of piety; who speaks of it, praises the Lord: who seeks it, adores God: who dispenses instruction in it, bestows alms; and who imparts it to its fitting objects, performs an act of piety and devotion to God. Knowledge enables its possessor to distinguish what is forbidden from what is not: it lights the way to Heaven, it is our friend in the desert, our society in solitude, our companion when bereft of friends; it guides us to happiness, it sustains us in misery; it is our ornament in the company of friends; it serves as an armour against our enemies. With knowledge, the servant of God rises to the heights of

goodness and to a noble position, associates with sovereigns in the world, and attains to the perfection of happiness in the next.

(Ibid.: 21)

The Quran bears testimony to the supreme value of learning, science and knowledge. The *Surah al-Alaq*, the first verses of the revelation to the Prophet, emphasize the following:

Read, read in the name of thy Lord Who creates
Creates man from a clot
Read and thy Lord is most generous
Who taught by the pen
Taught man what he knew not

The Islamic educational tradition in its ideal state exhorts a believer to be also mindful, using *'aql* (mind) in quest of *'ilm* (knowledge). In order to do this there is a need to rethink ideas about society and education, particularly in times of rapid change. Current rethinking in the Islamic world has led to the 'Islamization of Knowledge' agenda. Notwithstanding such agendas, within the Islamic intellectual and philosophical traditions there is ongoing rethinking regarding the nature of man, the nature of knowledge and the nature of mind, politics and education. While there are numerous articles on the role of teachers in the noble profession, there is little study of professionalism and religion.

The Spiritual Dimension of Change

To prevent a person from being an alienated thing, devoid of spirituality, with an empty soul, believers assert there is a need to develop God-consciousness, or at the very least, a consciousness of other realities beyond the material. There is a need to prevent isolation and disassociation and foster a sense of belonging, worth, self-confidence, wholesome identity and meaningfulness. Spiritual maturity demands a journey against mindlessness and a search for the human awareness and consciousness where existence bespeaks a psychic wholeness that cannot be explained by rationalistic terms. The secular, materialistic and mechanistic society is generally opposed to a thought tradition that fosters an inclusive spiritual self. It is evident that there are different levels of consciousness (Whitney 1995). What is called for is a balance between conscious rationality, inner intuitive knowledge and revealed knowledge. Writing on the spirituality of work, Treston states that:

Thus a spirituality of work embraces a religious view of the world. A religious view of the world celebrates both the fecundity of God's creation and work as sharing in the ongoing evolution of the creative energies of the universe. . . . As we have seen, the dominance of the social machine as a root metaphor in Western society has situated modern work within an economic frame of reference. The religious view of the world has been seriously challenged by global communications and scientific assumptions about our destiny. . . . But if our understanding of work is shaped solely by economic theories, then work itself is reduced in meaning. It becomes a mere instrument of production.

(Treston 1994: 28)

Arguments from scholars who adopt a religious perspective on work take the view that man is more than a machine; work is prayer-like and there is blessing in honest work beyond economic remuneration. In fact, such arguments support both the idea of 'pure' professionalism and the idea of servant leadership, or service to God or fellow beings (Berry 1995).

The Work of Teachers

Whether teachers are technical actors transmitting knowledge or applying rules, or moral actors transforming students, they are likely to be involved in interactive professionalism, contributing to building the ideal, highly energized 'learning-enriched school'. Notwithstanding this ideal state, it is reported that teachers experience classroom pressures that exert daily influence on their lives. These include the pressure for immediacy and concreteness, the pressure for multi-dimensionality and simultaneity, the pressure of adapting to ever-changing conditions or unpredictability, and the pressure for personal involvement with students.

Classroom pressure affects teachers in a number of ways. It leads them to focus on day-to-day effects or short-term perspectives; it isolates them from other adults, especially from meaningful interaction with colleagues; it exhausts their energy – 'at the end of the week, they are tired; at the end of the year, they are exhausted' (Crandall et al. 1982: 29); it limits their opportunities for sustained reflection about what they do – 'teachers tend to function intuitively and rarely spend time reasoning about how they carry out their jobs' (ibid.). Further, it tends to increase the dependence of teachers on the experiential knowledge necessary for day-to-day coping, to the exclusion of sources of knowledge beyond their classroom experience (Fullan 1991: 34).

Other challenges regarding the work of teachers include the challenges of overload, 'groupthink', untapped competence, narrowness of roles and failed reforms (Fullan and Hargreaves 1991). There seems to be a universality in the identification and description of classroom pressure. In Malaysia, letters to the newspapers, teachers' newsletters and memoranda submitted by the teachers' unions all give similar descriptions of teachers' work and the challenges to fostering a high sense of professionalism.

Forces that are Reshaping Ideas and Driving Changes: Personalities and Events

Underlying the rhetoric of educational restructuring are fundamental cultural scientific and technological changes which are reshaping our ideas of time, space (cyberspace), equality, democracy, the global village, the borderless world and our experiences of personal reality. The factors that have led to the restructuring of school education are complex. Of acknowledged significance is the accelerating pace of simultaneous change in a number of key dimensions in both the public and private domains of societies. Writers write, for instance, within the dominant economic rationalist paradigm, within the nationalistic political survival paradigm and within the new spiritualist paradigm. Elites and lay persons alike have to be on their guard against the basic insecurities of so much change happening so quickly, in order to prevent themselves becoming over-burdened with jargon, losing their ability to be critical with regard to both detail and larger issues.

Changes are, of course, personality driven or event driven – or both. To be sustained, such initiatives must be ideas driven. Those who hold on to ideas must fully comprehend their basis and justifications. It is possible to hold good policies with no idea of their rationale. This is why it is necessary to teach for cognitive excellence through cognitive apprenticeship in all domains of high-order human thinking.

The leader who is initiating changes must understand the forces by which the vision or changes are being driven. Changes may be:

- reform drive from other sectors;
- ideal-school-model driven;
- global standard;
- global-norm driven;
- infrastructure driven;
- market driven;
- local-resource driven;
- change-agent or personality driven;
- product driven.

In the field of quality improvement, it has been noted that the main change forces or triggers that precipitate a process of quality improvement in an organization, whether in manufacture, commerce or service, are the chief executive officer, competition, demanding customers (students or parents), a greenfield venture or a restart situation. In the field of education, we may add the stakeholders, the policy makers and community, professional groups as the main forces of change. Just as the CEO is regarded as the principal force of change, school principals and leaders are a critical change factor. As in the manufacturing sector, the school products in terms of academic and co-curricular performances, character building and other indices of school effectiveness are factors which indicate the 'fitness for purpose' and 'reliability' of school products in the scholastic competition between educational institutions. Demanding parents, teachers, employers and professional associations with high product and quality expectations can result in school people (suppliers) adopting a more effective quality system, developing advanced quality planning methods and systems, and introducing specific quality management tools and techniques.

The key ideas for educational change include the provision of equality of educational opportunities, the right to receive instruction to master the basic Rs and cultural literacy. Beyond the basics are the higher rights to expanding opportunities. The right to an education is held as a right for all. Other primary ideas in education are notions of the intelligence quotient that extend to multiple intelligences and from critical thinking to creative thinking and complex thinking.

Anticipatory Futures

The continuing challenges include the challenge to improve performance and the development of futures scanning and futures tools. In initiating changes, educators must address young people's needs, rights and responsibilities in the decades ahead. To develop foresight, they must undertake analyses of future trends in all domains of human activity and of the ways in which these trends will affect education, work, lifestyles and societal living. The development of an informed view of the twenty-first century in the process of dynamic global change will become an important source for development initiatives at the macro and micro levels. How global trends will change and redefine existing knowledge and know-how, and how these changes will affect individuals, families, institutions and cultures is a challenge that must be addressed.

The eleven forces considered to be driving global changes are population, food, energy, environment, science and technology, communications, labour, industry, education and training, the world economy, warfare and international alignments. Feather (1989) suggested that there are thirty-five forces restructuring our future. Slaughter (1994) suggests that eight factors have to be considered in identifying a trend: personal, institutional, professional, methodological, cultural, ideological, the level in the global system and the level of analysis. The sources of inspiration and hope identified are:

- the idea of a sustainable society and qualitative growth;
- the notion of a stewardship ethic: the environment as a community;
- the notion that the future is implicated in the present;
- the 'new science' reflecting an interconnected reality;
- the benefits of systematic foresight;
- the rebirth of the Sacred;
- the conservation and revaluing of native peoples and cultures.

Slaughter (1994) identified the following key issues and themes in relation to the needs of young people:

- self-knowledge;
- cognitive and ethical frameworks;
- practical and artistic skills;
- contextual insights;
- foresight and vision;
- informed optimism and empowerment;
- being part of a larger whole.

To develop insight and understanding at a more profound level, leaders could employ the following strategies:

- studying cultural education and understanding its creative potential;
- mastering the skills of critical futures study;
- renegotiating worldview assumptions;
- creating and supporting institutions of foresight;
- conceptualizing more advanced forms of social and economic life.

Educators make up one of a few groups of professionals who absolutely require a futures perspective in order to make sense of their work and fully discharge their responsibility to individuals and to society.

Delors (1996) asserts that 'Education throughout life is based on four pillars: learning to know; learning to do; learning to live together and learning to be.' To conceive education in a more encompassing fashion, including educational contents and methods, would clarify these four pillars.

New Leadership Roles

More than ever, leadership involves facing the management challenges of continuous change (Burns 1978). If educational leaders want to address the broader goals of society, they must provide leadership beyond technocratic skills. Features of leadership that are required to confront the forces of change include being accountable for the implementation of one's own initiatives or the prescribed initiatives of authorities. In addition, leadership demands include being responsible for the professional development of staff so that they may cope better with the complexity, dynamism and unpredictability that are the keystones of change. Consequently, teachers and educational leaders have to possess sophisticated, high-order cognitive skills. The key to the future of effective contributions by educational leaders lies in their ability to make sense of chaos, to remain confident, to help the members of their organizations to manage inherently complex and ever-changing situations of intensive role ambiguity, and to help others confront the anxiety they face individually and collectively. The new role of leadership must go beyond simply becoming efficient and effective under the old line-management, bureaucratic structures of the prevailing paradigms. The new roles are transformative and need to address the link between education and training and the goals of society. Shifting definitions of roles and leadership can be useful in helping leaders to clarify their goals and fit their leadership to the social setting in which they find themselves. Embedded in the new definitions are unexamined concepts such as shared visions, change facilitation, collaborative decision making and stake-holding. The challenge for transformative leaders is to see changes in emancipatory rather than controlling or manipulative ways. There has to be an appreciation that control that is devolved to organizations is merely bureaucratic if political and market control resides elsewhere.

The complexity and simultaneity of change has had a significant impact on the role of leaders. There is now an alternative power relationship in which there is greater expectation of collegiality and the endeavour to gain consensus. Educational leaders are required to work with a wide range of players, all of whom want to claim a larger stake in the educational setting. They are required to have a broad range of skills, including negotiation, group decision making and problem solving, and they have proactively to develop collaborative frameworks that are internally and externally responsive. There is a demand for more flexibility and cognitive adeptness. With increased managerial accountability, leaders have to balance top-down directives with sponsoring and organizing facilitative arrangements, building teams, being entrepreneurial, and doing forward planning. Leaders have to accept greater personal accountability, manage change positively and flexibly and contain their own misapprehensions and anxieties. The new educational leaders need to identify, define, elaborate and elucidate first-order changes based on first principles, those overarching principles of justice, equality, freedom and basic rights. First-order educational changes relate to the core business or the core technology of education, pertaining to educational principles of educability, potentiality, curriculum, pedagogy and evaluation. By focusing on first-order changes to the core technology of education, leaders could then accommodate and address second-order changes like developing collaborative decision-making processes, improving communication and developing shared vision. The administrative role of the principal vis à vis the professional pedagogical and academic role of the teacher would, of course, give a different focus to first-order changes.

Towards a Definition of Educational Leadership

Wherever challenges emerge from, whether from within or from outside, from the top down or from the bottom up, leaders continue to emerge and make the difference. Starratt observes that the third wave of reform and renewal:

> is now concerned with the leadership of schools, which centers on three major issues. The first concerns the management of the difficult transition from traditional style schools to schools for the twenty-first century. Due to the enormous complexity of such a transition, a different kind of administrator is called for than the one traditionally concerned with bureaucratic demands of managing the status quo (if there ever was a status quo for more than a week!). . . . The second issue deals with the purposes of schooling. These new educational leaders will have to be much more involved with shaping schools that are responsive to the emerging needs of the community and of the larger society, not only as regards the changing context of the world of work and employment, but also to the political, cultural, and social changes taking place . . . The third issue deals with the preparation and selection of these new leaders. What will be the standards and criteria for selection and preparation and ongoing education of such leaders?
>
> (Starratt 1993: 13)

Various ideas of the processes of leadership are presented by scholars and practitioners in the field. Kouzes and Posner (1995), for instance, suggest that leaders should challenge the process, inspire a shared vision, enable others to act, model the way and encourage the heart. Campbell-Evans and Begley (1996) suggest that profiles of school leadership be used as benchmarks for professional development. The key dimensions of professional practice include instructional, pastoral, management practices, problem-solving skills, school–community facilitatorship, school culture and educational management, advocacy and vision development. Blase et al. (1995) tell the stories of eight pioneers, democratic principals in action. Beck and Murphy (1994) discuss ethics in educational ethics programmes exploring rule ethics and dilemma resolution in training programmes. Starratt sums up his insight in the following statements:

> [L]eadership is fuelled by a vision of possibilities. That vision leads to a sense of the drama being played out every day in the school. It is a

drama of becoming a people, learning how to participate, how to negotiate, how to forgive, how to celebrate heroic ideals, how to give thanks to God. Within the large drama – the play within the play – is the drama of individuals struggling to be a somebody, learning about themselves through relationships, finding out how to be connected, and at the same time to be an individual. Leaders know that they are also players in this drama, know that the script as presently written is a flawed script, one that often leads to tragic outcomes. Leaders know that their responsibility – the whole company's responsibility . . . director, coaches, actors and critics – is to rewrite the script so that the drama can be more humanly satisfying. Leaders know that the essence of education is the rewriting and the rehearsal of a new script. Their way of playing in the drama is to invite others to the task.

(Starratt 1993: 57)

Clearly then, there is a rich and growing literature on leadership. And yet there are still some gaps in our understanding. These occur when, for instance, the dimensions of spirituality or advocacy are neglected or when the analysis and insights are academic and devoid of the actors' interpretations. Or they may occur because the model of leadership is based on a political model or on a business, corporate or industrial leadership model. The study of educational leadership should, ideally, maintain the integrity of the context and the profession, reflecting the ideals and motivations of the protoganists in an environment based on the purposes of education. For instance, if, typically, a political leader must maintain power, an educational leader surrenders power, without any loss of expertise or moral standing. If, typically, a business leader must make profits by competitive marketing, an educational leader may need to soft-sell, giving away the resources of knowledge and skills without the need to get immediate returns for self or organization. In both cases, educational leaders who surrender power or give away resources do not lose. On the contrary, the role and task of educational leaders as managers of knowledge, ethical role models and 'servants or service leaders' is to surrender and to give. In the surrender and the giving they are more successful and are enriched, becoming truer educational leaders, upholding the integrity of the profession. If these arguments are accepted, there will be a radical shift in thinking regarding the nature and purposes of educational leadership. It follows then that there will be changes in the selection and preparation of educational leaders.

Putting Things Together: The Quest for Frames

In classrooms and educational institutions teachers have to learn the ways and means of putting things together within a framework (Goffman 1981). This art and science of putting things together will help teachers to make sense of their profession and its purposes. The current challenge is the challenge of information technology. With the onslaught of the language and marketing of IT, teachers can feel paralysed or irrelevant. They may also give extraordinary reverence to IT advocates and the IT agenda. Only when teachers learn the joys and techniques of conceptualizing cumulative knowledge will they have the confidence of owning their personal knowledge. The ownership of personal knowledge, recognizing its relevance in the scheme of things, gives confidence to a teacher. Beyond the confidence, the act of putting things together provides a meaning and a purpose in every knowledge encounter. While experts in various fields provide their own conceptualizations of how things can be put together, each individual teacher can find his or her own unique joy in making sense of personal and professional realities. In one sense, the motivation consciously to act to put things together is the act of deliberate and continuous life-long education. The teacher then is a researcher not just about the teacher-learning process but about knowledge, about individual and group behaviours, about self and others, about life itself.

In Malaysia, Wan (1993), in attempting to develop the education system, suggested a frame which he termed the 'Educational Vision'. The Educational Vision focuses on eight pivotal concerns:

- national unity;
- management and leadership style;
- a caring education service;
- empowerment;
- a monitoring system;
- knowledge culture;
- caring schools;
- a culture of excellence.

To implement the Educational Vision much energy was expanded to mobilize all the teaching resources in unison to achieve national educational goals. To gain legitimacy for the Educational Vision, it was attached to the National Vision and the National Philosophy of Education. Among the dramatic strategies employed was that of *gerak gempur* (blitzkrieg focus) on an educational objective. This is an example of intervention at a national educational sub-system level.

Bajunid (1993) explains that one can look at the world as chaos or order. Whatever the implicit or explicit assumption of the way the world is, there is a level of small talk or trivia. Above this is the level of plain talk; above this the level of serious talk, and above this the level of professional discourse. Above the level of professional discourse is the level of the Great Conversation regarding the important and universal questions of life. In thinking and engaging in the Great Conversation one can relate one's stance to the relative frame of reference or to the absolute frame of reference. The relative frame of reference can be a received and mature corpus of knowledge from any of the disciplines of the humanities, social sciences or the natural sciences. The absolute frame of reference is usually a source of revealed knowledge or scripture considered sacred and absolute. In any discourse a mindful individual could be conscious of the level or levels at which a person is operating, sequentially or simultaneously. Beyond academic disciplines, and to be elicited from them, is Wisdom. When spiritual intelligence is considered, all knowledge leads to Blessing. In this frame of reference, the quest for and the significance of information in the educational scheme of things is only above the level of data and below the level of basic knowledge.

Foundational Notions In Education and the Development of Professionalism

A precondition for building strong professionalism is the mastery by professionals of the core knowledge bases of the profession. The core technology of education encompasses the corpus of knowledge on the educational foundations of philosophy, psychology, sociology, linguistics, anthropology, politics and the economics of education. Integral to the educational foundations is the corpus on the curriculum, pedagogy and evaluation. Teachers and teacher leaders usually master the methodology of teaching and some school subject areas, whether in the humanities, social sciences or physical sciences. Typically, the school curriculum should be integrative, comprehensive and subject based in its conceptualizations. Sometimes, however, there will be values, thinking and arts across the curriculum. Whatever the school, teacher education or educational management training curriculum, there are some important recurring concerns in education, such as those regarding the nature of knowledge, mind, intelligence, thinking, emotions, values, teaching, learning, which must be fully comprehended and addressed. There continue to be gaps in professional knowledge regarding phenomena such as the following:

- cognitive emotions;
- emotional intelligence;
- mature and profound knowledge in education;
- human potential;
- human intelligence;
- thinking in education;
- mindfulness;
- civilizational perspectives;
- world models and community-oriented models.

Do teachers and teacher leaders everywhere possess the intellectual and professional tools to continue to learn and keep abreast with developments in the field? How are teachers and teacher leaders keeping pace with new developments in the field and incorporating new discoveries and insights into their professional practice? How are these teachers and teacher leaders utilizing new understandings and mature knowledge and concepts to advance thinking, valuing and emotional maturity when they encounter the works of people like Gardner (1984), Langer (1989), Senge (1990), Lipman (1991), Goleman (1994), and Alder (1996) and Bronfenbrenner (1979)?

To ensure that there is strong professional credibility, there must be a universally acceptable knowledge base in the curriculum of teacher education. As is the case in other professions whose qualifications are recognized across different political, academic and professional systems, this must have comparable standards for measuring quality. By conforming to international standards, the professionalism of teaching will be strengthened. Today, the certificate- and diploma-level training of teachers, especially from educationally advanced countries and institutions, is often accepted as being equivalent for all teachers, although there are often different standards and focuses in the training. Certificates and diplomas for administrator training are often, however, not recognized because these are more culture-, system- and country-specific. The rethinking on professionalism regarding the training, qualifications and work of those in education must also therefore focus on developing some common core curriculum and mature foundational knowledge to be mastered by all those who are trained for and enter the profession to practise in classrooms and educational institutions. International and national accreditation mechanisms which will guarantee minimum standards for the profession must be established.

Errors in Philosophies, Policies and Practices

As in other domains of life, there are errors in philosophies, policies and practices in the education domain. Such errors can be idiosyncratic and limited in scope, but they may also be community or national errors. They may even be civilizational errors. These errors have to do with false assumptions or other kinds of mindless personal, professional or community behaviours reflecting mistaken certainties. Adler (1985) discussed the ten philosophical mistakes in western civilization. As there are these mistakes in the intellectual tradition, aspects of them remain in the educational tradition. In Islamic civilization, the one major mistake intensely discussed by scholars and leaders is that which deals with the 'closing of the door of *ijtihad*' (independent judgement). When a society does not possess its own indigenous intellectual tradition and there is no community of critical thinkers, and no tradition of critique, if it errs because of philosophies and policies imported from elsewhere, such errors will continue undetected and unquestioned. Evidently, each society needs its own critical thinkers. At the very least, a society needs to foster a critical tradition among its intellectuals and, specifically, within a particular professional practice. In the educational field there are several important errors, including the following:

- philosophical error;
- immature knowledge;
- partial knowledge;
- knowledge compartmentalization;
- the error of a single perspective (no cross-profession integration);
- errors in knowledge transmission, dissemination and utilization;
- the omission of indigenous wisdom;
- the omission of minority perspectives (those disadvantaged, by class or gender, special groups);
- errors in sequencing knowledge;
- dominance by self-perpetuating elites.

Globalization and Internationalization: A Strategic Agenda for Development

The cataclysmic changes in the political domain towards the end of the twentieth century herald the new era of internationalization and globalization. Notions of 'paradigm shifts', 'the age of unreason' and 'the borderless world' have captured the imagination of thinkers and leaders, leading them to plan differently for the future. Growing economies and the quest to ensure that targets will be met in all areas of development have unleashed new energies, hopes, aspirations and new elites. Schools are increasingly becoming the medium through which the new language of future worlds is articulated, encompassing the possibilities of internationalization and globalization. In the sweep of scientific and technological advances, typically, business people and people in industries are quick to innovate, seek new markets and sell their products ahead of their competitors. Typically too, schools which are the inheritors of the cultures and values of the past are slow to change and tend to remain conservative. Yet schools prepare for the future. When the two almost paradoxical purposes are pursued in tandem, meaningful development which does not disintegrate individual, familial and societal identities can occur. Schools can then develop shared values and ensure the acquisition of a common language of development.

With the formulation of the overarching Vision 2020 for the Malaysian nation, there has been an unleashing of powerful national aspirations (Mahathir 1991). The younger generations of Malaysians are called upon to prepare themselves to take over leadership in all domains and to continue to achieve the National Vision. Both the present leadership and the next generation of leaders are all called upon to share the Vision and to find their own roles in contributing to realize it. The Vision fosters a high self-esteem among Malaysians and provides hope that the country will become united, liberal, progressive and democratic. Somehow, most of the elite groups have come together to support and share the National Vision and to elaborate and enhance the implementation of programmes, projects and activities related to it. The majority of the population are also inspired by it, so that there is widespread support from all sectors. The power of the Vision has now mobilized the critical mass, enabling leaders to look beyond the shortcomings of today towards the possibilities of the future.

Of all the current educational reforms and changes that are being undertaken in Malaysia six are overarching and will have significant implications for the country:

- the creation of a teaching service in which all teaching personnel are university graduates. This policy will be implemented in phases, beginning with teachers in secondary schools;
- the commitment that all school administrators and others engaged in educational management will receive adequate training in administration, especially in basic core courses, Diploma, master's and higher-level courses in administration and management;
- the implementation of the policy of producing 60 per cent science graduates and 40 per cent non-science graduates from the school system;
- the provision of opportunities for 40 per cent of a cohort group to receive tertiary education, thereby democratizing higher education in Malaysia. This agenda has encouraged the establishment of private corporate universities and the expansion of private-sector involvement in tertiary education provisions;
- the establishment of Malaysia as a centre of excellence in education, an agenda that implies being competitive and recognizing the challenges of globalization and internationalization. The uncompromising pursuit of excellence, implies specifically, implementing Total Quality Management in education and encouraging educational institutions to attain MS ISO 9000 recognition or equivalent standards;
- the creation of 'Smart Schools'. The implementation of this policy will see that every student in every school will have access to a system of education that uses advanced technology. The traditional school curriculum, teacher education curriculum and the curriculum of educational management training will have to be radically reformed. In order to have access to information available in the outside world, students will have to master an international language, especially English.

These reforms mean the formulation of an overarching central and primary policies and of supportive secondary policies. In order to facilitate these, a series of educational legislation will have to be formulated and enshrined in the country's laws. Other administrative rules and regulations will have to be likewise developed to be responsive to all the changes. All these reforms call for concerted efforts to rethink educational provisions imaginatively and boldly, and depart from conservative and traditional ways. Many resources will have to be sought and provided. New kinds and levels of expertise are required to meet these challenges.

Today in Malaysia, teachers and educational leaders are challenged as never before by 'megatrends' (Naisbitt 1995). 'Mega' development projects like the Multimedia SuperCorridor create fundamental changes in infrastructure and must necessarily bring about rethinking regarding current situations and future policies and practices. The MSC project created the initiative to establish Smart Schools country-wide. The Smart School project is now a mega project in the education sector in terms of financial investment, intellectual capital investment, human resource investment and other related and necessary investments. It is likely to change the traditional and current philosophies, policies and practices of the curricular system, the educational delivery system and the educational evaluation system. The Smart School project is driven by the mega project outside the education sector. It is to the credit of educational leaders that they have responded fast and substantively, in such a way that the Smart School project has become the priority flagship application. As the curriculum, learning materials, teaching approaches, methods and techniques, and teacher and administrator education and teacher training are being reviewed, the stage is set for serious and radical rethinking of the work of teachers and school and educational leaders in an age of change. Malaysian teachers are beginning to be engaged in examining new possibilities, and a new language, which is beginning to constitute the collective professional language and memory of teachers and educational leaders in Malaysia, is being developed. The teacher is no more regarded 'as the sage on stage' but is seen as 'the guide by the side'. Educational leaders cannot work or lead in isolation any more, but will have to work closely with other knowledge workers, particularly those in the information technology industry. Changes promised by the introduction of Smart Schools will create unprecedented impact on the ways parents, teachers, students and society think and rethink about the role of education and schooling.

Conclusion

As the world enters the next millennium, teachers and educational leaders must play positive and effective leadership roles in society. Rooted in professional organizations, and using their knowledge base, teachers and teacher leaders are strategically placed to take leading roles in initiating and sustaining positive reforms in society. If teachers and educational leaders acknowledge that they are knowledge leaders and 'walk their talk', then, alongside other elites, educational elites will define the meaning of progress and development and the goals of education. If teachers and teacher leaders are reluctant to exercise knowledge-leadership roles in the wider society, then other knowledge workers and other knowledge elites will take over leadership. As individuals and as a profession, teachers will become followers and, at best, good team members in society. If as a profession teachers and educational leaders seize the moment for leadership, the new world order will be substantially different. Today, one of the largest groupings of trade unions is the teachers' grouping. The Educational International (EI) is the largest grouping of teacher leaders at the international level. If there is visionary leadership and effective and sustained follow-up action by teachers and their representatives, the teaching profession will make a difference to the new world order and to human civilization.

Beyond classrooms and educational institutions, teachers and educational leaders can make their stand regarding a number of significant ethical and development issues. Among the issues on which leadership by virtues is required are those of human cloning and genetic engineering, educability, ecological and environmental issues, poverty and disease, human rights and abuses of all kinds. Teachers and educational leaders must inspire themselves with great ideas such as goodness, truth, justice, liberty, equality and beauty (Adler 1981). As teachers and educational leaders are inspired by lofty ideas and ideals so will their students be inspired. As they clarify their thinking and opinions and take their stand based on knowledge and clarified values, they will educate a new generation of students who will be committed to making the world a better place, a more enlightened place where mankind exercises stewardship roles with human dignity and justice.

References

Abu-Sway, M. (1996) *Al-Ghazzaliyy: A Study in Islamic Epistemology.* Kuala Lumpur: Dewan Bahasa dan Pustaka.

Adler, M.J. (1981) *Six Great Ideas.* New York: Macmillan.

—— (1985) *Ten Philosophical Mistakes.* New York: Macmillan.

Alder, H. (1996) *NLP for Managers.* London: Piatkus.

Bajunid, I.A. (1993) Towards a Definition of Educational Leadership from the Educational Perspectives. Keynote Address at the Third National Educational Management and Leadership Seminar. Kuala Lumpur.

Beck, L.G. and Murphy, J. (1994) *Ethics in Educational Leadership Programs.* Thousand Oaks, CA: Corwin Press.

Berry, L.L. (1995) *On Great Service.* New York: Free Press.

Blase, J., Anderson, G.L. and Dungan, S. (1995) *Democratic Principals in Action.* Thousand Oaks, CA: Corwin Press.

Bronfenbrenner, U. (1979) *The Ecology of Human Development.* Cambridge, MA: Harvard University Press.

Burns, J.M. (1978) *Leadership.* New York: Harper & Row.

Campbell-Evans, G. and Begley, P. (1996) Using Profiles of School Leadership as Benchmarks for Professional Development. *Leading and Managing: Journal of the Australian Council for Educational Administration (Victoria),* 2(1):

Choudhury, G.W. (1993) *The Prophet Mohammad.* Kuala Lumpur: WHS Publications.

Crandall, D. et al. (1982) *People, Policies and Practice: Examining the Claim of School Improvement.* Vols 1–10. Andover, MA: The Network.

Delors, J. (1996) *Learning: The Treasure Within.* Paris: Unesco Publishing.

Feather, F. (1989) *G-Forces: Reinventing the World. The Thirty-Five Global Forces Restructuring Our Future.* Toronto: Summerhill Press.

Fullan, M.G. (1991) *The New Meaning of Educational Change.* London: Cassell Educational.

Fullan, M.G. and Hargreaves, A. (1991) *What's Worth Fighting For? Working Together for Your School.* Buckingham: Open University Press.

Gardner, H. (1984) *The Mind's New Science.* New York: Basic Books.

Gates, B. (1995) *The Road Ahead.* New York: Viking Penguin.

Goffman, E. (1981) *Frame Analysis.* Cambridge, MA: Harvard Univesity Press.

Goleman, D. (1994) *Emotional Intelligence.* New York: Bantam Books.

Kouzes, J.M. and Posner, B.Z. (1995) *The Leadership Challenge.* San Francisco: Jossey-Bass.

Langer, E.J. (1989) *Mindfulness.* Reading, MA: Addison-Wesley.

Lipman, M. (1991) *Thinking in Education.* Cambridge: Cambridge University Press.

Mahathir, M. (1991) *Malaysia: The Way Forward.* Kuala Lumpur: Centre for Economic Research and Services, Malaysian Business Council.

Naisbitt, J. (1995) *Megatrends Asia: The Eight Asian Megatrends that are Changing the World.* London: Nicholas Brealey.

Novak, P. (1995) *The World's Wisdom.* San Francisco: Harper Collins.

Roff, W.R. (1967) *The Origins of Malay Nationalism.* Kuala Lumpur: University of Malaya Press.

Rusk, R.R. (1965) *The Doctrines of the Great Educators.* New York: St Martin's Press.

Senge, P.M. (1990) *The Fifth Discipline.* New York: Doubleday.

Slaughter R.A. (1994) *From Fatalism to Foresight: Educating for the Early Twenty-first Century.* Australian Council for Educational Administration (ACEA) Monograph Series. Melbourne: ACEA.

Starratt, R.J. (1993) *Transforming Life in Schools.* Melbourne: ACEA.

Treston, K. (1994) Work and Spirituality. In F. Crowther et al. *The Workplace in Education: Australian Perspectives.* Rydalmere, NSW: Edward Arnold Australia.

Tsai Chih Chung (ed.) (1991) *The Sayings of Mencius.* Singapore City: Asiapac.

Ulich, R. (ed.) (1971) *Three Thousand Years of Educational Wisdom* (second edition). Cambridge, MA: Harvard University Press.

Wan, Mohd Zahid Mohd Noordin (1993) *Wawasan Pendidikan: Agenda Pengisian.* Kuala Lumpur: Nurin Enterprise.

Whitney, D. (1995) Spirituality as a Global Organizing Potential. Paper presented at the Organization Dimensions of Global Change, No Limits to Cooperation Conference. New Mexico.

12 Steering In and Steering Of the School

Gunnar Berg

This chapter provides a synthesis of a number of key concepts currently being used in the field of organizational and curriculum theory to deepen our understanding of school development. Using changes in the Swedish school system as an example, schools' steering sources are discussed. The available scope of action for professional activities of schools is examined through macro and micro processes linked to school culture. A distinction between the school as an organization and the school as an institution is suggested.

Introduction

The purpose of the project 'Steering, Leadership and the School's Work/ Activity' (SLAV 2), is to study whether the change in Swedish schools constitutes a school-political shift of system (Englund 1996) in a real sense, and in that case how this shift influences school–municipal activity on a municipal-political as well as a professional level. This chapter provides an overview of some of the main features of the changed steering structures within the sphere of the school. Further, some parts of the project's problem areas, as well as its conceptual apparatus, are discussed. For the purpose of exemplification, some discussions from SLAV 2's predecessor, the project SLAV 1 ('School Leaders' Work and Working Conditions'), are also included.

Theoretical Frame of Reference

In a deeper sense, the concept of steering is primarily tied to the school as an institution, while leadership focuses more on the school as an organiza- tion (Berg 1993). Against this background, this chapter begins by discussing the concepts 'institution' and 'organization' in general, and the school as an institution and an organization in particular, partly separately and partly in

relation to each other. The word 'institution' derives from the Latin verb *instituere*, which means approximately 'to install' and 'establish'. Thus, in general terms an institution can be characterized as an established installation. In an overview of the concept of institution, Sirjamaki (1967) points out that the term has existed in the English language since the mid-fifteenth century, and that two definitions are: 'time-worn praxis in the social and political life of people' and 'prescribed order and regulation of human activity'. As Sirjamaki mentions, some sociologists have found it constructive to make a distinction between institutions and organizations. Organizations are seen as the associations through which people act, and institutions as embodying interest-group-related norms and conditions for action which people have to follow.

The school as an institution can be seen as a formal system for conducting activity that deals with fostering and education and can also be regarded as the agency responsible for the reproduction of society, that is, for the instilling of, of example, society's system of norms and for the transmission of knowledge necessary to the individual and society (Berg 1989).

'Organization', roughly implies a tool or instrument with which to carry out specific work (Berg and Söderström 1988). If an organization is viewed in terms of function then among other things the organizational culture will come into focus. If the organization is viewed as form, the administrative apparatus, or work organization (ibid.), will stand more in the foreground. (For a more detailed discussion of organizations viewed as function and form, see Abrahamsson 1993.) An organization can be said to strive towards becoming an institution. Organizations are established for the purpose of representing values and can thus be seen as instruments for institutionalization. Institutionalization can in other words be viewed as a value-consolidating process, the aim of which is to transform an organization into an institution.

Problem Area

The change in Swedish schools that occurred during the post-war period can be understood from the perspective of the school's *steering sources*, which is a collective term for the state's as well as society's steering *of* and *in* the school (Berg 1995). Officially, the main direction of state steering during this time was towards changing the school from a selective to a civic, democratic school. This change has, however, not been very effective with regard to the school's functions and traditional value bases. Available data indicate that the schools' and teaching occupation's traditions in practice dominate the content of activity, thereby making up the core of the actual value bases established within the school as an institution (see further Berg 1992).

The range between and within the school's various activities implies that its practice can be formed in different ways, without violating the state steering or the existing conceptions and value systems within and outside the school.

The tasks of the school personnel are very complex as a result of the various missions and functions of the school. This complexity has been increased by the changes in the steering of the Swedish school during the last decade, through the state's decision to undertake decentralization, deregulation and municipalization, which was manifested in the 1994 curricula for the compulsory and the voluntary school. Through these changes, certain centrally formulated, detailed rules have been replaced by framework rules.

The question is why the state replaced such detailed rules with more general framework rules. The real reason for this should be sought not only within the narrow perspective of the school. Rather, it seems to be rooted in a development whereby various societal institutions gained ground at the cost of other institutions closely linked to the state. The latter represent earlier established value bases which can be expressed in terms linked to the Swedish model, such as 'welfare state'. The former institutions, on the other hand, represent values which by all accounts are more directly connected with market-economic key words. The economic and political collapse in eastern Europe at the end of the 1980s, and the European common market's expansion towards monetary union, give indications of the kinds of values that will dominate the future development of and within western societies, at least. The general change in the relations between the state and society has effects on the school as an institution. More explicitly, the comprehensive school is on the way to being replaced by a more market-oriented school, where career directions are given increased emphasis at the cost of equality and a school for all.

An Outline of the Educational Reform: Changed Distribution of Responsibility

Generally speaking, the educational reform implies that the steering structure aims more at evaluating and controlling, rather than giving direct instructions as to how the school's daily activity should be formed. Further, one can say that the change of the state steering of schools reflects the fact that the view of school's equality which is linked to the Swedish welfare model has been replaced by a more pragmatic, and perhaps also more market-oriented, concept of equality. This implies that the educational reform in question must be understood in its social-structural *as well as* its education-institutional context. Given this, concepts such as state, society, institution, politics, bureaucracy, etc. become the necessary analytical tools in our research work. 'An effective conceptual apparatus in this connection

is the distinction between "*stateifying the society*" and "*societifying the state*"' (Petersson 1988; my italics and translation). These concepts can be linked to the social-structural changes that characterized Swedish society in the 1980s and 1990s. The key words in this transformation process are such terms as deregulation and restructuring. These concepts are often used interchangeably. In Söderlind and Petersson (1988) an attempt is made to bring some order into this conceptual chaos:

> Decentralization implies that the decision-making power is transferred from the state to some other legal body. . . . De-concentration means that competence is transferred from one state agency to another, subordinate, state agency. Delegation implies the transference of the right to make decisions from a superior official to a subordinate official within an agency.
>
> (Ibid.: 116; my translation)

If the concept definitions in the quotation are taken *ad notam*, the implication is that decentralization expresses a changed relationship between the state and society, while de-concentration and delegation imply a corresponding, unchanged relationship. The change in the relationship entailed by decentralization can generally be described as a shift of power from the state to society, which is synonymous with a transformation process oriented toward the societification of the state. This implies that it is an empirical question as to whether decentralization actually does result in a societification of the state. It is, in fact, fully possible that the power that the state formally gives up via decentralization can be taken back – and even strengthened – by means of various control measures. Thus in extreme cases, decentralization, on the official rhetorical level, can give expression to a societification of the state. Concretely, the control measures linked to decentralization might imply an increased *stateification of society* in relation to the original situation. In this case the state has 'covertly' increased rather than reduced its position of power. Thus, the point of departure for our construction of analytical models is that the school's steering, especially during the post-war period, has been very composite as a result of the school's different missions and functions.

Steering Systems and the School's Steering Structures

Relations between Politics and Bureaucracy

The SLAV 2 project focuses on the concepts of *politics* and *bureaucracy* within the sphere of the school. In general, one can say that parliamentary democracy in a strict sense is based on a distinction between politics and bureaucracy, insofar as politicians make decisions that are then loyally

carried out by the bureaucracy in accordance with the political intentions. This absolute distinction can hardly be made in decision making within public life, however – and especially not within complex, 'people-related' spheres of activity such as health care, education and welfare, where decisions of a more or less political nature are made also on the bureaucratic level. In research on implementation processes, a distinction is made between, among other things, *top-down* and *bottom-up* strategies (see, e.g. Sannerstedt 1993). The former imply that the main interest in the implementation process is focused on the political level, while 'bottom-up' implies that interest is focused more on the level where the professionals, or in Lipsky's terms '*the street-level bureaucrats*' (1980; my italics), act.

The conceptual framework developed below is based on relations between politics and bureaucracy in general, and between school politics and school bureaucracy in particular:

1 *Politics in a general societal sense, and bureaucracy in the sense of the school as a state-established institution whose mission is to carry out activity in society.* Here the variable of politics is problematized in the relation between the 'strong' (stateified society) and the 'weak' (societified state) state. Bureaucracy is problematized in the form of the school as one (of several) societal institution(s), which in turn is focused in the range between a centralized and a decentralized school system. The latter concepts acquire their implications in accordance with the above-mentioned conceptual definition, which implied that centralization/decentralization is a question of transference of decision-making power between a centre and a periphery and vice versa.

2 *Politics in the sense of 'school politics', and 'school bureaucracy' in the sense of the type and degree of scope of action within whose framework the street-level bureaucrats carry out actions of a bureaucratic–political nature.* This point can be regarded as a special case of the first-mentioned point, and it lies at the centre of the SLAV 2 project's research interest.

The relation between school politics and street-level bureaucrats is dealt with later. First there is concentration on the general problematics which are included in point 1. Different power relations between politics and bureaucracy in the general sense referred to above, pave the way for different combinations of *steering forms*, a term borrowed from Lundquist (1992). Under the influence of an earlier work by Ramström (1963), four interesting steering forms in this connection can be described as follows:

1 *Rule steering* implies that street-level bureaucrats get direct directives, instructions, and/or orders from superior political levels within the organization. In the extreme case, these instructions do not leave any actual scope for the street-level bureaucrats' own independent actions.

An example of such steering within the sphere of the school is steering by means of rules concerning course division, work schedules, lecture hours, allocation of resources, etc.

2 *Result steering* implies that the desired behaviour of the street-level bureaucrats is specified in, for example, regulations of various types. Examples of result steering within the sphere of the school are decisions about acceptable results with regard to grades, tests, national exams and other evaluative activities. The fact that official activity during recent times has focused on concepts such as 'quality development' and 'quality guarantee' can probably be seen as an expression of an increased focus on result steering. The same is true of the widely used international concept of 'accountability', which focuses on an evaluative activity with quantitative overtones.

3 *Frame steering* is oriented toward the specification of different frameworks, and/or areas of responsibility, which the street-level bureaucrats are not allowed to overstep and/or side-step. Examples of some basic questions, which in this connection are emphasized on account of the school system's formal deregulation, are: 'Where do the boundaries lie between the school's political and professional steering?' and 'Where do the boundaries lie between the responsibility of the state as an employer and the responsibility of the municipality as an executor?'

4 *Goal steering* implies that the desired goals and/or behaviour are given in more or less operational terms, and the street-level bureaucrats themselves choose the methods for achieving these goals or, alternatively, for acting in accordance with the goals. The concepts of equality/a school for all, which were mentioned above, formally compose the core of the goal-steering system, which makes up the basis of the deregulated school system. Politically coloured goal-concepts of this type must, however, be the object of further political and, above all, professional interpretations, if they are to be utilized as more operative guidelines for the daily work of the school.

Generally speaking, the various steering forms relate to the paired concepts of 'politics–bureaucracy' in such a way that rule and frame steering mainly put the focus on the significance of politics in the top-down structured process of implementation. In contrast, result and goal steering focus more on the street-level bureaucrats as the principal actors in the implementation process (see Figure 12.1).

This reasoning leads to the conclusion that the more the power in the implementation process is concentrated at the political level, the greater the opportunities for applying rule and frame steering. Further, if the street-level bureaucrats have a relatively strong position in the implementation process, and the political level's power is relatively weak, then there

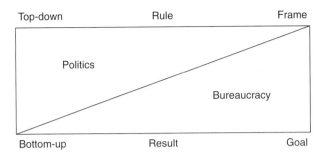

Figure 12.1 Politics and bureaucracy in relation to different forms of steering

are greater opportunities to apply result and goal steering. The above-stated is further developed in what follows.

Owing to its dominant position and control of power, the stateified society has the ability to regulate the institution's activity. This can occur within the framework of a centralized as well as a more decentralized bureaucracy. In the centralized bureaucracy, the state has (by definition) the power to make decisions about the content of the mission as well as about the way in which it is carried out. In practice the relations between politics and bureaucracy are regulated by the state's issuing of more or less detailed rules. The bureaucracy functions in practice, then, as a transport route, where rules are mediated between the institutional and the organizational level (case A in Figure 12.2). The strong state steering can, however – in principle – also be conducted in a more decentralized bureaucracy. In this case the strong state's power is linked to the content of the mission ('the limits'), while the forms for carrying out the mission (i.e., for carrying out operative tasks within the limits set by the state) are handed over to peripheral agencies (the street-level bureaucrats) who independently make the decisions, implement, and follow up. The state formulates, in other words, more or less uniform boundaries for the content and form of the activity, and within these boundaries the bureaucracy is given considerable scope for its own, independent actions (case C).

The weaker state (the societified state) can in principle exist in relation to the centralized as well as the decentralized bureaucracy. In the former case (cell B in Figure 12.2) the state only has the ability to formulate certain minimum criteria for a desired result of the institution's activity. The operative bureaucracy's activity is then limited to the control of these stipulated criteria. In the school's case this can be a matter of ensuring that, for example, schedules, competence criteria and principles for allocating resources are upheld. The relation between the (relatively speaking) weak state and the more decentralized bureaucracy (case D) is a matter of the state having only the ability to express its ambitions in general, ambiguous

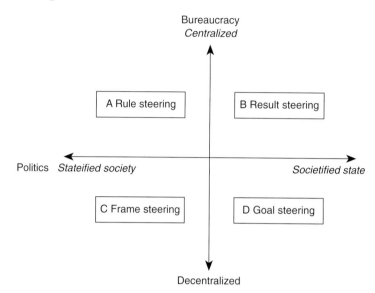

Figure 12.2 Politics, bureaucracy and types of steering systems

and perhaps even contradictory formulations. This paves the way for various local political and professional actors (street-level bureaucrats) to directly or indirectly interpret these generally formulated goal descriptions. The type and degree of the (local) societal pluralism – rather than explicit state ambitions – will thus, in the last instance, decide the content and forms of the actual activity.

Against this background, the reasoning that is summarized in Figure 12.1 is further developed in Figure 12.2, where an attempt is made to illustrate, in a general sense, the different 'ideal-typical' cases of steering relations between politics and bureaucracy using the term 'ideal-typical' in the Weberian (1947) sense.

The Changed State Steering of School in the Light of the Different Steering Systems

Having discussed the general relations between politics and bureaucracy, we can now narrow the discussion to our actual problem area – school politics and school bureaucracy.

As emphasized earlier, the state steering of school has undergone a change. In the official rhetoric, this change is often described as the transition from a rule-steering structure to a goal-steering structure. But in actuality, earlier it was more a matter of an ambiguous steering structure which contained a great number of detailed rules. This rule steering, however, also had pronounced features of result steering (grades, national exams), as well as goal steering (general writings on democracy, co-operation, solidarity, etc.) and frame steering (subject goals, course schedules, etc.). On a formal level, the situation today implies that this earlier, largely rule-steered school has been replaced by what is largely a result- and goal-steered school. Certain detailed rules still exist (e.g. course division). Result steering has escalated (increased emphasis on municipal and national supervision). General goal formulations which focus on democracy and human perspectives are still given a prominent place in curricular texts. Frame steering also occurs in the form of writings on 'the student's choice' and 'the school's choice', etc.

Using Figure 12.2 as a point of departure (the axes have the same desig-nations as in this figure), this can be illustrated as shown in Figures 12.3 and 12.4. Figure 12.3 shows that the largely detailed-rule-steered (marked as a square with continuous lines) school is (was) centralized in its basic character, and that rule steering is (was) complemented by certain features of frame, result and goal steering. Figure 12.4 illustrates the largely goal-steered school system; goal and result steering dominate, but there are still features of rule and frame steering in the steering structure. The steering

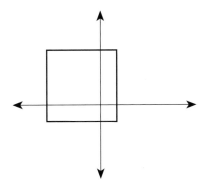

Figure 12.3 The largely rule-steered school

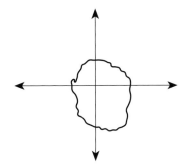

Figure 12.4 The largely goal-steered school

structure is more decentralized and the limits more diffuse in their basic character (marked by the 'dotted cloud').

If the 'square' and 'cloud' are removed from Figures 12.3 and 12.4, respectively, one can say that different compositions and proportions of rule, result, frame and goal steering compose the *outer limits* of the respective steering structures. These limits are synonymous with the school system's formal *political missions*. Within the limits of these respective steering structures, there is room for the street-level bureaucrats to formulate their *bureaucratic–political* tasks. These tasks compose the basis of the actual activity's content and forms. Both steering structures thus contain more or less extensive scope for activity on the bureaucratic level, even though the type and degree of this scope differs in significant respects within the respective steering structures.

Steering Structure and Occupational Roles

If we take the 'square' and the 'cloud' in Figures 12.3, 12.4 and 12.5 as a point of departure, we can say that both steering structures contain more or less extensive scope for locally formulated actions. Additionally, regarding the street-level bureaucrats, if we focus on the type of occupational roles that are accepted by and in these respective steering structures, we find there are relations between

- the largely rule-steered school system and a top-down perspective;

and

- the largely goal-steered school system and a bottom-up perspective.

Rule steering, therefore, paves the way for the decision-making level to exercise a high degree of power and influence vis à vis the operative work. A more result- and goal-steered activity implies that the 'weak' state can only express its intentions with vague, ambiguous and perhaps contradictory steering means. This provides an opportunity for the street-level bureaucrats to interpret these vague intentions (the mission) and, with a significant degree of autonomy, transform the mission into tasks. This implies that the street-level bureaucrats acquire different roles in the respective steering structures. In the largely rule-steered school system, interest is focused on the decision-making political level, and the street-level bureaucrats' roles are reduced to plain and simple implementation of the politically formulated mission. In the largely goal- and result-steered school system, the interest in the implementation process is directed toward the street-level bureaucrats as active and relatively independent groups who make

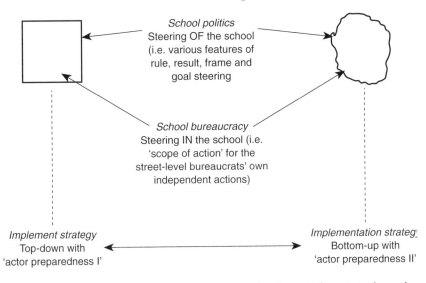

Figure 12.5 School-political steering structures and implementation strategies and preparedness among the school's street-level bureaucrats

their own (bureaucratic–political) decisions in connection with transforming the rather vaguely formulated mission into operative tasks. This reasoning leads to the conclusion that, if the street-level bureaucrats are to function as loyal executors of the political level's decisions – or if this group has its own, actual influence over the content and form of the implementation work – then possibilities arise for different kinds of actor preparedness among these groups.[1] Later I will discuss how these apply to the occupational group of school leaders. At this point, however, they will simply be referred to as 'actor preparedness I' and 'actor preparedness II'. This can be summarized as shown in Figure 12.5.

It should be emphasized that this is a matter of 'pure' relations between politics and bureaucracy, and not *a priori* assumptions about the actual situation under study. This implies that, if schools are studied empirically from a bottom-up perspective, this can lead at best to evaluations as to where the dominant actor preparedness lies in the range between actor preparedness I and II. The collection of data itself occurs, in other words, on the level of the school as an organization, but in order to acquire deeper understanding of why the professional actor preparedness can vary from school to school, the results of the empirical studies are 'lifted' from the organizational to the institutional level. This implies that the focus is placed on the type and degree of the institutional value bases in which the respective kinds of actor preparedness are anchored.

School Leaders as Street-Level Bureaucrats

At the time of writing, an analysis is underway of the SLAV 2 project's empirical studies which were carried out in ten Swedish municipalities. This project is a development and expansion of the problem area that was treated within the framework of the project 'School Leaders' Work and Working Conditions' (SLAV 1) (Nytell 1994; Berg 1995), and we can take our ideal-typical examples from that project.

If we thus focus on school leaders as an occupational group and regard this group in the perspective of actor preparedness II, the way is paved for an educatively and administratively responsible school leader. On the other hand, if school leaders are regarded in the perspective of actor preparedness I, the role can instead be characterized as that of a pure administrator. The tasks of the educatively and administratively responsible school leader consist in making sure that the actual activity corresponds to the institutional mission, whereas the administrator's tasks are more specifically to manage the activity on its own terms, i.e. in conformity with traditional conditions (Berg 1995).

These divergent demands from the surrounding world can be viewed as extreme points of a measure which express the different demands on, in this case, school leaders. The administrator role is based on the school leaders carrying out the work that the teachers – in their capacity as the main bearers of the traditional school culture – expect them to, in accordance with a concept developed in the SLAV 1 project, namely, the so-called *invisible contract* (Berg 1996). Simply put, this implies a more or less strict division of work between the school leaders and the teachers. The school leader's main responsibility is here limited to managing the school's administrative apparatus (task distribution, formation of schedules, etc.) for the purpose of giving the teachers the administrative prerequisites to carry out traditional instruction. The teachers are responsible for the activity in the classroom, and the school leaders for the activity that occurs outside the classroom; the parties intervene to a limited extent in each other's area of activity. The educatively and administratively responsible school leader has, basically, a different occupational role, which presupposes that school leaders adhere to, and act in accordance with, the fundamentally more diffuse institutional mission that is marked as the 'dotted cloud' in Figures 12.4 and 12.5. Given this, it follows that each school leader must have deeper insight into this mission's background, development and (ambiguous) content. This is the same as having insight into how far the limits for permissible school activity extend.[2] With these insights as a point of departure, the task of the school leader is then to check that the actual activity is kept within these limits. This rather supervisory school leader role ought to be complemented, however, by a supportive role, which implies that the school leader encourages and stimulates the personnel in relation to the problems which can and do arise from the school's activity. This is the same as encouraging the school's personnel to make use of the scope of action that exists within the limits. The occupational code here is thus a matter of acting as a boss (control–evaluation) as well as a leader[3] (support–development work). Against this background, the educatively and administratively responsible school leader's work area encompasses the school's activity – including the work in the classroom – in all its aspects. Further, the fundamental knowledge base needed by a school leader to be able to cope with an occupational role of this type can be described as a broad knowledge of the surrounding world with a focus on steering *of* as well as steering *in* the school.

The educatively and administratively responsible school leader must, in other words, interfere in some way in the strictly divided work relationship between teachers and school leaders which is expressed in the 'invisible contract'. In this 'battle for the classroom' there is a hint of a potential conflict between the school leader and the teaching profession.

By linking the pair of concepts 'steering of' and 'steering in' the school to the educatively and administratively responsible school leadership and the purely administrative leadership, respectively, the SLAV 1 project was able to distinguish some critical areas for the respective school leadership roles. It was apparent that educatively and administratively responsible school leadership is a matter of *leading* the activity within the limits ultimately set by the type and degree of 'steering sources' that are encompassed in the concepts of steering of and in the school. Further, this leadership is a matter of taking offensive action in relation to the existing cultures and the types of actor preparedness linked to them. The administrative leadership is basically a question of *being led*. More precisely, this ultimately implies carrying out activity in accordance with the existing system of rules, and striving to 'tame' the existing school culture so that its content corresponds to the content and meaning of the system of rules. The core of educatively and administratively responsible leadership is thus a matter of discovering and utilizing the *opportunities* that are available, whereas the core of administrative leadership is a question of forming the activity in relation to the *limits* prescribed by the system (see Figure 12.6). Thus, Figure 12.6 integrates the earlier discussions that focused on steering *and* leadership.

Final Comments: Steering System, Steering Structure, and Steering Form

Now and then in this work I have used the concepts in the heading above, and therefore it may be helpful to try to define them in a composite way.

By *steering form* is meant the formal means with which to influence, such as rule, result, frame, and goal steering, which are applied on a political level and whose purpose is to get the relevant bureaucratic level to put the

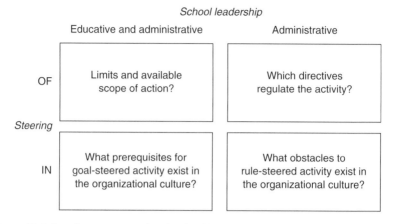

Figure 12.6 Steering as opposed to leadership

political mission into practice. *Steering structure* refers to the combinations of steering forms, which as a whole constitute the outer limits within which the activity is carried out (steering 'of'), and that thereby mark the type and degree of the scope of action for the bureaucratic–political actions of the street-level bureaucrats (steering 'in'). *Steering system* is the most comprehensive concept in this connection, and it refers to the potential of the means of influence that – given the actual institutional context (state-society) – are available in the formal and informal interaction between and within the main actors of the implementation process, that is, the politicians and street-level bureaucrats. Figures 12.1 and 12.2 illustrate the steering system's general potential, while Figures 12.3–12.5 give two pictures of the school's steering structures, which encompass different combinations of steering forms.

Notes

1 The concept of actor preparedness was coined and further elaborated in Berg (1989).
2 Cf. the discussion on the scope of action model, presented in Berg (1983, 1993).
3 Cf. the distinction between boss and leader in Stålhammar (1984).

References

Abrahamsson, B. (1993) *Why Organizations?* Newbury Park, CA: Sage.
Berg, G. (1983) Developing the Teaching Profession: Autonomy, Professional Code, Knowledge Base. *Australian Journal of Education*, 2.
—— (1992) Changes in the Steering of Swedish Schools: A Step towards 'Societification of the State'. *Journal of Curriculum Studies*, 24.

—— (1993) *Curriculum and State Schools as Organizations: A Scandinavian View. An Integration of Research into the School as an Organization and Institution Conducted at the Department of Education, Uppsala University.* Uppsala Reports on Education, 30. Uppsala: Department of Education, University of Uppsala.

—— (1995) Steering of the School, the School as an Institution and the School Culture. In K. Hämäläinen, D. Oldroyd and E. Haapanen (eds), *Making School Improvement Happen.* Studia Paedagogica, 7. Helsinki: Department of Teacher Education, Vantaa Institute for Continuing Education, University of Helsinki.

—— (1996) Steering, School Leadership and the Invisible Contract. In J. Kalous and F. van Wieringen (eds), *Improving Educational Management.* Educational Policy and Administration Series. Academisch Boeken Centrum, ABC. De Lier.

Berg, G. and Söderström, M. (1988) Work Organization in School – What it is About? *School Organization,* 2: .

Englund, T. (ed.), (1996) *Utbildningspolitiskt systemskifte?* Stockholm: HLS Förlag.

Lipsky, M. (1980) *Street-Level Bureaucracy: Dilemmas of the Individual in the Public Services.* New York: Russell Sage.

Lundquist, L. (1992) *Förvaltning, stat och samhälle.* Lund: Studentlitteratur.

Nytell, U. (1994) *Styra eller styras? En studie av skolledares arbete och arbetsvillkor.* Doktorsavhandling. Uppsala Studies in Education, 58. Uppsala: Acta Universitatis Upsaliensis.

Petersson, O. (1988) *Metaforernas makt.* Stockholm: Carlssons.

Ramström, D. (1963) *Administrativa processer.* Stockholm: Sv Bokförlaget.

Sannerstedt, A. (1993) Implementering – hur politiska beslut genomförs i praktiken. Im B. Rothstein (ed.), *Politik som organization. Förvaltningspolitikens grundproblem.* Stockholm: SNS Förlag.

Sirjamaki, J. 1967. Education as Social Institution. In D.A. Hansen and J.E. Gertl (eds), *On Education: Sociological Perspectives.* New York: John Wiley.

Söderlind, D. and Petersson, O. (1988) *Svensk förvaltningspolitik.* Uppsala: Diskurs.

Stålhammar, B. (1984) *Rektorsfunktionen i grundskolan. Vision-verklighet. Akademisk avhandling.* Uppsala Studies in Education, 22. Uppsala: Acta Universitatis Upsaliensis.

Weber, M. (1947) *The Theory of Social and Economic Organization.* New York: Free Press.

13 School Principals in Transition
Conflicting Expectations, Demands and Desires

Jorunn Møller

This chapter focuses on how a group of Norwegian principals cope with the devolution of greater responsibilities to schools. When asked, principals state their preference for addressing curriculum and instructional issues, but they feel imprisoned by a problematic working context, and a managerial agenda seems to dominate. Not only does time push against the realization of their wishes, but they experience conflicting demands and expectations from superiors, teachers, parents and students. Participating in action research seems to strengthen an educational agenda, but in the short run it may result in an intensification of work, because spaces for critical reflection upon practice have been curtailed. However, principals are daily involved in a struggle for negotiating their legitimacy as leaders, and in this process analytical competency and reflection on action among peers may become crucial.

Contradictions in Policy

Decentralization has been a key word in educational reforms in Norway since the 1970s. The basis of the main arguments has been that greater decentralization would mobilize resources that were not available under more centralized conditions, and that decentralized systems could utilise available resources more efficiently. Management by objectives is said to be a central principle of governance, and new national curriculum guidelines have been launched, in which the goals are more clearly articulated and tied to a national assessment programme. In White Papers from the government there seems to be a strong belief that better leadership and assessment in school are the keys to school improvement.

However, contradictions are detectable. For instance, school democracy and teacher professionalism are emphasized in national curriculum guidelines. Here the professional teacher seems to be the key to school improvement. At the same time, in moving from central control towards more local control, the question of who should have the responsibility is raised, and the struggle between political and professional power over education has been intensified. New constructs in which principals are seen as managing directors are growing in prominence and power. In policy documents dealing with in-service training, the notion of the 'reflective practitioner' has emerged as a desired goal of continuing professional development. Reflective practice among educators has been underlined as the answer to increasing the quality of leadership, teaching and learning. An expectation is placed on school-based development, and there is a focus on collective as well as individual learning. At the same time, work intensification has increased dramatically, so that space and opportunities for critical reflection upon practice have been curtailed for both principals and teachers. Moreover, there is a tendency to exert control over teachers' work and teachers' time, and reforms launched at municipal level seem to be driven by concerns for effectiveness, productivity and accountability.

Seen from the perspective of principals, the devolution of greater responsibilities to schools has contributed to a number of changing demands upon them. They are expected to be instructional leaders, role models for teachers, innovators, change agents, negotiators and managers. Each role contains desirable values, but often they compete with each other. For instance, managing means keeping the organization working efficiently towards its goals. In order to do that, the ability to reduce conflicts is highly prized. To focus on leadership, on the other hand, means seeking changes, taking risks by introducing new programmes, and accepting conflict as a natural state. There are certainly dilemmas inherent in these roles[1] (Cuban 1996).

In this article, I will explore how some school principals in Norwegian compulsory schools, have attempted to cope with the devolution of greater responsibilities to schools, and some of the dilemmas inherent in their role.[2] The analysis is based upon qualitative data drawn from a two-year action research project involving twenty-seven school leaders from three municipalities in Norway (cf. Møller 1995, 1996). The action research project offered an opportunity to reflect systematically on actions with colleagues and external researchers.

The School Principal as an Instructional Leader

In the Norwegian context neither external nor internal accountability issues have emerged onto the agenda until recently. There has been a strong norm of non-interference in the teacher's classroom activities, and individual autonomy is part of the tradition in schools. When principals and teachers have discussions, they talk about ad hoc problems like student discipline or parental complaints, rather than curriculum policies or anything else related to instructional efforts. Trust in teachers' work has for long been a tacit dimension in principals' approach to leadership, or maybe in reality it has to do with accepted zones of influence. This can be related to the history of teaching in Norway. During the period from the late decades of the nineteenth century to the early 1970s, teachers had high status, and teaching attracted the brightest people, especially in rural areas. Historically, the status of Norwegian teachers probably rested a good deal on their role in public life (cf. Lauglo 1990).

However, established zones of control are now challenged. People outside schools question the autonomy each teacher has in his or her classroom. In the media teachers are often depicted as antagonistic to change. The Ministry of Education, Research and Church Affairs has responded by placing the principal in a key role in change efforts and school improvement. As a result the opposition between control and autonomy in schools seems to have been accentuated, and principals experience a dilemma of top-down steering versus professional autonomy. The following situation[3] can be used to highlight this dilemma:

> The staff at Skogen have, through a long process, developed a shared vision and formulated a shared policy. Glasser's 'School without Failure' has inspired teachers to organize their relationship with students in specific ways, involving students in curriculum planning and problem solving. They are trying to break down the boundaries between the different classes, having a shared responsibility for all students at the school. When new teachers are employed, both the principal and the teachers are engaged in sharing their vision and motivating for commitment.
>
> When Mr Hansen got tenure at this school, he received a lot of information about how the school was working, what goals it had set, and how it had tried to accomplish them. In conversations with the principal, Hansen says he will be committed to the school's vision. There is, however, often a gap between espoused theories and theories in use. The principal soon understands that Hansen does not involve students in curriculum planning in his class. He is also unwilling to accept shared responsibility for all the students. His concern is his own classroom and his own students. He does not care for other students.
>
> The principal decides that he has to do something, and initiates several conversations with Hansen. He gives him pedagogical literature to read, and he ensures that experienced teachers at schools are willing to share their knowledge with Hansen. However, nothing seems to have any effect. Now Hansen insists on teaching in his own way. The principal has a dilemma, which he frames in the following questions: can I accept that a teacher refuses to follow the school policy? For how long shall I accept this when this teacher declared that he would be loyal to the school's vision when he started working at the school?

When is the time for support, and when is the time for confrontation and demands? When do you use sanctions? What kind of sanctions do I have? The principal fears that non-interference will have a negative effect on the rest of the staff. Is it a good idea to try to persuade this teacher to move on to another school where individual autonomy is still accepted?

The importance of developing a vision has been emphasized in recent years (cf. Hoyle 1986). Research on leadership has particularly dealt with strategies used by school administrators to influence a more collaborative culture in schools (Leithwood and Jantzi 1990; Leithwood and Steinbach 1993). A shared vision and commitment building among staff are perceived to be crucial to school improvement. The rationale behind shared vision building has to do with the creation of meaning, ownership and mutual trust. But as Fullan and Hargreaves (1992: 94) have pointed out in their analysis, there is a peril to beware of here: 'While commitment to collaboration is important, over-commitment or compulsion can be damaging.' Vision without voice very easily results in bureaucratic control, but the opposite makes it impossible to validate education.

As the situation at Skogen school shows, building a shared vision does not solve the dilemma of steering. The stability of staff members may change. New people are coming in without the same commitment to the vision. The principal and the teachers are left with the challenge of how to include new members of staff in the established culture without disempowering them. How can one balance between mandates and menus? Maybe the established culture needs critical voices? The many conversations with the teacher referred to in this example, have the purpose of convincing the teacher that changing practice is to the benefit of the students. But we do not know if the students think Mr Hansen is an under-performing teacher: we only have the principal's perception and description of the situation.

The dilemma is connected with what it means to be a professional teacher, who is going to define standards for good teaching, and when the principal has the right to interfere. The dilemma can be analysed through the lens of legality (the formal steering of schools) versus legitimacy (the informal control mechanism embedded in traditions and culture). No doubt, seen from the perspective of legality, the principal has the right to interfere with classroom activities in this situation. But the question is whether this will be of any help to the students. The principal can influence employment policy only to a very small degree.[4] Hiring is done by the school board at the municipal level; the opportunity to influence firing is even less. Thus, in reality the principal lacks sanctions. He is left to rely on argumentative authority.

Teacher autonomy has long been interpreted as the right of each individual teacher to make independent judgements about classroom practice (cf. Little 1988). However, teachers have many more collective tasks now compared to earlier days. Thus, the need to develop a collective knowledge base and to reflect on teaching among peers has increased. In addition, the system is only partially independent. As a profession, teachers have freedom of movement within the limits defined by what society expects of its schools, but these boundaries for action are abstract, indistinct, and often contradictory (cf. Berg 1993; Lundgren 1986). It is hardly correct, though, to interpret the autonomy given by society as an individual freedom: the autonomy is given to the profession. It means that the teaching profession has the right to construct and uphold standards of good teaching; and critical reflection with colleagues can serve as a protection against arbitrariness in teaching and also a guard against the power of the profession. At the same time, one needs to maintain a balance between individuality and collaboration and recognize that there must be room for individual ways of teaching.

From the arguments above, it should follow that the principal should choose top-down steering in this case, but the dilemma does not disappear with that. To change a culture of 'privacy' in teaching requires a long-term strategy in which in-service training should be combined with support, challenge and patience. In addition, structural frames which prevent collaboration at school level should be changed.

Reflecting further on the situation, one will discover dilemmas related to issues of loyalty in the situation at Skogen school. As a middle manager, the principal has the responsibility to implement the national curriculum guidelines. In this case, according to the principal, the teacher did not differentiate his teaching in proper ways, in spite of having a mixed ability group in the class. Consequently, one could say that the principal should interfere. He would find support in the school law: nevertheless, the potential to act seems much more limited. At the same time, as an employer, the principal has a caring responsibility for everyone on his staff. What is the best way of caring in this situation?

The School Principal as a Change Agent

Principals are expected to act as change agents, but the study reveals that principals' approach to change is very cautious, even when they are under strong pressure from superiors to act as change agents. It seems best to be on the safe side, not disturbing everyday practice too much. There is, though, an acknowledgement among school leaders of the need for changes in schools. As an example I will refer to what the principal at Oakridge school, a lower secondary school with 350 students, wrote in her journal:

> I really want to be a visible and assertive principal, but very often I do not succeed. . . . The staff are used to having a voice in every decision

making, and I can recognize this as important for raising enthusiasm and commitment. But there is a limit. This whole year I have been thinking about how to initiate peer review and a more collaborative culture when it comes to teaching at this school. But the staff want to give other things priority. I have chosen not to insist on my proposition, but I am not satisfied with it. How can people give something priority if they don't know what it means? I have tried to use an implicit strategy, starting to talk about this more informally, and I can see interest awaken in some. Everything would have been so much easier if only the superintendent could say: You must implement peer review! Then I could use my time on the motivation phase instead of this very slow process. The district office should be more demanding! (Or is this another excuse for me not being able to do what I want?)

The principal at Oakridge school wishes for more support from the superintendent. But the question still remains: will it be of any help? Looking at schools from a micro political perspective, there are a lot of ways to resist steering. The principal has to convince staff that change is necessary, good both for the students and for the school. At the same time, it is important to emphasize that our choices are not always based on altruistic behaviour. Many may have private privileges and interests to defend.

Other studies show similar tendencies. There seems to be a strong pressure towards conservative attitudes and stability within the school system. Lortie (1987) is rather pessimistic about the principal's potential to be a change agent. In his study of principals in Chicago, he found that there were four powerful tendencies towards stability, related to recruitment, role constraints and psychic rewards, constraint of system standardization and career contingencies. Stålhammar's (1985) study shows similar tendencies. Very few principals initiated changes at the school level; pressure towards stability was far more important.

The Principal as Manager

Managing means keeping the school working efficiently toward its goals, and historically principals have given priority to administrative duties and housekeeping. But are principals effective managers? My study shows how principals often organize their days in a rather ad hoc fashion. The following description, based on field notes from observation of the principal of Flatland school in his office, can be used to highlight this issue. The observer was a consultant from the School Director's Office. Before the observation started, the principal said that he planned to write a summary from a meeting with parents.

The office hour is characterized by discontinuity and several inter-ruptions in which the principal tries to respond to emergencies and housekeeping. The office door is open. First he has a meeting with the caretaker of the school. They are discussing the economics of a building project. The principal wants to work out the economic details, and he gives reasons why this is important. The caretaker is unclear about the economics, and it is difficult to understand how expensive the project is going to be. In a way they never end the discussion, and they do not make an appointment for a follow-up meeting. [*It seems to the observer that economics was not the real issue at hand. Rather, it was important for the two parties to confirm their relationship to each other.*] When they start the meeting, the principal shows interest in the caretaker's work, asking questions, and when their discussion comes to an end, the principal says: 'It seems that you are very satisfied with working at this school.' The caretaker confirmed it with a smile.

A teacher suddenly rushes into the office and begins talking about three students with whom she has serious problems. The principal accepts that the moment for discussion is convenient, even though he has an external observer listening to the conversation and even though the door to the hall is open. It takes time before the principal under-stands what the problem is and is able to give a few words of advice. They talk for approximately twenty minutes, and the teacher is stand-ing beside the principal's desk.

Two men who are unknown to the principal, are suddenly standing in the doorway. They want to discuss the alarm system with the principal. The principal starts talking to them, but he seems a bit surprised and confused at their arrival. He says that there is a possibility that the school could be interested in buying a new system, but he needs to dis-cuss this with his deputy head and suggests that they arrange a meeting later. It has now become clear that the visitors are selling alarm systems. The discussion continues. After fifteen minutes the principal repeats, and this time it is clear: 'Can we arrange for a meeting about this? Call me later!'

The school bell announces that the office hour has passed. No summary from the meeting with parents has been written. For the next hour the principal is going to teach grade four (10–11-year-old) students. The principal tells the observer that what she has observed has been a typical office hour. He is always interrupted, and is seldom able to do what he has planned.

This summary from observation field notes gives only a glimpse of the principal's job, but other field notes give a similar picture. In a working context filled with contradictory expectations, principals are strongly action oriented and seem to be constantly responding to the needs of the moment (Møller 1995).

Later the same day the principal reflected with peers and an external facilitator on his way of taking care of his duties. What had happened that day was part of what the principal experienced as a pattern. In his reflection the principal focused on what he had managed to do. He thought it was right to listen to the angry teacher and help her to deal with her problem, but he was dissatisfied with having given so much time to the salesmen.

In the conversation the external facilitator encouraged the principal to reflect more on his own reconstruction of experiences and asked why he chose to do what he did. At first it was difficult to articulate reasons. Then he argued that teachers always expected him to be available. Why he had been available to the salesmen in the same way, he could not explain. It had just happened. The tacit knowledge that the principal had allowed to develop over time was identified as a norm of his being available for every-one all the time. The principal understood that he tacitly allowed other people to decide the agenda of the day. He became aware that alternative courses of action were needed to fulfil the mission of the school. However, when it came to dealing with students' problems, the principal found it right and important to be available. An ethic of caring was dominant in his understanding of his mission. Reflecting more on this issue, the principal realized that he could probably be of more help for his teachers and students if he gave himself more time to analyse the situation before giving advice.

In this case the external facilitator contributed, through her questions, to another way of framing and understanding the experiences. As a result the principal proclaimed that he wanted to organize his days differently. He had not been aware of the way in which he always let other people decide what he should do. No wonder it was difficult to give priority to addressing curriculum issues. A *motivation* to change his actions emerged, but that does not mean that he was better *able* to deal with contradictory expectations in the future.

A Managerial Imperative?

Time is central to the formation of both school leaders' and teachers' work (cf. Hargreaves 1994). A new agreement between the Ministry of Education, Research and Church Affairs and different teacher unions concerning the tasks of teaching personnel was put into effect on 1 January 1994. The agreement implied an increased amount of scheduled time available for teachers outside the classroom. The Ministry saw this agreement as a tool to enable principals to take responsibility for implementing the new national curriculum guidelines and make plans for collaboration. They referred to educational research which emphasized collaboration among teachers as important for school improvement, and the agreement would make it possible to break down teacher isolation and develop norms of collegiality.

Many principals appreciate this new agreement on work time for teachers. Seen from their perspective, collective time is important in order to initiate more collective work in school. Teachers assess quite differently the way collective time is organized (Klette 1996), and defend their right to use preparation time more flexibly. Principals have experiences of the way in which conflicts arise when they designate preparation time for particular purposes like collaborative planning, but at the same time they feel they have to be loyal to their employers at the municipal and central level. They are engaging in coping strategies to comply with legal mandates. Yearly they have to send a report to the education officer on how the collective work-time is organized. They are both oppressors and oppressed. For some principals a dilemma of identity has been created. They want to be considered as professional leaders among both their teachers and their superiors, but what does it mean to be a professional in a job where they feel they continually have to respond to daily emergencies? It seems as if the criteria used by the municipality are different from the criteria used by teachers. In-service training for principals[5] is the responsibility of the municipal level, and when in-service programmes initiated by municipalities are analysed, it seems as if an understanding of leadership as management is dominant.

The question is whether the education policy lays down a managerial rather than an educational agenda for its exercise. According to many school leaders, decentralization has come to mean an opportunity to manage dwindling budgetary resources, and there has been a great increase in paperwork as a result of greater emphasis on accountability and evaluation. The position of principal has become less attractive, and there are few applicants for the jobs available in many cities.

Reflective Inquiries as an Approach to Professional Development

Action research is connected with professional development. But do principals manage to address curriculum and instructional issues in a better way than before, after they have been involved in reflective inquiry? Do they deal with work intensification in a better way than before? Or is this just a strategy to legitimize the allocation of less money to in-service training?

In their own review, the principals emphasized that participating in action research resulted in a greater awareness of their responsibility as educators. They referred to situations on which they had managed to address curriculum and instructional issues in a better way than before.

But sometimes the process of reflecting on what was happening in their practice caused more frustrations than emancipatory feelings, as journal entries, interviews and field notes from peer review reveal:

> I have become more and more aware of how important reflective activities are. It is a way of developing one's competency. You can't be a supervisor to teachers without having competency. But to find time for systematic reflection in everyday practice is problematic. We always have too little time.
>
> (Principal at Flatland school)

> When you are engaged in daily work and routines, and a lot of things are happening, to find time for reflection becomes a burden. There are always tasks you *must* do. . . . In fact, I found writing in a journal very time consuming. It is a burden. However, I have experienced some benefit from it. Participating in this project has stimulated more reflection. Usually I never write down my reflections, but I do reflect on what is happening.
>
> (Principal at Bygda school)

> I give priority to being available for my staff. My door is always open. This means other tasks have to wait if teachers need to talk with me. Maybe that is a wrong priority? Maybe I should sometimes close my door in order to do some paperwork and more long-term planning? I always have to do paperwork at home. I know I haven't managed to be an initiator of pedagogical change, even though I know the staff expect me to do it. I don't have enough time to do all of the tasks. . . . By participating in this project, I have discovered new aspects of leadership, and I think I have developed both my thinking and my skills. I am now motivated to take more education; I think I need it to become a real educator. But time is a problem. I am so dissatisfied by having so little time for administration and leadership.
>
> (Vice-principal at Flatland school)

These reflections might have a connection with leaders' aspirations to be considered as professionals in a job where they continually felt that they had to respond to daily emergencies. The leaders' descriptions could have been a way of defending themselves against expectations that they should have been more reflective. The principals knew the 'right' answers. They had 'learned' that long-term planning, having a vision for their school, and reflection on action were important for calling oneself professional. Did this mean that engaging in reflective inquiries in fact resulted in an intensification of work? In addition to all other duties and demands, they were expected to plan for reflective inquiries. Maybe in the short run reflective inquiries meant an intensification of work, particularly because spaces and opportunities for critical reflection upon practice had been curtailed owing to the contemporary conditions of schooling. But principals will be involved in a struggle for negotiating and maintaining their legitimacy as leaders. In this process analytical competency and reflection on action among peers may become crucial.

Conclusion

The data from the action research project referred to in this chapter, inhibit generalizations, but the findings give leads to future areas of investigation. First, there is certainly a tension between principals' desire to be instructional leaders and demands from the municipal level for them to be managers. Undoubtedly, the paperwork has greatly increased, owing to greater emphasis on accountability issues. Very often principals find themselves engaged in coping strategies to comply with legal mandates that sometimes seem impossible to implement. Contradictions within reform initiatives and society are an integral part of the explanation of the patterns explored in the research project.

Second, being a principal in Norwegian compulsory schools has historically been linked to housekeeping and maintaining order. It is naive to assume that policy statements towards the restructuring of schools will alter these relationships and zones of influences in the short run. There are many ways to resist steering if one examines schools from a micro political perspective, and neither the actions of principals nor the actions of teachers are always based on altruistic behaviour. The legitimacy of leadership cannot be commanded, it can only be granted. To change a culture of privacy in teaching requires a long-term strategy, and vision without voice can easily result in bureaucratic control (cf. Hargreaves 1991). In the field of educational administration there seems to be a tacit ideology of political neutrality, and the range of contextual factors that restrict and condition the way principals and superintendents act in specific settings are often neglected. Moreover, the tendency to see school culture as an organizational variable that can be shaped and manipulated by administrators misses the point that culture is contested and lies beyond rational control (Bates 1986).

Third, it is true that principals have power as part of their formal position. Vis-à-vis students, and sometimes teachers and parents, they do wield power. Yet they are often victims of dysfunctional institutional arrangements and are engaging in coping strategies to comply with legal mandates that are sometimes impossible to implement. More correctly, one could say that educational administrators are both oppressors and oppressed (cf. Anderson 1991; Burbules 1986). Both the actions of subordinates and the actions of superiors influence the structures of domination. At the same time all actors are constituted by the structures in which they find themselves (Giddens 1984).

Action research as an approach to professional development among principals seems to have great potential for strengthening an educational agenda in schools. It helps principals to focus on their responsibility as educators. However, in the short run it may result in an intensification of work, because spaces for critical reflection upon practice have been curtailed, owing to the conditions of schooling. To initiate change in schools probably presupposes a combination of change in structural frames and culture, and a continuous education for principals and teachers. This education should include an understanding of the type of control that state and society exercise on the school, reflections on actions among peers, and focus on understanding and thriving in dilemma-ridden settings.

Appendix

The Education System in Norway: An Overview

In Norway, the National Assembly, the Storting, has the legislative power and overall responsibility for education. The Storting consequently sets the principal objectives of education and the frames of its administrative structure. The government exerts its authority in matters of education through the Ministry of Education, Research and Church Affairs. This ministry covers all levels of education from primary and secondary to higher education, including adult education and Norwegian research policy. In 1997, in the legislative reforms known as Reform 97, the Storting decided to lower the school starting age from 7 to 6, and to extend the period of compulsory schooling to ten years instead of nine. Pre-school education and child-care institutions are the responsibility of the Ministry of Children and Family Affairs.

There are three main levels in the education system:

1 compulsory school (ages 6–13 and lower secondary, ages 13–16);
2 upper secondary education, including apprenticeship training (ages 16–19);
3 tertiary education: colleges and universities.

The private sector in Norwegian education is small (1.6 per cent of pupils in compulsory school, and about 4 per cent in upper secondary). Private schools are regarded as a supplement to state schools rather than as competitors. Most private schools are based on a particular religious denomination or philosophy of life. As a rule, private schools receive a grant that covers 85 per cent of their running costs. (Cf. *The Development of Education 1992–94, Norway*. National Report. Oslo: The Royal Ministry of Education, Research and Church Affairs)

Notes

1 Dilemma is used as a concept to capture the alternative or contradictory orienta-tions the leaders experience (cf. Berlak and Berlak 1981; Cuban 1992).
2 The appendix (p. 221) gives a brief account of the education system in Norway.
3 The description from Skogen is based on the principal's presentation of a case which was discussed with peers at a meeting. The principal needed advice about what to do in this specific situation. Skogen school is a primary school with 220 students and 19 teachers. Pseudonyms are used throughout.
4 This is an issue that is under debate in the Norwegian context at present. Many politicians call for a change whereby principals can appoint teachers. Some municipalities, for instance Oslo, have decentralized the appointment of teachers to school level. However, appointments and firing are still strictly regulated by law, and teacher unions have an important voice.
5 Norwegian principals do not have to participate in a formal preparation pro-gramme of school administration to become school leaders. Neither is there a system of apprenticeship with an experienced and competent administrator. Three years of practice as a teacher is sufficient to enable a teacher to apply for a leadership position. Having once secured the position, principals are offered six to twelve days a year of in-service training.

References

Anderson, G. (1991) Studying Up: Critical Inquiry and the Study of Teaching and Administration. Paper presented at the annual meeting of the American Educa-tional Research Association, April. Chicago.

Bates, R. (1986) *The Management of Culture and Knowledge*. Victoria, Australia: Deakin University Press.

Berlak, A. and Berlak, H. (1981) *Dilemmas of Schooling: Teaching and Social Change*. London: Methuen.

Berg, G. (1993) *Curriculum and State Schools as Organizations. A Scandinavian View*. Uppsala: University of Uppsala, Department of Education.

Burbules, N.C. (1986) A Theory of Power in Education. *Educational Theory*, 36(2): 95–114.

Cuban, L. (1992) Managing Dilemmas While Building Professional Communities. *Educational Researcher*, 21(1): 4–12.

—— (1996) Reforming the Practice of Educational Administration through Mana-ging Dilemmas. In S.L. Jacobons, E.S. Hickcox and R.B. Stevenson (eds), *School Administration: Persistent Dilemmas in Preparation and Practice*. London: Praeger.

Fullan, M. and Hargreaves, A. (1992) *What's Worth Fighting For? Working Together for Your School*. Toronto: Ontario Public School Teachers' Federation and New York: Teachers College Press.

Giddens, A. (1984) *The Constitution of Society*. Berkeley and Los Angeles, CA: University of California Press.

Hargreaves, A. (1991) Restructuring Restructuring: Postmodernity and the Prospect for Educational Change. Paper Presented at the annual meeting of the American Educational Research Association, April. Chicago.

—— (1994) *Changing Teachers, Changing Times: Teachers' Work and Culture in the Postmodern Age*. New York: Teachers College Press.

Hoyle, E. (1986) *The Politics of School Management*. London: Hodder & Stoughton.

Klette, K. (1996) Working Time Blues: How Norwegian Teachers Experience *Restructuration in Education*. Paper presented at the European Conference on Educational Research, September. Seville.

Lauglo, J. (1990) A Comparative Perspective with Special Reference to Norway. In M. Granheim, M. Kogan and U. Lundgren (eds), *Evaluation as Policymaking: Introducing Evaluation into a National Decentralised Educational System*. London: Jessica Kingsley.

Leithwood, K. and Jantzi, D. (1990) Transformational Leadership: How Principals Can Help Reform School Cultures. Paper presented at the annual meeting of the Canadian Association for Curriculum Studies, June. Victoria.

Leithwood, K. and Steinbach, R. (1993) Total Quality Leadership: Expert Thinking plus Transformational Practice. Paper presented at the annual conference of the Canadian Society for the Study of Education. Ottawa, Ontario.

Little, J.W. (1988) Assessing the Prospects for Teacher Leadership. In A. Lieberman (ed.), *Building a Professional Culture in Schools*. New York and London: Teachers College Press.

Lortie, D. (1987) Built in Tendencies Toward Stabilizing the Principal's Role. *Journal of Research and Development in Education*, 22(1): 80–90.

Lundgren, U. (1986) *Att organisera skolan*. Stockholm: Liber Utbildningsförlaget.

Møller, J. (1995) Rektor som pedagogisk leder i grunnskolen – i spenningsfeltet mellom *forvaltning, tradisjon og profesjon*. Avhandling til dr.polit. graden. (Ph.D. thesis) Pedagogisk Forskningsinstitutt, University of Oslo.

—— (1996) Rethinking Educational Leadership. *EERA Bulletin*, 2(3): 13–24.

Stålhammar, B. (1985) *Skolledning i förändring*. Stockholm: Liber.

14 Preparing for External Inspection

School Leadership as a Continuing Project in Identity Construction

Colin Biott and Franz Rauch

The purpose of this chapter is to show how the role of headteacher has been enacted contingently in a large urban primary school in England during a six-month period prior to an external inspection by the Office for Standards in Education (OFSTED). The case study was carried out during a European Union funded project 'Management for Organisational and Human Development'[1] which, in part, has investigated individual agency at different hierarchical levels in organizations. It traces interplay between a headteacher's urgent requirement to prepare a school for inspection and her aim to enable staff to contribute to organic school development. The chapter is not concerned with success or failure, and what we have outlined here may represent focused effort in special circumstances rather than a long-term orientation to work or enduring personal change. The chapter explores some dilemmas the headteacher experienced in her work, and shows how she transformed external regulation into a resource to reduce her own uncertainty, suggesting that school leadership can be understood as a continuing project of identity construction in the face of contradictory demands. Despite intense concentration of effort to meet inspection criteria, the headteacher continued to feel that she could make things happen; seeing herself as a shaper and developer, with an eye on the future, rather than being merely reactive to imposed mandates.

Increasing Demands on Headteachers

Headteachers in the UK have been 'encouraged to be more self-determining, entrepreneurial, cost effective and consumer orientated' (Bowe et al. 1992: 140). They have become targets as well as agents of change in a drive for improved standards in schools, and a recent survey by the National Association of Headteachers in the UK has revealed 'probably the worst recruitment crisis in living memory' (*TES* 1997). Between 1996 and 1997 the number of vacancies for primary school headships in England has risen by 29 per cent. Similar problems have also been reported in the USA, for example, by Oberman (1997) on drop-out of principals in Chicago and by Portin and Williams (1997) on the effects of increasing pressures in Washington State.

It remains to be seen whether a solution to the problems of recruitment and retention will be found mainly in improved training through the new National Professional Qualification for Headteachers in England; in better support; in changes to workloads and the job itself, as in experiments of collaborative co-principalships in New Zealand (Court 1997); or in changes in the political contexts in which it is carried out. In the meantime, we do need to know how headteachers currently try to cope with an increasingly demanding job. Woods, for example, has provided an account of how a creative headteacher left the profession five years before he had intended, because the coping strategies he had 'fashioned and used throughout his life were not capable of counteracting the massive alienation that now confronted him in the system' (Woods 1995: 152). This headteacher reacted against the commodification and depersonalization of education. He was having to spend more time on administration and finance, instead of concentrating on what he had always done: supporting and inspiring his staff in their teaching. He 'found himself doing a whole range of jobs somewhat inadequately'. Previous HMI inspections had been constructive, critical and fair, but a traumatic OFSTED inspection 'that involved the publication of the inspectors' report, policy documents and action plans left no room for manoeuvre and undermined morale' (ibid.: 155).

Alison, the headteacher in our case study, also felt relentless pressure to present the school favourably in the competitive market-place. In her concentrated effort to get things ready for inspection, she showed tendencies similar to Troman's (1996) middle-school headteacher who saw himself as a 'managing director', and Hellawell's (1990) primary heads who had come to see themselves as 'line managers'. Yet, simultaneously and tenaciously, she held on to her preferred identity as a shaper and developer: a leading professional in a collegial school.

Distinctions have often been made between concepts of leadership and management, with the former being concerned with promoting moral values and beliefs, and the latter concerned mainly with how to get things done. More has been learned, however, by studying how the concepts become interrelated in actual work, for example, in paradox and simultaneity (Deal and Peterson 1994), as evolution from management to moral and cultural leadership (Sergiovanni 1995) or as achieving a balanced mix (Rolff 1997). Cascadden (1997), referring to the effects of recent reforms in the USA, has described principals' roles as essentially oxymoronic. The eight principals in his research study, nominated as outstanding by superintendents and professors, all perceived themselves as leaders of their schools but under the influence of central office. For Cascadden, simply describing their roles 'as a mix of management and leadership does not really capture the paradoxical and oxymoronic nature of the role':

> Participants felt that they had been called upon to enact more top down mandates, and that they were expected to do this more collaboratively. Participants also indicated an oxymoronic role when they described being proactively reactive by scheduling unscheduled time and planning for unplanned contacts and issues. They also described contrary expectations of being the primary shaper of a communal culture.
>
> (Ibid.: 9)

Møller (1996) has noted a similar trend following restructuring in Norway, where new constructs of educational leaders as school entrepreneurs have given rise to two main kinds of dilemmas, those related to control and steering issues and those related to loyalty and professional values.

Caught between contradictory demands, headteachers, like classroom teachers, may feel either de-skilled, through what Jeffrey and Woods (1996) refer to as deprofessionalization and assault on the self, or re-skilled into a kind of new professionalism with pain (Hargreaves 1994) and through creative strategies (Woods 1995; Woods and Jeffrey 1996). As Altrichter and Salzgeber (1996) have argued, change can have two faces, in that new rules on the structural side can give rise to new resources, skills and abilities being mobilized on the side of personal agency.

Our case study offers a clue to the relationship between structure and agency through exploring how uncertainty is foreshadowed, created, experienced and dealt with in the school. We have tried to uncover ways in which structure, power, personal agency and identity are interrelated and shaped in subtle and changing ways.

Research Process

The field work was conducted between November 1995 and April 1996. It was based on ethnographic methods with participative elements, agreed with the headteacher and deputy headteacher. Like Møller (1996) in her Norwegian study, we have tried to bring together insiders' and outsiders' perspectives. Through discussions with the headteacher about our earlier analyses, drafts and feedback reports we have tried to generate a 'third framework' of her situation (Elden and Levin 1991).

The data for the case study consist of school documents, interviews and observation field notes recorded in a diary. Semi-structured interviews were conducted with the headteacher, deputy headteacher, eight teachers, a classroom assistant, secretaries, a member of the governing board, and an external consultant from an industrial company. The headteacher's interviews were extended to allow for narrative accounts involving reflexive

reconstructions which alerted us to the syntax of narrative and its value in understanding school leadership in personal, organizational and broad structural terms. Observations were made of meetings of the management team, various curriculum teams and the whole staff, as well as of classes in progress. Informal talks with teachers and general field observations were also recorded in a research diary.

The school was inspected in May 1996 (one month after our field work) by a team of eight OFSTED inspectors. In our paper we have made some reference to the subsequent official report as additional documentary evidence.

The School and its Catchment Area

At the time of the field work, the school had 514 pupils (257 boys, 257 girls) and 34 teachers. The headteacher was appointed in 1993 when the school was formed by the merger of the infant and junior schools. It is housed in two separate ninety-year-old brick buildings in a large city in northern England. Most of the pupils come from the nearby community, which is of mixed social and multicultural backgrounds. There is a high proportion of private rented accommodation in the area. About 42 per cent of pupils are eligible for free school meals. Nearly 290 pupils come from homes where English is an additional language, and up to fifteen languages are spoken in the community. Although on entry to the school some pupils have poorly developed language and social skills, and others do not understand English, some pupils are able to tackle the National Curriculum and are above average ability. In 1995, 59 per cent of pupils did not have nursery education.

School Aims, Values and Standards

Alison's aspirations for the school are expressed, on the one hand, by the motto 'One world. One family. Our school', which suggests plurality and learning together and, on the other hand, by her emphasis on individual achievement. Her dual concern for both social justice and market-led competitiveness – 'I want to have the best school in (the city) . . . high standards' – was reflected in the subsequent OFSTED inspection report which refers in positive terms both to the caring reputation of the school in the community:

> The overwhelming response of the parents' meeting was one which was supportive of the school, with particular reference by the parents to its outstanding multicultural ethos, its happy and welcoming atmosphere where they felt their children achieved their full potential. They felt this was because of the clear understanding by the school of the

direction in which it was moving and the caring headteacher and her staff.

(OFSTED Report, para. 145)

and to its standards of achievement, which are described in the report as 'satisfactory or better in nearly three-quarters of the lessons seen (126) and of these a minority are very good or excellent'.

> The school is very well led by the headteacher. In particular, she gives strong curriculum development for the school's aim for a curriculum which meets the needs of the school and is promoting a vision of the curriculum which actively promotes the cultural and social development of the pupils.

(OFSTED Report, para. 52)

Dilemmas

Like Møller (1996) and Bowe et al. (1992), we found that Alison experienced a number of dilemmas. We have selected four examples to illuminate choices and contingencies amongst a mix of personal and contextual aspects of her work. She was, at times, caught between

- 'looking down from the top' and belonging as a member or fellow professional;
- responding to individuals' professional development needs and steering whole staff development;
- seeking external affirmation and avoiding external threats;
- reducing uncertainty and encouraging participation (between control and contribution).

Between 'Looking Down from the Top' and Belonging as a Member or Fellow Professional

Alison was aware of 'looking down from the top' to carry out a kind of surveillance of standards, while at the same time she was also trying to belong, as a 'curriculum leader' or professional leader, amongst colleagues:

> Well, I manage by walking around, watching and looking . . . and for me I want to have the best school in the city . . . high standards, and to move towards my goal I walk around . . . I walk into classes, I talk to children, I talk to parents, and gather views from that . . . I take the helicopter view: just sit back and think of myself from the top and I look down to see what's happening and I watch people, I watch people

in the staffroom, I watch for groups and I manage a lot by intuition . . . I sense many things . . . and within that I do believe a lot in people making their own destinies. . . . I want a system whereby people can develop with innovation and wherever they do that I will back them . . . but I am aware it's the culture and I think we are coming into the stage where the culture is ready to support future things where people think for themselves . . . another (part of my) style of management is that I do read a lot. I read a lot of research papers and things about the curriculum. I still see myself as the curriculum leader, I am very involved in the curriculum.

The teachers value their headteacher's 'knowledge of educational practice' and of how to get things done, two of the six categories of knowledge that Eraut (1994: 75–99) cites as being important for heads and which give them a leading professional role. Combining these kinds of knowledge with pervasive membership, Alison tries to articulate her values and vision through her own participation in the daily life of the school. As teachers say:

[S]he treats people well, talks to people, shares everything with people . . . she is very open . . . she is very well organised in the way that she got things like the quality system going . . . management meetings . . . communicating ideas and giving people all sorts of information . . . feedback from courses, just keeping . . . I think she is really good and knows a lot.

She gave us a lot of feedback of what she would like to see in place . . . very helpful with any problems with children.

Both the headteacher and the deputy are ever watchful, maintaining close contact with colleagues, pupils and, where possible, with parents and the community, too. For example, Alison observes classes, talks with children, gives feedback to teachers, and moves about the school to snatch brief conversations, interconnected over time, with children, teachers and parents: what Cascadden (1997) has called 'being there' and Fernandez (1997) has referred to as 'visibility' and 'modelling' in 'walking the talk'. Alison describes this as 'professional communication', knowing at the same time, and herein lies the dilemma, that she is also likely to be judgemental:

I would think very carefully about how I would approach things with staff. I have seen absolutely poor lessons, rubbish, I can't believe that was our school. Now I have to be very careful how to feed that back to those teachers.

In retrospect, she is conscious of when she has tried to foster reflection and emphasize provisionality, and when she has told teachers what she wants them to do. Sometimes she has found herself suggesting contrived reflection, so that when she says 'Have you thought about this' she is really pinpointing something she wants to see changed:

> I think I use a great variety . . . I use 'Have-you-thought-about-this-bit' . . . I use, 'Well-I-am-sorry-but-you-have-got-to-do-this-bit' . . . I do try to keep staff informed [about] a lot of things which we have no control over, all the external influences . . . well, I need to talk to them quietly.

The dilemma we have tried to convey here is woven densely into the fabric of headship, especially before a looming external inspection. It underlies a seemingly straightforward sentence in the subsequent OFSTED report about monitoring and intervening:

> The headteacher monitors the progress the pupils make in the core subjects and *intervenes* when necessary to ensure they reflect the skills and knowledge required.
>
> (OFSTED Report, para. 54)

Between Responding to Individuals' Professional Development Needs and Steering Whole Staff Development

> The school aims for a closer integration between staff responsibilities, appraisal and staff development. A strength of the school is its allocation of time for individual staff to develop their professional skills and apply them directly to their own work. Their response is positive and reflects the esteem in which staff development is held by the staff; however it needs to be more closely monitored to ensure its outcomes and their application to the quality of teaching and the curriculum are realised to a greater extent. Teachers are well supported and encouraged by the head and deputy head to improve weaknesses and all teachers bring to their work quality some of which is very high.
>
> (OFSTED Report, para. 56)

In this school, each teacher is granted half a day per week release from teaching, to be used for professional development. This is arranged by providing some specialist teaching.

In the first year following amalgamation, Alison and her deputy had conducted interviews with each of the teachers to enable them to identify their own development needs and, at the same time, to get a feel for the

overall picture. At that time they anticipated little tension between teachers' personal concerns and those of the school.

As a consequence, a training and review programme was arranged to embed action research into the work of curriculum teams. When the programme was set up, however, few of the teachers actually took part in it: 'What I have to say is that (the deputy) and I were disappointed by the people . . . the chat, on paper and the reality were mismatched. . . . We realised that we had given them too much choice.'

Since then, staff development has been more closely tied to the immediate needs of the school. One factor influencing this decision has been the report of an invited audit by a member of the school's board of governors who is also an industrial consultant. The main conclusion of her report was that:

> There is no doubt that the Managers and staff of —— Primary School are committed to Training and Development. The work already carried out is most appreciated by all staff interviewed and from the results of the questionnaires. What does seem unclear is how this links in with the overall development of the school as an entity in its own right.
>
> (Confidential, internal report)

Between Seeking External Affirmation and Avoiding External Threats

Our interviews have revealed buoyant views of the external environment of the school. First, OFSTED inspections, the National Curriculum and increasing difficulties in the local catchment area are seen as partly threatening and partly as an impetus to generate greater effort. Second, agencies such as local businesses and universities are approached for co-operative links, consultancy, training and ultimately for external endorsement and reassurance.

Constructive responses to external challenges are evident, for example, in several curriculum initiatives, new materials and policy documents. Openness to sources of external support is evident in several close contacts with local universities in connection with initial teacher training, INSET programmes and small-scale research projects. In addition, some business practices are being introduced as a way of trying to integrate financial planning with school development and of clarifying chains of decision making. One example of the latter is the establishment of a Quality Management System which has been adapted from the business sector with the help of an industrial consultant. By inviting a range of industrial consultants to assess training and to introduce and audit 'quality' procedures, Alison has symbolized her concern for external comparison. According to Pava (1986), this use of 'outside witness' is common in change processes which are non-synoptic.

Looked at in one way, external comparison and audit may be helping Alison to develop what Eraut (1994) has called 'control knowledge' to enable her to control her own behaviour rather than that of others. By inviting in outsiders she has confirmed her own sense of agency as a school developer rather than a compliant implementer of external mandates. Looked at another way, seeking external witness has talked up the school, kept teachers on show, 'on their toes' and vulnerable.

Between Reducing Uncertainty and Encouraging Participation: Between Control and Contribution

Participation is both encouraged and limited, so that working and learning together becomes a mix of truncated teamwork and genuine contribution, ranging across formal, semi-formal and informal arrangements. Both Alison and her deputy use the concept of collaboration frequently, especially in references to their own 'shared journey'. This contrasts with the sense of isolation often ascribed to a headteacher's role. Connectedness, rather than her isolation, is a recurring theme in Alison's narrative.

She established 'a very very clear structure [of teams]' to get people working together. These teams form a kind of nested arrangement. 'Year group teams' of three teachers arrange their own semi-formal meetings for the day-to-day running of their part of the school. Every teacher also works in one or two curriculum teams. The school management team includes year group leaders, curriculum team leaders, and other teachers with specific responsibilities. In addition, all the staff come together twice each month for meetings. Whilst the intention of this structure of groups is 'to flatten the hierarchy', Alison has mentioned several problems that have arisen from seeking contributions from all staff:

> [W]ithin that system of allowing everyone to be involved in everything – it was very difficult to move forward and what we began to identify was that often we would come to policy decisions which really didn't suit anybody because there were things that we had to do and you would get 'No, I don't agree with that!' and so you met in the middle. Policies were put together and then were put in the file and people went back to the classroom and did their own thing.

This is seen differently from the teachers' viewpoint:

> I think [the headteacher] has a lot of good qualities. She is very strong, very efficient, has a lot of good ideas. If my criticism would come at all, it is that I think she wants to have her own ideas going through.

> I think there are times when just any member of staff feels they want to say something or ask something, and not always go through these channels.

This illustrates the difficulties that arise when participative groups are expected to react urgently to imposed change as well as to edge towards likemindedness through experimentation and discussion. The structure sets parameters for controlled teamwork geared, in the short term, to products rather than processes. For example, to save time, performance standards were introduced rapidly into the school without discussion with the teachers. Instead, the head and deputy adapted national guidelines and incorporated elements of schedules used by a local university for assessing students:

> If we took this out to consultation which we have done with similar things before and everybody has a different opinion and what tends to happen is that you end up with a very mediocre half way measure . . . but [the deputy] and I want high standards, we are people with very high ideals and high standards.

She saw herself steering towards a school culture that will 'combine co-operation with high standards of individual achievement'; a complex mix of her own control and staff contribution. We have defined 'control', for the purposes of this chapter, as reduction of uncertainty and 'contribution' as what Churchman (1968) has called responsible action to construct a desired future for the whole organization, a form of involvement beyond co-

operating with others on immediate work tasks. It would be crass to suggest simply that the headteacher might be less controlling or manipulative, or that the staff should be enabled and encouraged to contribute more, without taking into account various pressures upon them at this time. What does seem likely is that the relationship between contribution and control will continue to have both personal and situational dimensions.

More needs to be known about complex relationships between head-teachers' power and control and staff contribution, especially prior to arbitrarily scheduled external inspections. As Bowe et al. have noted, one consequence of recent reform 'is as much about the redistribution of power and privileges *within* institutions as it is about redistribution *between* them' (1992: 142; authors' emphasis).

In changing times, control and contribution may take many forms. For example, Nias et al. (1992) formed a revised view of the role of head-teachers, prior to the introduction of the national curriculum and OFSTED. They found that, in 'whole schools', headteachers exercised a controlling influence upon developments in ways that the authors had formerly assumed were incompatible with collegial and democratic decision making. More recently Woods and Jeffrey have discerned the growth of an embryonic professional discourse 'to counter and neutralise the effects of managerialism' (1996: 50) and to reaffirm values underpinning teachers' practice. It involves transformations, rather than total condemnation, of tenets of managerialism, so that teachers may have begun to shift meanings rather than simply reject external regulation.

Transforming External Regulation into a Resource

The imposed framework of external inspection 'rules' has been used by Alison as a resource to reduce predilection of individual teachers and, at the same time, to reassure them that she is able to deal with foreshadowed uncertainties. This transformation of external regulation into a resource can be understood through exploring how uncertainty is created, experienced and dealt with in the school.

Her use of external 'rules' of inspection is not being seen crudely as a way of overcoming recalcitrance amongst the school staff, but, as Salaman has argued, to 'co-ordinate situations where organisational members lack adequate knowledge of events and processes' (1980: 141). Teachers did have access to copies of official inspection criteria, but grapevine stories, media reports of other schools' weaknesses and public naming and shaming all combined to generate confusion, self-doubt and worry as they awaited their turn for scrutiny. Woods and Jeffrey (1996) have reported how OFSTED inspection is sometimes experienced, even weeks after the event, as an assault on the self which pervades whole lives. As this school waited for emotional and professional upheaval, Alison's forecasting antennae were becoming critically important. In this sense, her power was structural rather than personal. Hickson et al. (1973) have pinpointed three main factors which lead to high levels of structural power: a central position in relation to the key task (in this case, preparing for inspection), a low degree of replaceability (being the only one with the necessary strategic overview) and ability to cope with the main area of uncertainty facing the organization.

The headteacher's guidance was sought to help with basic tasks such as classroom management and lesson preparation. This conveys the depth of uncertainty felt by experienced teachers for whom, under normal circumstances, such things had become relatively secure parts of their everyday work. In responding to them, Alison was able to reshape the framework of 'external rules'. She was able to stress her own priorities when she assigned varying degrees of importance to different aspects. It also confirmed her centrality and pervasiveness. In this way Alison was transforming her own anxieties about external control into a form of contingent internal control, at the same time as she reassured and gained the teachers' trust.

Accomplishing an Acceptable Self-Identity

Alison's narrative reconstruction of the build-up to inspection reveals not only an extraordinary energy but also a marked duality. Through an intensification of activity she has symbolized business efficiency and external market awareness, and this has been mixed with continuous reference to participatory development, collective caring, moral reponsiveness and doing the best for all children: 'one world, one family, our school'.

According to the subsequent inspection report, decision making could be improved by having clearer structures and processes in place, and by subject leaders being more effective in carrying out formal responsibilities. A contrasting perspective would be to acknowledge the contributions that teachers have been making to school development as they tried things out, solved practical problems, gave and showed things to each other and talked about their work. The former view derives from the discourse of inspection and managerialism, while the latter belongs to workaday discourse, emphasizing continuity within change and valuing contributive membership rather than formal leadership. Connections between continuity and imposed change, and between the competing discourses of managerialism and professional leadership, are woven into Alison's stories of what she did and what she thought: her actions and her beliefs.

School development has been made up of a shifting mix of regular scheduled meetings, daily giving, showing, talking and watching, unexpected opportunities, directives, imported systems, separate initiatives and whole-staff projects. Taken together, 'doing-development' and 'talking-out-beliefs' have been integral and entangled parts of change itself, even though their meanings and impact have not always been clearly interrelated at the time. As Pava has indicated, in non-synoptic change it is hindsight that 'allows the theme and action to inform each other' (1986: 621).

Layers of individual and shared experiences are accumulating in the school, and for Alison herself the interplay between 'what was thought' and 'what was done' becomes part of her 'emplotment'; her narrative account of the school which helps her to learn what the school says about itself and what it does. It forms a thread in the telling as she connects various events and episodes into a storyline. Somers and Gibson stress the importance of 'emplotment' in constructing social identities and in making 'a significant network or configuration of relationships' (1994: 60). This 'emplotment' is more than a non-theoretical sequencing of events, but it is beyond the scope of our field work to make any claims about how headteachers in general might construct new professional identities. It is a task to which we intend to return using a broader biographical canvas. Pahl (1995) has recently given a lead in his case studies of how self identities are accomplished among those who have been highly successful in the late modern world. Each of his cases exemplifies:

> [T]he iterative interaction between ontological narratives of actors – the way they make sense of their personal lives, defining what they should do in the context of whom they think they are – and the meta-narratives of the historical conjuncture in which they live – the end years of the Thatcher government and the collapse of the Berlin wall and all that followed from that. The main theme is the interrelations of the public and private.
>
> (Ibid.: 121)

In our sub-heading for this section of the chapter we have used the verb 'accomplishing' to catch a dynamic process of identity formation, and to avoid the notion of a stable, unified self or public category status of 'school headteacher'. Identity is seen by Calhoun as a personal and political project 'in which we participate, empowered to greater or lesser extents by resources of experience and ability, culture and social organization' (1994: 28).

We have come to see the importance of investigating school leadership as a continuing project in identity construction. So far we have offered an analysis of the build-up to a critical event in Alison's career. Next we will try to understand how she has made sense of this event in retrospect and what is happening to her perceptions of her work within her whole life. In doing this, we may help to illuminate continuities and change in contemporary headship, but, as Goodson (1992) has observed, quoting the folk song collector Robin Morton, it is important to get to know 'the singer not the song', for if we are to understand the song more fully we need to know the song in the life of the singer.

One engaging puzzle will be to try to understand the extent to which headteachers make their own narratives and the extent to which the narratives reinvent their authors. Alison's narrative confirms the kind of person she wants to be, interwoven with the kind of person she feels she has had to become. It conveys creativity in difficult circumstances, and it combines professional and managerial discourses both in the range of concepts used and in its concerns about dilemmas of substance, style and strategy.

Note

1 The Management for Organisational and Human Development Project was funded by the European Union, Human Capital and Mobility Fund in 1995–96. It was co-ordinated from the University of East Anglia, and the other institutions in the network were the Universities of Northumbria, Malaga, Innsbruck and Klagenfurt, the Scottish Council for Research in Education and the European Centre for Educational Innovation and Research in Frascati, Rome.

References

Altrichter, H. and Salzgeber, St. (1996) Zur Mikropolitik schulischer Innovation. Wie Schulen durch das Handeln verschiedener Akteure mit unterschiedlichen Interessen Struker gewinnen und sich entwickeln. In H. Altrichter and P. Posch (eds), *Mikropolitik der Schulentwicklung*. Innsbruck and Vienna: Studienverlag.

Bowe, R., Ball, S. and Gold, A. (1992) *Reforming Education and Changing Schools*. London Routledge.

Calhoun, C. (1994) Social Theory and the Politics of Identity. In C. Calhoun (ed.), *Social Theory and the Politics of Identity*. Oxford: Blackwell.

Cascadden, D.S.T. (1997) Principals as Managers and Leaders: Implications for Teaching Educational Administration. Paper presented at the American Educational Research Association, March. University of Chicago.

Churchman, C.W. (1968) The Case Against Planning. In *Management Decision*, 2: 74–77.

Court, M.R. (1997) Reconstructing 'The Principal': Professional/Parent Partnerships and Devolution Dilemmas. Paper presented at the Sixth Norwegian National Conference in Educational Research, May. University of Oslo.

Deal, T.E. and Peterson, K.D. (1994) *The Leadership Paradox: Balancing Logic and Artistry in Schools*. San Francisco: Jossey-Bass.

Elden, M. and Levin, M. (1991) Cogenerative Learning: Bringing Participation into Action Research. In W.F. Whyte (ed.), *Participatory Action Research*. Newbury Park, CA and London: Sage.

Eraut, M. (1994) *Developing Professional Knowledge and Competence*. London and Washington DC: Falmer Press.

Fernandez, A. (1997) Leadership in an Era of Change. Paper presented at the Sixth Norwegian National Conference in Educational Research, May. University of Oslo.

Goodson, I. (1992) Sponsoring the Teacher's Voice: Teachers' Lives and Teacher Development. In A. Hargreaves and M. Fullan (eds), *Understanding Teacher Development*. New York: Teachers College Press.

Hargreaves, D.H. (1994) The New Professionalism: The Synthesis of Professional and Institutional Development. *Teaching and Teacher Education*, 10: 423–38.

Hellawell, D. (1990) Some Effects of the National Dispute on Relationships Between Headteachers and School Staffs in Primary Schools. *British Journal of Sociology*, 11: 397–410.

Hickson, D.J., Hinings, C.R., Lee, C.A. and Schneck, R.E. (1973) A Strategic Contingencies Theory of Intraorganizational Power. In G. Salaman and K. Thompson (eds), *People and Organisations*. London: Longmans.

Jeffrey, B. and Woods, P. (1996) Feeling Deprofessionalised: The Social Construction of Emotions During an OFSTED Inspection. *Cambridge Journal of Education*, 26(3): 325–43.

Møller, J. (1996) Rethinking Educational Leadership: Critical Perspectives on the Norwegian Case. Paper presented at the European Conference on Educational Research, September. University of Seville, Spain.

Nias, J., Southworth, G. and Campbell, P. (1992) *Whole School Curriculum Development in the Primary School*. London and Washington, DC: Falmer Press.

Oberman, G. (1997) A study of Principal Turnover in the Chicago Public Schools. Paper presented at the American Educational Research Association Annual Meeting, March. University of Chicago.

Pahl, R. (1995) *After Success: Fin-de-Siècle, Anxiety and Identity*. Cambridge: Polity Press.

Pava, C. (1986) New Strategies of Systems Change: Reclaiming Nonsynoptic Methods. *Human Relations*, 39(7): 615–33.

Portin, B. and Williams, R.C. (1997) The Changing Role of the Principal in Washington State. Paper presented at the American Educational Research Association Annual Meeting, March. University of Chicago.

Rolff, H.G. (1997) *Bild von Schule und Schulleitung*. Dortmund: IFS.

Salaman, G. (1980) Roles and Rules. In G. Salaman and K. Thompson (eds), *Control and Ideology in Organisations*. Milton Keynes: Open University Press.

Sergiovanni, T.J. (1995) *The Principalship: A Reflective Practice Perspective*. Boston: Allyn & Bacon.

Somers, M.R. and Gibson, G.D. (1994) Reclaiming the Epistemological 'Other': Narrative and the Social Construction of Identity. In C. Calhoun (ed.), *Social Theory and the Politics of Identity*, Oxford: Blackwell.

TES (1997) *Times Educational Supplement*, 5 September: 1.

Troman, G. (1996) Headteachers, Collaborative School Cultures and School Improvement: A Changing Relationship. *Educational Action Research*, 4(1): 119–44.

Woods, P. (1995) *Creative Teachers in Primary Schools*, Buckingham: Open University Press.

Woods, P. and Jeffrey, B. (1996) *Teachable Moments*, Buckingham: Open University Press.

15 Leadership in an Era of Change

Breaking Down the Barriers of the Culture of Teaching

Alicia Fernandez

The culture of teaching, long characterized by conservatism, presentism, privatism and individualism, may prove to be one of the major barriers to change and improvement in schools. In a grounded study of teacher professionalism, leadership has emerged as one of the overarching influences in transforming this culture into one which supports the changing needs of learners and teachers. Leadership seemed to have the potential for creating a professional community of teachers who were committed to continuous learning, who did not fear change, and who worked in collaborative ways to create shared goals, visions and standards for their schools. Evidence from interviews with Canadian school teachers suggests that there is a commonality in the set of traits and behaviours displayed by principals that supports, energizes and inspires the building of a professional community in schools by developing a sense of self-efficacy and self-worth amongst teachers.

Introduction

In the last decade, educational reform has taken a more indirect route to school improvement by emphasizing the development of teacher professionalism. In an effort to improve teacher competence, restructuring policies focused some attention on improving the present condition of the teacher's workplace and the organization and management of teachers who are already in schools, as well as the preparation of those who are contemplating a career in teaching. This has not been an easy task. Most efforts at professionalizing teachers are embedded within policies that restructure either time and space, curriculum and pedagogy, or accountability measures. The proliferation of new policies that bombard schools has been putting quite a stress on teachers. As front-line workers, not only are they given the main responsibility for implementing change, they have also become ultimately accountable for the outcome of implementation. Teachers' resistance to change is well documented (Lightfoot 1983; Elmore 1990; Schlechty 1990). Although there has been evidence that some schools have been able to embrace change, a majority of teachers do not readily 'jump on the bandwagon', so to speak. Having found stability in the 'old ways of doing things', teachers' approach to any kind of change has naturally tended towards scepticism, mistrust, and even fear. Transforming these attitudes into more receptive and positive ones requires not only changes to curriculum or pedagogy but, most importantly, changes in the context in which teachers teach. This study draws on teachers' experiences of a restructuring policy. It is grounded in data derived from fifty-three teacher interviews during a two-year period. Preliminary analysis unearthed several factors that influence the development of teacher professionalism in the schools, amongst the strongest of which is leadership.

The Changed Nature of Leadership

In this study Max Weber's comparative notion of traditional authority and bureaucratic authority as legitimizing beliefs that support the exercise of control in an organization provides a means of comparing the past and present method of management used by school administrators (Weber 1947).

Leadership has always been one of the important factors in school improvement and effectiveness. However, in the current environment of change and upheaval in education, leadership, particularly that of the school principal, has taken a more critical role in providing a local context in which change can occur. But alongside the many changes in education has also emerged a change in the role of principals. In the past, principals were able to rely upon traditional authority and bureaucratic authority to support and exercise control in their respective schools. Today, with policies that espouse greater teacher and community voice in matters that affect the school, principals often find themselves pinned amongst the demands of district and state institutions, teachers, and parents. Their role can no longer be sustained by tradition or bureaucratic authority legitimized by law. As sole or ultimate decision makers they had a powerful means of controlling both teachers and students. In the last decade, however, teacher militancy has grown, and teacher unions have been more proactive in seeking to improve the conditions of teachers' workplaces. For example, teachers have demanded more voice, not only in matters of curriculum pedagogy and evaluation, but also in traditionally centralized policies of professional development, the allocation of budget and resources and the structure of school space and time. Developing alongside these demands has been research that claims that increased autonomy and participation in decision making have the potential for greater teacher ownership of innovations, and therefore more positive attitudes to change. Moreover, the fast pace of social, economic and technological change has made traditional and bureaucratic authority in schools ill suited to supporting various adaptations that schools have had to make (Murphy 1990). In short, vested authority has become increasingly challenged and threatened by teachers, students and the community.

Nowadays, although a principal may appear to have means of control, he or she may have very little actual power. Even before the appearance of site-based decision making, principals' authority had began to show signs of weakening. It has been a fact for a long time now, that principals cannot really make others carry out their wishes unless staff consent to do so of their own accord (Holmes and Wynne 1989). The role of the principal has increasingly become grounded on influence and persuasion rather than control and management. Interpersonal transactions have become more effective at bringing about change in schools than the conventional power of legitimate authority.

Purpose and Rationale

In light of these developments, the research on principals' influence and leadership has become all the more important to the study of educational change. That leadership has emerged as a strong factor in our initial analysis of teacher interviews suggests that principals in the study may have been able to navigate amongst the many changes and consequent demands on their role well enough to effect a supportive context in which teachers could work and develop professionally. As suggested by the grounded theory method espoused by Strauss and Corbin (1990), once the major themes of the investigation have emerged, a more thorough analysis of each theme should follow. The purpose of this study is to describe the influence of the principal in developing teacher professionalism in the schools. Two questions framed the study: (1) How did principals influence the development of teacher professionalism? (2) On what school factors did they have influence on?

Results of the Study

The principals in the study had varying leadership styles, personalities and beliefs. However, a common thread emerged from teachers' perception of principal behaviours and strategies that impacted on their work and their workplace. Principals were able to support the growth of teacher professionalism largely through visibility, modelling, support, high expectations, and decisiveness and courage. These behaviours had a positive impact on the development of teachers' professional orientation, characterized by greater sense of shared purpose and standards of practice, commitment to continuous learning, greater belief in teacher self-efficacy, and a shared sense of responsibility for student outcomes.

Visibility

The importance to teachers of the principal's physical presence in the school was best exemplified by one school's experience:

> Our principal was . . . really overdue for retirement. He kept stringing along for several years, so he really did not know what was going on in terms of school leadership. Our principal was also involved in outside activities, which took him out of the school. He was a very capable person while he was here, but in the last couple of years his time was absorbed outside of the school. Consequently, we were quite leaderless and directionless. This combined with the ten-year cynicism made things not that great around here. People started going off in different directions.

A principal who was actively involved in the affairs of the school had a big influence on staff cohesion of purpose and direction. Being visible meant being part of the team. It closed the gap between those who worked and those who only supervised. It meant that the principal knew what was going on in the school and was able to act on whatever gaps of practice there might be, on the one hand and give praise for a job well done, on the other. One teacher claimed that there were very few major problems in the school because they had a principal who was always present to help solve problems and facilitate teachers' work.

Visible leadership from principals helped teachers stay in focus. Communication was more open so that things were not allowed to be mis-understood. It was typical for schools to experience bouts of uncertainty and confusion when implementing new initiatives. In one school, the principal brought into context any concerns and was able to emphasize what the school stood for and what school goals were at issue. Visible leadership did not mean only physical presence: it also meant visible vision. However, visibility did not mean 'barging in' with a vision. Although principals in the study had their own strong vision of what the school should look like, their strategy of sharing the vision took on more democratic and persuasive ways. They articulated the vision to staff, students and community con-stantly through words and actions. This meant that everyone became aware of expectations: for students, expectations of behaviour; for staff, expectations of high-quality practice; and for community, expectations of support for what the school was trying to do.

Teachers felt a stronger sense of security when the principal was around. They felt good knowing that there was someone there who could help them in case there were incidents they could not handle. But the most important effect of principals' involvement in teachers' work was the assur-ance that what they were doing was meaningful and important. Teachers' sense of efficacy was ultimately fortified by the knowledge that their immediate superior knew and supported what they were doing.

Although visible principals were in and out of classrooms and hallways, most of the teachers' experiences of the principal's presence were positive. They did not see his or her constantly being around as curtailing their autonomy:

> He likes to be involved, but only enough to know what is going on. He wants to have his fingers in everything and be aware of it, but not have to be responsible for getting a lot of it done. He likes to know what is going on but lets us do our work.

As long as the principal was careful not to meddle in the domain of curriculum and pedagogy, which was perceived as mainly teachers' responsibility, his or her presence was welcomed.

Visible leadership took many forms. One description from a teacher summarized it this way:

> The principal is involved and has a keen interest in all aspects of schooling. She takes initiative when she sees there is a need for improvement in certain areas. She is available to discuss problems with. She visits different staff rooms and talks to people. She does little things like take the phone off the hook so that conversation is uninterrupted. She has frequent informal visits to classrooms. The principal comments on what people do in their courses. If she thinks there is room for improvement, she does not hesitate to say so. She acknowledges successes through public forums such as staff meetings. She gives token rewards, like a box of chocolates. She also announces extraordinary successes through the PA [public announcement system] or student bulletin. She does the same for students and teachers. The principal has high expectations. When she sees high calibre work, she acknowledges it.

Modelling

Modelling, or leading by example, is probably one of the best mechanisms for building trust among staff and for creating standards of excellence. One teacher credited the numerous achievements in the school to both the past and present school administrators:

> [T]he last two senior administrators that have been here have made a real effort to get this feeling of trust and excellence, and have done so by example.

Another explained why she and the staff worked so hard, and why they were committed to continuous improvement of teaching skills and knowledge:

> She leads by example. She is hardworking. She is dedicated. She spends hours and hours of her time – so many hours it is unbelievable – until she actually runs herself down. Anything that she asks you to do you know is important. She leads by action. She would not ask you to do anything that she would not do herself and try her best at. Everything she does has to be topnotch, otherwise it is unacceptable.

Principals' vision and expectations were exemplified more through actions than words. Respondents called it 'walking the talk'. Tired of administrators or policy makers who espouse one thing and do another, teachers described characteristics of their principals that restored their motivation, their energy and their commitment to their work. These were actions described as caring, positive, fair, hardworking, democratic and empowering.

Caring

Unlike other occupations where professionalism is characterized by detached and impartial treatment of clients, those who work in education have to care genuinely for their students. Teachers derived some assurance that school practice would always be for the benefit of students when principals themselves displayed caring for students. This was manifested in the way principals talked to and talked about kids:

> She always has something really strongly positive to say to the kids to project an appreciation of the value of their accomplishments. That to me is a big leadership role. It is letting the kids be informed of how we value their accomplishments – be it in the classroom or in special performances. . . . I feel the ultimate leadership is the valuing of the kids. . . . My view of a leader is somebody who facilitates workers. That is how I try to be a leader.

It also showed in one principal's priorities:

> Students do go and talk to him. Students will talk to him on a confidential basis and know that it is confidential. He is very interested in the counselling processes and in the students that are seen. We have what is called a confidential binder in the office with confidential information on students who are going through difficult times or having problems.

That was set up at his insistence. I would say he is a strong support for our students.

Positive

Optimism is a generally positive attitude towards the challenges of the job, whether they be easy or difficult. The joy of coming to work, job satisfaction, and general feelings of well-being among staff were attributed to the tone set by the principal. In one school, a teacher described her principal as a person who would always think her cup half full instead of half empty. In another, problems were seen not as insurmountable barriers, but as challenges that could be overcome:

> He tries to be positive and encouraging. He says it is going to work; we can work around the problems; we can make it work; we can make it fit our situation. He tries to make it sound like it is going to be possible.

Optimistic attitudes are contagious. In these schools, uncertainty, fear and cynicism brought about by the burden of new initiatives were neutralized or diluted by positive leadership.

Fair

Privatism is a persistent norm in schools (Hargreaves 1980; Little 1990; Lortie 1975). The presence of fear in being judged and criticized by other adults is a pervasive feature of teaching. The egg-crate organizational structure has not helped in alleviating competence anxieties among teachers who are sensitive to one another's differences in educational philosophy and pedagogical preference (Hargreaves l980). In the study, many respondents claimed that principals who modelled fairness and non-judgemental attitudes were able to develop trust among staff and transformed the norm of privatism into openness to critical evaluation of teacher practice. This was qualified by their respect for the principal's professionalism – meaning trust in the expert judgement of a superior:

> She is open to any kind of input. She treats you like an equal. She is very professional and very approachable. She is a very well rounded person and a great administrator. . . . [The feedback on my work comes from] meeting with my principal on my professional development. I really respect her opinion. She is very professional, if she gives me the green light, that is good.

The role of evaluator is not an easy one. For principals charged with the task of evaluating teachers, it was important that they were seen as 'expert teachers' themselves. Coupled with the previously discussed characteristics of visibility, principal evaluation became an important factor in shoring up teacher self-efficacy as well as opening up discussion for teacher development and learning.

Hardworking

Teachers felt that they had to work harder to implement any new initiative. Teachers were more willing to invest time and energy in these endeavours when they saw the principal working just as hard. For the teachers, professionalism was not confined to their ranks alone: principals who worked alongside teachers brought a stronger message of professionalism than those who merely paid lip service to it. One teacher equated professionalism with the characteristics displayed by her principal:

> She models professionalism. If she requires something to be done of her staff, she does it herself as well. She does not have expectations that she would not expect of herself. She expects professionalism from all of us and demonstrates it herself.

Thus, professionalism became defined as a quality of practice that was characterized by hard work and competence. It was practice that had high expectations of oneself and of others. Professionalism meant setting a common standard of quality for all.

Democratic

Democratic behaviour included allowing teachers opportunities to make decisions. Principals modelled collaboration and collegiality by respecting the wishes of the group or by making acceptable compromises. Although some principals were more shy and authoritative, they rarely made decisions without consulting the staff first.

> She does not take it upon herself to run the whole show; she will get everybody involved to a certain extent and values everyone's input. . . . She does not stand up and make the rules. She meets with us and will ask what we think and then make the decisions from there, so it is a staff decision. It is not something that she will decide and then put forward.

Modelling a collaborative model of decision making created a climate of cooperation in the school. Problems were solved together or in consultation with one another:

She lets us come up with a workable solution because she feels that we have to do it. She herself models a cooperative climate, so it naturally follows that the rest of us would do that.

Having the opportunity to exercise professional judgement in the company of peers affirmed many teachers' perception of self-efficacy. One teacher found that although her principal might not be crucial to collaborative activity, she nevertheless set the tone for collaborative and collegial work and therefore made exposure of practice in front of colleagues a more positive experience.

Another dimension of democratic behaviour was not barging in with a vision. For example, one astute principal did some research before putting forward her ideas for innovation:

[S]he is not someone who is forcing a vision on everybody. She more or less arrives at the complementary vision by asking people how they do things – how they can fit into the picture.

In any kind of change effort it is important to determine the readiness of those who are going to implement change. Each context has its own culture, its own way of doing things, its own varied set of skills and its own kinds of personalities. Although not all principals in the data were sensitive to context, it was apparent that teachers preferred sensitivity to individual situations. Only two of the principals seemed to consider the history and the level of competence of their staff. One principal, in particular, was perceived to model greater sensitivity to the needs of her staff:

[S]he has gone to the staff to see where they are coming from and what level they are at in terms of change . . . her vision is meeting the balance; we are all coming together and balancing in the middle.

The result was a true sense of shared vision in the school, and higher levels of cohesion, coherence and congruence of purpose and direction.

Empowering

Empowering behaviour included trusting teachers as experts in their field. It encouraged risk-taking and experimentation, while offering as much support as possible. Teachers were more encouraged to try new innovations when they perceived the principal as taking the same risk as they were:

The next stage is something new and it is a new game. I go into all these things wondering if it will work. But the nice thing is that the administration says it does not matter if it does not work; but we have to experiment. That is the biggest single change in my life since our principal has come here. It is a risk-free situation.

Being allowed to try something new is, in itself, a learning process. It increases the depth and breadth of experience and allows teachers to expand their repertoire of teaching skills. Many teachers involved in innovative projects were able to see beyond the present. Those who experienced success were more eager to try other ideas and no longer resisted change. In fact, most of them looked forward to more challenges. One teacher even admitted to being energized, despite being near retirement. Long accustomed to a culture where teachers were told what to do and being made solely responsible for the success or failure of policies, principals who were able to relinquish power and authority in order to expand leadership in the school had more success with changing teachers' attitude towards change.

Support

Colleagues, students, friends and community form an important source of support in teachers' work. In an occupation characterized by immediacy and fraught with uncertainties (Lortie 1975; Grimmett and Housego 1985), support is an overarching necessity. Support from a superior is especially important because it has the power to facilitate practice by removing barriers, or easing constraints. A supportive atmosphere could have an energizing effect, in that teachers enjoyed coming to work more:

> [The principal] has built up this really friendly kind of atmosphere in the school. Last year, I was burnt out; with her coming in with her enthusiasm and especially that support, I have my energy back and I really enjoy coming and working here.

It may also be a source of affirmation of practice, and therefore a source of positive perception of self-efficacy.

Principals in the data provided support in a number of ways. I used some of Blase's (1991) dichotomy of leadership support to describe teachers' perceptions of the many ways that support was manifested in their schools.

Emotional or Personal Support

One principal attended to making staff feel good about themselves:

> Her main concern is our well-being. She wants us to feel good about ourselves. Self-esteem is important to her among her staff as well as among the students. That filters down; if the staff feels good then the students feel good.

Another personally acknowledged school successes and accomplishments in a public way. By doing so, she developed a general sense of well-being in the school.

Another teacher felt supported emotionally, when she was having a crisis with one of her students just by talking to her principal and having someone back up her decisions:

> I have had some bad interactions with real problem children – not children, eighteen-year-old kids. That is a very emotional thing. I do not know if you have ever had these things when you have a student who is in difficulty . . . the principal has always been very supportive one way or another.

Many studies have documented the sink-or-swim socialization of beginning teachers. They are the ones who are especially vulnerable to feelings of uncertainty and isolation. A principal's personal support could help in a newcomer's attempts at specific strategies or methods of teaching. In this study, a second-year teacher found her frequent contact with her principal a great help in her learning:

> She is very supportive. . . . I feel like if I went to her with a particular problem, she would not ignore it, she would not blame, she would help me problem-solve. She would try to ease whatever [the problem] is for that particular teacher.

So did another colleague:

> She is very supportive emotionally, and that has been a big help. Anything you ask her for, she will tell you either that is possible or that is not possible. 'Here is how I can help you.' She gives us a lot of support.

A large part of having emotional support from their principal was having those nagging doubts about their ability to do the job considerably eased. It gave those fairly new to teaching both the self-confidence and the courage to forge ahead.

Administrative Support

Administrative support refers to principals' attempts to protect teachers' teaching time (Blase 1991), as well as create time for teachers to pursue professional development activities. Teachers in one school appreciated the fact that the principal did not involve them in decisions that had to do with the running of the school.

> We are not asked to make decisions about the everyday life of the school. He does not do anything by committee, which I think is a waste of time. He allows us to be involved in things that are important. But when it come to things that he should be doing himself, he just does them.

In schools where collective decision making was taken literally, a proliferation of committees ensued. Teachers' involvement in all aspects of school life took them away from their job – that of teaching. This was resented by most teachers who felt that their primary role was being railroaded by time spent on 'imposed collegiality' structures such as committees. Principals who were able to minimize these intrusions through creative management of time did so by making administrative decisions themselves and left the creation of committees to teachers whenever they felt they needed collective input.

Time is a scarce resource in teaching. Teachers have so many added responsibilities that it is important for them to have a principal who does not waste time. One of the biggest time consumers for teachers were the staff meetings. It was therefore greatly appreciated when principals were able to manage staff meetings well. One teacher expressed it this way:

> She always handles meetings really well. They move quickly. She does not get off topic. She will not let us get off topic. You appreciate that, because you have a certain amount of time that you would like to be at a meeting, and then after that it wears out. . . . She is strong enough that she can help to steer everything, and that you have to meet the agenda. You have to try to get those things done.

Student-related Support

Principals in the study created an atmosphere conducive to teaching and learning by having high expectations of student behaviour. All five principals were proactive in setting the tone of discipline in their schools. Teachers felt assured that there would be support from the office whenever a possibly explosive situation with students or parents arose. Although in most cases the job of enforcing discipline was delegated to the vice-principal, it was the principal, nevertheless, who communicated the code of behaviour to the students and community. There was a general agreement that students learned best when they were not distracted and that teachers taught best when their students were not distracting them from their teaching:

> His leadership style is based on a personal philosophy of allowing teachers to teach and doing whatever he can to make that happen.

Creating a school environment for that, by keeping a lid on things as he puts it, and not letting the wheels come off the car – which means that your students are not going crazy. . . . He very clearly outlines what the behaviour expectations are, and will follow through by and large when those expectations are not kept.

Financial or Material Support

Despite educational cutbacks, principals in our data seemed to find money to meet instructional and professional development needs of teachers through creative resourcefulness. They were all encouraging and positive of teachers taking advantage of opportunities to develop and expand their skills:

In terms of his leadership, it is a matter of him making available things that we need.

The principal is a money manager. She had managed to build the resource for us. When we have real needs, we can go and get books, for instance. We have had to replace of couple of sets of books lately because they were just worn out. On top of our instructional fund, she has given us the resources to do that.

Having the resources to do one's job is an essential factor in the development of teacher professionalism.

Professional Support

Principals who were perceived to have the expertise to guide teachers in their undertakings were more effective in providing teachers with professional support. One principal was especially adept at guiding her teachers without making them feel that they were being pressured or obliged into doing things. As she was also perceived and respected by her teachers as having some expertise, the school was more readily able to take the plunge towards change:

She leads very well without making you feel like you are having to do something or without feeling any pressure. She leaves a lot of options open; she leaves it up to us, but yet at the same time, she guides us.

Beginning teachers, especially, often looked up to their principals or in some cases, their department heads, for specific directions of practice. Unlike their more experienced colleagues, they were often unaware of the resources and opportunities available to them. The principal was often their link to outside expertise, or information on sources that were only available to administrators. Teachers in the study perceived principals as having more time to do research and therefore being more up to date on pedagogical and curriculum issues. Professional support was manifested in terms of providing teachers with articles or journals tailored to their current interest or need. Other principals linked their teachers to other schools or universities. Two schools had university–school partnership projects. All these linked both beginning teachers and experienced teachers to sources of professional development.

High Expectations

All the principals in the study had high expectations. These schools had many innovative projects going on because the principals were proactive in seeking ways to improve the quality of learning and teaching there. A typical response from teachers was:

> [The principal] would not like to run the kind of school where things were mediocre or where things were the same as they had been before he got there.

Decisiveness and Courage

Teachers considered decisiveness and courage to be good qualities in a principal. They perceived the principal role as one bombarded by situations which need immediate attention and, in some cases, immediate action. In one school, the principal had her staff's respect because:

> When a crisis comes up, the principal is very quick on the mark. She does not organize a committee. She is able to take an active role. . . . She is not afraid to make fast decisions and hard decisions when it comes to something that is important.

Large secondary schools are especially prone to altercations, so that even common occurrences such as playground disputes could be quite disconcerting to most teachers and possibly affect the way they do their work. When conflict occurs at the staff level, it becomes all the more important that there is leadership to help resolve the problem. Principals who were able to manage conflict, as well as empower staff to develop conflict resolution skills, were seen as displaying the ultimate leadership in administration. As one teacher asserted:

> There are always large group situations with confrontation. You have to have the leadership style to provide that, but that is the ultimate leadership in administration, I think.

Conclusion

Principals have the potential to influence the quality of student learning experiences in the school by building the capacity of staff to effect change. This is not an easy task. Schools have constantly and consistently been buffeted by waves of change in efforts to finally 'do it right'. These experiences have not been altogether pleasant for those who have had to implement change. Duke (1994) suggests that the drift and detachment that plague schools today is the result of such experiences. Drift is described as the condition of lack of clarity about what needs to be done, while detachment refers to the lack of motivation to accomplish the task even when it is fully understood. Teachers' cynical and sceptical stance towards many reform policies stems from confusion about what schools are for and what their role is within the general framework of education. Steeped in the many demands on them, many teachers have managed to 'survive' the intensification of their work by burrowing deeper into the culture of isolation characterized by privatism, individualism, presentism and conservatism. Duke (1994) asserts that when such conditions exist, leadership becomes a critical factor. Combating drift and detachment in schools needs leadership that generates confidence and courage amongst staff. Early research on teaching and teachers' work concedes the presence of a culture of teaching characterized by privatism, conservatism, presentism and individualism (Waller 1932; Jackson 1968; Lortie 1975). These elements are interwoven in mutually supportive ways to create a medium through 'which many innovations and reforms must pass . . . [and] in that passage they frequently become shaped, transformed or resisted in ways that were unintended and unanticipated' (Hargreaves 1980: 126). The challenge of many principals is how to transform the culture into one that is collaborative, communal, progressive and more future oriented.

Waller suggests that the nature of an occupation determines the norms of practice within that profession (1932). Many features of teaching affect the behaviours, beliefs and attitudes of those who teach. Structural arrangements, social organization and school processes have important influences on teachers' perception of themselves as empowered professionals (Dreeben 1970; Firestone 1993; Lortie 1975; Rosenholtz 1989). Leadership, particularly that of the principal, has the potential to influence changes in these factors. The five principals in this study were perceived by teachers to have made, in one way or another, an impact in their professional orientation – a shared sense of purpose, shared standards of practice, commitment to continuous learning and sense of personal efficacy, and a shared sense of responsibility for student outcomes. Although they conceded that changes in the school were not entirely dependent on the principal's leadership, the actions, behaviours and continuous support of school leadership had allowed them to move from isolation to collaboration, from conservatism to progressivism, from presentism to a more future orientation and from privatism to a more public orientation.

Although other contextual and cultural variables interact in varying ways within the local context of schooling, the leadership factor could not be ignored as one of the overarching influences on initiating, developing and sustaining change. Leadership takes on an especially important role in the development of the expertise and skill of those who are front-liners in the implementation of any restructuring policy. As many commissioned studies in America have claimed (Carnegie Task Force 1986; Holmes Group 1986), schools already have the essential resource to effect change – the teachers. The role of school systems, then, is to find ways to help teachers develop into competent professionals. Principals who are in the proximal position not only of authority but also of influence have the potential to open up spaces and opportunities for teachers to learn and develop into the professionals that schools of today need.

References

Blase, J. (1991) The Micropolitical Perspective. In J. Blase (ed)., *The Politics of Life in Schools: Power, Conflict and Cooperation*. Newbury Park, CA: Corwin Press.

Carnegie Task Force on Teaching as a Profession (1986) *A Nation Prepared*. New York: Carnegie Forum on Education and Economy.

Dreeben, R. (1970) *The Nature of Teaching: Schools and the Work of Teachers*. Glenview, ILL: Scott, Foresman and Company.

Duke, D. (1994) Drift, Detachment and the Need for Teacher Leadership. A paper presented at the American Educational Research Association (AERA), April. New Orleans, USA.

Elmore, R. (ed.) (1990) *Restructuring Schools: The Next Generation of Educational Reform*. San Francisco: Jossey-Bass.

Firestone, W.A. (1993) Why Professionalising Is Not Enough. *Educational Leadership*, 50(6): 6–11.

Grimmett, P. and Housego, I. (eds) (1985) *Teaching and Teacher Education: Generating and Utilizing Valid Knowledge for Professional Socialization*. Vancouver, BC: University of British Columbia Press.

Hargreaves, D.H. (1980) *The Occupational Culture of Teachers*. In P. Woods (ed.), *Teacher Strategies and Structure*. London: Croom-Helm.

Holmes, M. and Wynne, E.A. (1989) *Making the School an Effective Community: Belief, Practice and Theory of School Administration*. London: Falmer Press.

Holmes Group (1986) *Tomorrow's Teachers: A Report of the Holmes Group*. East Lansing, MI: Holmes Group, Michigan State University.

Jackson, P.W. (1968) *Life in Classrooms*. New York: Holt, Rinehart & Winston.

Lightfoot, S.L. (1983) *The Good High School: Portraits of Character and Culture*. New York: Basic Books.

Little, J.W. (1990) The Persistence of Privacy: Autonomy and Initiative in Teachers' Professional Relations. *Teachers College Record*, 91(4): 509–36.

Lortie, D. (1975) *Schoolteacher: A Sociological Study*. Chicago: University of Chicago Press.

Murphy, J. (1990) The Educational Reform Movement of the 1980s: A Comprehensive Analysis. In J. Murphy (ed.), *The Reform of American Public Education in the 1980s: Perspectives and Cases*. Berkeley, CA: McCutchan.

Rosenholtz, S. (1989) *Teachers' Workplace: The Social Organization of Schools*. New York: Longman.

Schlechty, P.C. (1990) *Schools for the Twenty-First Century: Leadership Imperatives for Educational Reform*. San Francisco: Jossey-Bass.

Strauss, A. and Corbin, J. (1990) *Basics of Qualitative Research: Grounded Theory Procedures and Techniques*. Newbury Park, CA: Sage.

Waller, W. (1932) *The Sociology of Teaching*. New York: Sage.

Weber, M. (1947) *The Theory of Social and Economic Organizations*. New York: Free Press.

16 Reinventing School Leadership for Lasting Reform in the Third Millennium

Brian J. Caldwell

This chapter draws on research that over fifteen years examined a major element of reform, namely, the local management or self-management of schools, defined as the systematic decentralization to the school level of authority to make decisions on the allocation of resources, defined broadly, within a centrally determined framework of goals, policies, priorities, standards and accountabilities. The chapter pays particular attention to what lies 'beyond the self-managing school', drawing implications for the work of school leaders. Major themes from Beyond the Self-Managing School *are introduced, with research drawn mainly from the Collaborative Research Project in Victoria that makes clearer than has been the case in many other studies the direct and indirect effects of a capacity for self-management on improved outcomes for students. These effects are laden with roles for school leaders. The intention is, however, to look beyond the present, to schools of the third millennium, for it is clear that major change lies ahead, largely due to the effects of technology.*

Introduction

The span of fifteen years' research divides into three periods of five years. The first, from 1983 to 1987, was based on studies of school effectiveness in a Project of National Significance in Australia. The outcome was a model for management centred on learning and teaching that formed the basis of training programs for parents, principals and teachers in Victoria, culminating in a book called *The Self-Managing School* (Caldwell and Spinks 1988).

The second period, from 1988 to 1992, involved a continuation of the training programs, but on an international scale, as governments in a number of countries began a program of major restructuring in public education, all of which involved a simultaneous shift in the centralization–decentralization continuum, creating systems of self-managing schools within centrally determined curriculum and standards frameworks. Further research was conducted, resulting in a second book, *Leading the Self-Managing School* (Caldwell and Spinks 1992).

The third period, from 1993 to 1997, involved the design and implementation of one of the most comprehensive approaches to school reform ever undertaken. With 1,700 schools, Victoria is the largest system of public schools anywhere to have decentralized as much as 90 per cent of its education budget to schools. Towards the end of this time, it became clear that the major features of Schools of the Future, as the reform was known, were largely irreversible, at least in the foreseeable future, in similar fashion to what has emerged in Britain in respect to the local management of schools, and that other matters ought to move to centre stage. The outcome of this work is a third book, *Beyond the Self-Managing School* (Caldwell and Spinks 1998).

Tracking Change in School Education

If an international perspective is adopted, it is apparent that reform is proceeding on three tracks:

- Track 1: building systems of self-managing schools;
- Track 2: unrelenting focus on learning outcomes;
- Track 3: creating schools for the knowledge society.

These are tracks rather than discrete or sequential stages. Evidence of each may be found in different settings: schools, school systems and nations vary in the distance they have moved down each track.

Track 1: Creating Systems of Self-Managing Schools

The shifting of significant responsibility, authority and accountability to the school level within a curriculum and standards framework, with new alignments of personnel and other resource functions, will probably become the norm for the management of schools in the public sector. No system that has moved in this direction is likely to return to arrangements that provided good service over much of the last century but are now apparently obsolete.

The experience of Britain illustrates this expectation, given that each of the major political parties went to the 1997 election intending to maintain the key elements of reform that centred on the local management of schools within a centrally determined curriculum and standards framework. Despite the contentious nature of their introduction, and the fact that many issues remain to be resolved, it seems that the National Curriculum and, especially, the local management of schools have been among the success stories of the 1988 Education Reform Act and will be maintained by New Labour.

Brian J. Caldwell

Knowledge and skill in the management domain were prominent in the new role for school leaders because this was where their role changed most profoundly. The model for management in *The Self-Managing School* (Caldwell and Spinks 1988) proved helpful, with its focus on goal setting, policy making, priority setting, planning, budgeting, implementing and evaluating (Figure 16.1). The preferred mode of operation was for members of the school and its community to work in teams based around programs of learning and teaching and the support of learning and teaching.

Further research and consultancy resulted in a refinement of the model and the specification of four dimensions of leadership. It became apparent at the end of the 1980s and in the early 1990s that expectations for change were becoming very high indeed; schools needed a mechanism to buffer

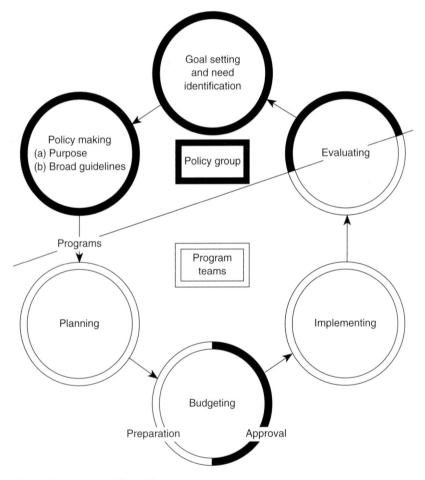

Figure 16.1 A model for self-management

them against continuous change on all fronts and governments required a mechanism to make clear their expectations for schools. In *Leading the Self-Managing School* (Caldwell and Spinks 1992) a school charter was proposed, with a deeper capacity for strategic planning (Figure 16.2).

A four-dimensional model of school leadership was proposed:

- *cultural leadership*, referring to a culture of excellence underpinned by the values of quality, effectiveness, equity, efficiency and empowerment, and effecting a shift from a culture of dependence in a centralized system to a culture of self-management;
- *strategic leadership*, referring to a capacity to understanding emerging trends in society at large and in schools generally, discerning their likely and preferred impact on their school;

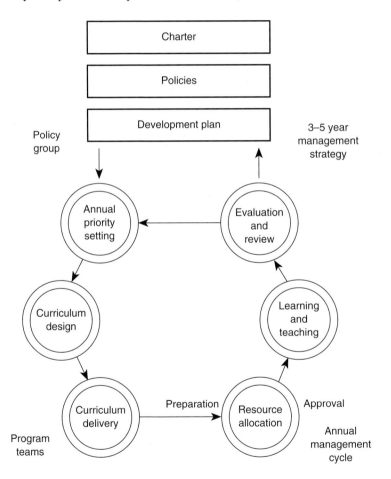

Figure 16.2 A refined model for self-management

- *educational leadership*, referring to the building of capacity among teachers, parents, and students by 'nurturing a learning community';
- *responsive leadership*, effectively 'coming to terms with accountability' by recognizing the right of different individuals and institutions to know how well the school is doing.

Track 2: Unrelenting Focus on Learning Outcomes

With settlement of the major dimensions of school reform as far as organizational arrangements are concerned, at least as they involve the local management of schools, as illustrated in Britain, it is likely that momentum will build for reform on Track 2 of change in school education. This calls for an unrelenting focus on learning outcomes.

In effect, movement on Track 2 recognizes that reform on one track alone will not, by itself, have an enduring impact on the quality of schooling. New responsibilities, authorities and accountabilities must be used to improve learning and teaching. Evidence of how this has been accomplished is now emerging. Really significant change now depends on schools taking up and applying knowledge about school and classroom effectiveness and improvement, and this body of knowledge is richer and deeper than ever. There are some imperatives around which consensus is building, including literacy, numeracy, adoption of approaches that smooth the transition from primary to secondary, and managing increasingly complex arrangements in programs at senior secondary level. 'Unrelenting' is an appropriate word to describe the commitment that will be required to ensure that all students learn well, with new learning and re-learning through teacher education and professional development.

Linking Self-Management and Learning Outcomes

Approaches to leadership and management in *The Self-Managing School* and *Leading the Self-Managing School* placed learning and teaching, and the support of learning and teaching, at the heart of these processes. Simply shifting responsibility, authority and accountability to the school level will not, by itself, have impact on learning and teaching unless explicit linkages are made.

Much has been written about the extent to which Track 1 reforms have had impact on outcomes for students. It seems obvious that, if explicit links are not made in the manner suggested above, there will be no impact, and that is precisely what the research has shown (see Summers and Johnson 1996 for a meta-analysis of research findings).

The need to shift attention from Track 1 to Track 2 was made clear in a comprehensive account of local management in Britain. Alison Bullock and Hywel Thomas conclude:

If the standard and quality of learning is to be at the centre of education – and it is surely the key test of decentralization – it is not apparent
that the processes and practices of decentralization we have discussed in
this book are adequately geared to its achievement.

(Bullock and Thomas 1997: 222)

How this can be done is illuminated by recent research in Victoria,
Australia, where the Schools of the Future (SOF) reform afforded an
opportunity to explore the impact of self-management, because linkages of
the kind described were part of the design of that reform.

How the Links are Made in Schools of the Future

Education in the public sector in Australia is the constitutional responsibility of the states, although the national (commonwealth or federal) government plays an important role, since it provides grants to the states from
revenue derived from taxation. About 70 per cent of students attend
government or public schools, while 30 per cent attend non-government or
private schools, with the majority of the latter in systems of Catholic education. The nation's public school system consists of eight state or territory
systems of education. Public education in Australia has traditionally been
highly centralized, with little discretion for school-based decision making.
There has, however, been a steady shift to school-based management in
recent decades.

In Victoria, a package of reforms to restructure the system was designed
in early 1993, and released under the banner of Schools of the Future.
In broad terms, this package has four dimensions as illustrated in
Figure 16.3. A curriculum and standards framework (CSF) was established
for all years from preparatory to year 12, designed by the recently established Board of Studies. About 90 per cent of the state's school education
budget was decentralized so that each school had a 'global budget' for
virtually all areas of recurrent expenditure, including teaching and non-
teaching staff, the only exceptions of note being capital expenditure and
certain categories of expense for system and school support. Regional and
central offices were downsized. Local selection of teachers was introduced,
though permanent teachers continued to be employed by the Education
Department. The capacity to select teachers at the school level and to
develop a school workforce plan was curtailed in the early years by the
fact that the total number of teachers in the system was still considered in
excess of requirements, so many schools carried a number of 'over-
entitlement' teachers. A Professional Recognition Program was introduced
to provide a new career structure for teachers. A performance management
framework was established for principal class personnel. The accountability
system provided for annual reports to the Education Department and

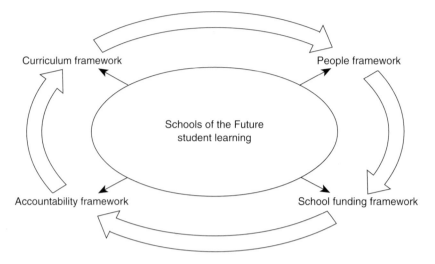

Figure 16.3 The four dimensions of Schools of the Future

school community and a process of triennial review. A Learning Assessment Project was established at the primary level, with all students being tested in literacy, mathematics and science at years 3 and 5. Results were used for school-level planning and report to parents; 'league tables' of results were not introduced, in contrast to practice in Britain. These features were all implemented within a framework of a school charter, a short document that sets out the priorities, programs and special characteristics of each school, being an agreement between the school, its community and the Education Department that will shape its operations for a period of three years.

Schools of the Future was the focus of a major investigation known as the Co-operative Research Project, established in early 1993 as a joint endeavour of the Department of Education, Victorian Association of State Secondary Principals, the Victorian Primary Principals Association and the University of Melbourne. Its purpose was to monitor the processes and outcomes of Schools of the Future as perceived by principals. The project was managed by a steering committee of two representatives from each of the four participating organizations. There have been annual surveys of principals and a range of more focused studies on particular aspects of the reform (see Co-operative Research Project, 1994, 1995a, 1995b, 1996, 1997 for reports of the surveys).

Noteworthy findings in 1996 relate to the views of principals about whether they would wish their schools to return to the arrangements that existed prior to the implementation of Schools of the Future. The overwhelming majority did not wish their schools to return to pre-Schools of the Future arrangements, consisting of 82 per cent for the curriculum framework, 89 per cent for the funding framework, 77 per cent for the people framework, 77 per cent for the accountability framework, and 86 per cent in an overall sense. These findings are surprising, given powerful concerns about workload, declining levels of job satisfaction, dissatisfaction with a principal performance management scheme, and frustration at 'bureaucratic interference' and inadequate resources.

Modelling the Links

Particular attention was paid to findings related to outcomes for students, since it was the view of the majority of principals that there had been gains in the areas of curriculum, teaching and learning, either in improved outcomes or improved capacities to carry out the work of the school. For example, 85 per cent of principals gave a rating of 3 or more on a 5-point scale of 'low' to 'high' regarding the extent to which the expected benefit of 'improved learning outcomes' had been realized in their schools.

It is possible to undertake analysis of responses in the survey to determine the direct and indirect effects of selected factors on learning. The approach known as structural equation modelling was employed, using LISREL 8 (see Jöreskog and Sörbom 1993). This approach allows the analysis of ordinal-scaled variables such as those utilized in the items of this survey.

The first step was to take clusters of related items in the survey and to treat these as constructs. Seven constructs were formed:

- curriculum and learning benefits (3 items);
- personnel and professional benefits (7 items);
- planning and resource allocation benefits (9 items);
- school and community benefits (6 items);
- curriculum improvement due to the curriculum and standards framework (CSF) (7 items);
- CSF curriculum support (4 items);
- confidence in attainment of schools of the future objectives (9 items).

A one-factor congeneric measurement model was used to examine the relative weight that each item contributes to a particular construct. All but eight of the forty-five items contributed to the various constructs, with those contributing the most being consistent with an intuitive explanation of which capacities in Schools of the Future ought to impact on curriculum and learning. These included greater financial and administrative flexibility, enhanced capacity to attract staff, higher community profile, planning the provision of curriculum, course advice in support of the curriculum and standards framework, and confidence in an objective of Schools of the Future to encourage continuing improvement to enhance learning outcomes.

Further analysis was conducted to determine the 'goodness of fit' between the data and a model formed by the constructs described above. Figure 16.4 contains the explanatory regression model that shows the interdependent effects among variables (in this instance, latent variables that represent the constructs) on the variable curriculum and learning benefits. Standardized path coefficients are shown, representing the direct effects (all paths are statistically significant beyond the $p < 0.05$ level by univariate two-tailed test). The fit between data and model is very good indeed, with an Adjusted Goodness of Fit Index of 0.947, indicating that about 95 per cent of the variances and co-variances in the data are accounted for by the model.

The path coefficients may be interpreted in this manner. The direct effect of 'school and community benefits' on 'personnel and professional benefits' is indicated by a path coefficient of 0.479. This indicates that an increase in the measure of 'school and community benefits' of 1 standard deviation produces an increase in the measure of 'curriculum and learning benefits' of 0.479 of a standard deviation.

While these findings are based on the perceptions of principals, the direct, indirect and total effects are consistent with expectations for the successful implementation of a scheme of self-management. The structural features of such reforms such as the shift of authority, responsibility and accountability

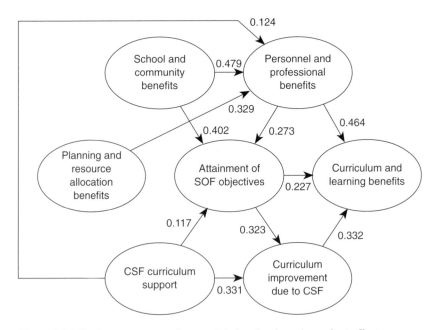

Figure 16.4 Explanatory regression model showing interdependent effects among factors influencing perceived Curriculum and Learning Benefits showing standardised path coefficients

to the school level are unlikely, by themselves, to have either a direct or an indirect effect on curriculum and learning unless the capacities that may be nurtured within such arrangements are developed. Clearly, the principals who report curriculum and learning benefits tend to be those who have reported benefits in other domains of the Schools of the Future program, including the capacity to select staff, increased flexibility in the use of resources, and involvement of the community.

Interpreting the Findings for School Leaders

The model in Figure 16.4 suggests pathways for the exercise of leadership in self-managing schools. While further research is under way to determine the manner in which these pathways are travelled in schools that have evidence of improved outcomes for students, they appear trustworthy and are consistent with a 'theory of action' for the self-managing school. Referring to items on which constructs were derived, such action in respect to direct effects concerns, for example, better personnel management, increased staff satisfaction, enhanced professional development, shared decision making, enhanced capacity to attract staff (these being in the personnel and professional domain); and planning the provision of a curriculum program, establishing levels and standards in key learning areas, focusing attention on key learning areas, basing curriculum around intended learning outcomes, responding to the range of student needs and reporting outcomes to parents (these being in the curriculum domain). In respect to indirect effects, for example, these concern a higher level of self-management, increased financial and administrative flexibility and better resource management (these being in the planning and resource allocation domain).

Building a capacity to accomplish these tasks is clearly a role for school leaders on Track 2 of change in schools. Such a capacity should be deeply embedded in a school, for there ought to be many leaders engaged in such work, not just the school principal. Contrary to concerns, or perhaps in response to research evidence that suggests that work to date has not been so focused, the direct effects of action in the curriculum domain should be noted. Leadership and management should be balanced, with a focus on learning, curriculum and the people resources of the school.

Raising the Stakes in Standards-Driven Reform

While these findings are helpful in describing a preferred role for school leaders, they do not capture the scope and sense of urgency for change on Track 2. The word 'unrelenting' was used to describe the focus on learning and teaching. Robert Slavin uses the word 'relentless' to describe an imperative for action in schools that seek to succeed in early literacy. His Success for All and Roots and Wings programs are among the nine designs in the

New American Schools program that raise the stakes in terms of work to be done in the USA (see Stringfield et al. 1996 for an account of these designs).

New Labour in Britain and authorities in other countries are making clear that standards-driven reform must lie at centre stage. In political terms, there is bipartisan support on this issue. This means that school leaders on Track 2 must be first and foremost educational strategists, for they will need to know much about what works and why in an era when the levels of knowledge on these matters is higher than it has ever been. Working with teams of teachers to gather data on student achievement, on entry and in relation to standards for different levels of schooling, is central to this task. The concept of 'value added' in respect to the contribution of the school will preferably replace raw-score-based 'league tables' in some countries, notably Britain.

These are demanding and highly skilled roles for school leaders, with capacities dispersed in the school rather than focused in the person of the principal. The implications for the preparation and ongoing professional development of teachers and their leaders are profound.

Track 3: Creating Schools for the Knowledge Society

Developments in recent years suggest a third track for change in school education. Track 3 cannot be described in detail but may be presented as a vision, illustrated in a gestalt in Figure 16.5, that is, 'a perceived organized whole that is more than the sum of its parts' (Concise Oxford English Dictionary). This gestalt and its elements, as described below, are drawn from *Beyond the Self-Managing School* (Caldwell and Spinks 1998).

Each element in this gestalt may be found at present, although their manifestation in a single school is still rare. As suggested at the outset, the precise manner in which the following will unfold will become clearer over the next decade, with variation from setting to setting.

- Dramatic change to approaches to learning and teaching is in store as electronic networking allows 'cutting across and so challenging the very idea of subject boundaries' and 'changing the emphasis from impersonal curriculum to excited live exploration', to use the words of Papert (1993) in *The Children's Machine*. At risk is the balkanized curriculum that has done much to alienate children from schooling, especially in the middle years of the transition from primary to secondary (G1, 'Connectedness in curriculum').

- Schools as workplaces are transformed in every dimension, including the scheduling of time for learning and approaches to human resource management, rendering obsolete most approaches that derive from an industrial age, including the concept of 'industrial relations' (G2, 'Workplace transformation').

- The fabric of schooling is similarly rendered obsolete by electronic networking. Everything from building design to the size, shape, alignment and furnishing of space for the 'knowledge worker' in the school is transformed. In one sense, of course, the school has no walls, for there are global learning networks, and much of the learning that calls for the student to be located at school in fact occurs in many places – at home and, in the upper years of secondary schooling and for life-long learning, in the workplace (G3, 'School fabric and globalization').

- A wide range of professionals and para-professionals support learning in an educational parallel to the diversity of support that may be found in modern healthcare. The role of teacher is elevated, for it demands wisdom, judgement, and a facility for managing learning in modes more complex and varied than ever. While the matter of intellectual capital must be resolved, the teacher is freed from the impossible task of designing from his or her own resources learning experiences to challenge every student: the resources of the world's great teachers will be at hand (G4, 'Professionalism and great teaching').

- A capacity to work in teams is more evident in approaches to learning, given the primacy of the work team in every formulation of the workplace in the knowledge society. This, of course, will confound those who see electronic networking in terms of an outdated stereotype of the loner with the laptop. The concept of 'pastoral care' of students is as important as ever for learning in this mode, and in schools that quite literally have no boundaries (G5, 'Teams and pastoral care').

- Dale Spender's challenge in *Nattering on the Net* (Spender 1995) to formulate 'cyber-policy of the future' is a priority. The issues of access and equity will drive public debate until such time as prices fall to make electronic networks as common as the telephone or radio, and that may soon be a reality, given trends in networked computers (G6, 'Cyber-policy, access and equity').

- The concept of the virtual organization or the learning network organization is a reality in the knowledge society. Schools take on many of the characteristics of such organizations, given that learning occurs in so many modes and from so many sources, all networked electronically (G7, 'Virtual schools').

Rethinking the Work of School Leaders

The work of the school leader has certainly changed in profound ways in recent years. The role was relatively stable and straightforward until the last quarter of the century. For the principal, it was largely a matter of administering a standard curriculum that did little to accommodate a range of student aptitudes and interests. Many students failed to reach the end of secondary school and most secured employment in their local

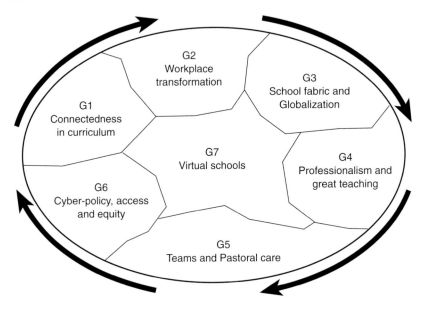

Figure 16.5 A vision for schooling in the knowledge society, illustrated in a gestalt
Source: Caldwell and Spinks (1998)

communities. There was little involvement of parents, except for minor fund-raising and social activities, and no substantive role in decision making. Resources were allocated to schools by formula, and no funds as such were decentralized to the school level. The principal was expected to 'run a tight ship' as far as staff were concerned, be a model teacher, and regularly visit the classrooms of the school.

The role began to change in the 1970s and early 1980s as policies to redress disadvantage and empower communities were enacted. Funds were allocated to particular purposes and, in some cases, these were decentralized to schools with a more powerful role for teachers and parents in decision making. For the most part, however, these funds were retained centrally in an increasing array of organizational units in an expanding bureaucracy. A model derived from research on school effectiveness helped define a new role for school leaders in goal setting, policy making, priority setting, planning, budgeting, implementing and evaluating, with these activities based around programs of learning and teaching and the support of learning and teaching (Caldwell and Spinks 1988).

This role became important as governments around the world restructured their systems of public education, with local management within a centrally determined framework becoming the norm (Track 1). Cultural leadership, strategic leadership, educational leadership and reflective leadership were important dimensions of the work of school leaders in a period of rapid change (Caldwell and Spinks 1992).

The most important aspect of the emerging role is concerned with improving the quality of learning for all students, with standards-driven reform now gaining bipartisan support in most places (Track 2). School leaders must be educational strategists, working with others to develop a capacity for state-of-the-art learning. Work in this area is best illustrated by the priority given in most places to improving standards of literacy for all students in primary schools. Certainly the role is changing to a more strategic one, at least on the part of school principals. Gurr's research with secondary principals in Schools of the Future in Victoria confirms this. The principal may be spending less time in classrooms and working alongside teachers, but he or she is spending more time on 'bigger picture' strategic matters in ways that reflect the contemporary view of transformational leadership (see Gurr 1996a, 1996b, 1996c). For these reasons, the concept of 'educational strategist' should be pre-eminent in the new role.

At the same time that these matters have settled (Track 1) or have gathered momentum (Track 2), there is evidence that school education is being reinvented, largely driven by advances in technology. One cannot be certain about the detail of reform, but a capacity for strategic management will become increasingly important for school leadership on Track 3.

The transition is not easy, because the changes are profound and resources are scarce, in school education as in other fields of public and private endeavour. Taken together, though, these sound like rich and rewarding roles for school leaders at the dawn of the third millennium.

References

Bullock, A. and Thomas, H. (1997) *Schools at the Centre? A Study of Decentralisation.* London: Routledge.

Caldwell, B.J. and Spinks, J.M. (1988) *The Self-Managing School.* London: Falmer Press.

—— (1992) *Leading the Self-Managing School.* London: Falmer Press.

—— (1998) *Beyond the Self-Managing School.* London: Falmer Press.

Cooperative Research Project (1994) *Base-Line Survey.* Report of the Cooperative Research Project on 'Leading Victoria's Schools of the Future', Directorate of School Education, Victorian Association of State Secondary Principals, Victorian Primary Principals Association, The University of Melbourne (Fay Thomas, Chair). (Available from Department of Education).

Cooperative Research Project (1995a) *One Year Later.* Report of the Cooperative Research Project on 'Leading Victoria's Schools of the Future', Directorate of School Education, Victorian Association of State Secondary Principals, Victorian Primary Principals Association, The University of Melbourne (Fay Thomas, Chair). (Available from Department of Education).

Cooperative Research Project (1995b) *Taking Stock*. Report of the Cooperative Research Project on 'Leading Victoria's Schools of the Future', Directorate of School Education, Victorian Association of State Secondary Principals, Victorian Primary Principals Association, The University of Melbourne (Fay Thomas, Chair). (Available from Department of Education).

Cooperative Research Project (1996) *Three Year Report Card*. Report of the Co-operative Research Project on 'Leading Victoria's Schools of the Future', Directorate of School Education, Victorian Association of State Secondary Principals, Victorian Primary Principals Association, The University of Melbourne (Fay Thomas, Chair). (Available from Department of Education).

Cooperative Research Project (1997) *Still More Work to be Done But . . . No Turning Back*. Report of the Cooperative Research Project on 'Leading Victoria's Schools of the Future', Department of School Education, Victorian Association of State Secondary Principals, Victorian Primary Principals Association, The University of Melbourne (Fay Thomas, Chair). (Available from Department of Education).

Gurr, D. (1996a) The Leadership Role of Principals in Selected 'Schools of the Future': Principal and Teacher Perspectives. Unpublished doctoral thesis, The University of Melbourne.

—— (1996b) On Conceptualising School Leadership: Time to Abandon Transformational Leadership? *Leading and Managing*, 2(3): 221–39.

—— (1996c) Reply to Gronn and Lakomski. *Leading and Managing*, 2(3): 246–48.

Jöreskog, K.G. and Sörbom, D. (1993) *LISREL 8: User's Reference Guide*. Chicago: Scientific Software, Inc.

Papert, S. (1993) *The Children's Machine: Rethinking School in the Age of the Computer*. New York: Basic Books.

Spender, D. (1995) *Nattering on the Net: Women, Power and Cyberspace*. North Melbourne: Spinifex.

Stringfield, S., Ross, S.M. and Smith, L. (1996) *Bold Plans for School Restructuring: The New American Schools Design*. Mahwah, NJ: Lawrence Erlbaum Associates.

Summers, A.A. and Johnson, A.W. (1996) The Effects of School-Based Management Plans. In E.A. Hanushek and D.W. Jorgenson (eds), *Improving America's Schools: The Role of Incentives*. Washington, DC: New Academy Press.

Notes on Contributors

Ibrahim Bajunid is Director of Institut Aaminuddin Baki, Malaysia. He has initiated 'twinning' Masters' degree programmes and contributed to collaborative research projects with universities in Britain, the USA and Australia and is Chair of the National Committee for the Promotion of Professionalism in Training and Consultancy Management. His educational management experiences encompass concerns for and contributions to all phases of education, and he has presented several keynote addresses at international policy conferences.

Gunnar Berg is a Professor of Education at the University of Uppsala and the University of Dalarna, Sweden. His major interests are organization theory, and the relation between educational research and organization theory in particular, leadership and management in general, and school leadership and school management in particular. He has for many years been responsible for different programmes of in-service training for principals/heads, teachers and educational policy makers, as well as leaders for other public organizations. He has also been involved in several international projects, for instance the OECD International Improvement Project, and has been a board member and a chair in European Network for Improving Research and Development in Educational Management (ENIRDEM).

Colin Biott is a Professor of Professional Education and Development at the University of Northumbria, England. His particular interests are in practitioner research and the impact of change on the lives and work of teachers. Recent projects have focused on induction for newly qualified teachers, training needs of community children's nurses and identity construction in school leadership. His books include *Working and Learning Together for Change* and *Collaborative Learning in Classrooms and Staffrooms*.

Stewart Bonser is a Senior Research Associate with Murdoch University for the 'Restructuring Australia's Schools' Project. He has extensive experience as a teacher educator in Western Australia, Queensland and New South Wales. His research interests include language arts education and the teaching of reading as well as the processes associated with school improvement and reform.

Brian J. Caldwell is Dean of Education at the University of Melbourne where he holds a Personal Chair in Education. His major interests are leadership, resource allocation and the management of change, particularly under conditions where significant authority, responsibility and accountability are decentralized to schools. His books have influenced developments in several nations. He recently completed a trilogy with Jim Spinks, published by Falmer Press: *The Self-Managing School* (1988), *Leading the Self-Managing School* (1992) and *Beyond the Self-Managing School* (1998). His book with former Minister for Education Don Hayward, based on landmark devolution in Victoria, was published by Falmer Press in 1998 under the title *The Future of Schools: Lessons from the Reform of Public Education.* He was President of the Australian Council for Educational Administration from 1990 to 1993.

K.K. Chan was an Associate Professor and is presently Honorary Associate Professor of the Department of Curriculum Studies, The University of Hong Kong. Her research interests include curriculum policies, reform and change; curriculum evaluation; integrated and cross-curricular studies. She is presently Chief Executive, Curriculum Development Institute, Education Department of the Hong Kong Special Administrative Region, China.

Christopher Day is a Professor of Education, a Director of the Centre for Teacher and School Development, and Head of Humanities Division, Graduate School, University of Nottingham. Prior to this he worked as a teacher, lecturer and local education authority adviser. He is widely published, and edits *Teachers and Teaching: Theory and Practice*, an international journal. He is convenor of the European Education Research Association's Group on research into the continuing professional development of teachers and general secretary of the International Study Association on Teachers and Teaching (ISATT). His abiding interest is in contributing to understandings of and improvements in the professional lives of teachers and headteachers. His most recent publications include *Developing Leadership in Primary Schools* (1998, with Hall and Whitaker, Paul Chapman) *and Developing Teachers: The Challenges of Lifelong Learning*, (1999, London, Falmer Press).

Alicia Fernandez is the current PACT (Professional Actions and Cultures of Teaching) Administrator. She has had extensive experience as a teacher, consultant and administrator in the Canadian public school system. Her research interests lie in the areas of teacher professionalism, educational leadership and leadership development, and school effectiveness and change.

Ivor Goodson is a Professor at the Warner Graduate School, University of Rochester, New York and also holds a Chair of Education at the University of East Anglia in his native England. He is an author of a range of books on curriculum and life history studies. They include *Studying Curriculum: Cases and Methods* (1994), *Schools Subjects and Curriculum Change* (3rd edition, 1995), *Biography, Identity and Schooling* (with Rob Walker) (1991), *Studying Teachers' Lives* (1992) and *Teachers' Professional Lives* (1996). He is the founding editor and North American editor of the *Journal of Education Policy* and the international editor of the *Journal of Qualitative Studies in Education*.

Shirley Grundy is an Associate Professor in the School of Education, Murdoch University, Western Australia. She directed an ARC-funded research project: 'Restructuring Australia's Schools: Organizational, Management and Pedagogical Practices'. Her research interests include curriculum theory, policy analysis, organizational leadership and management, school-based research and development, and school/university partnerships for teacher professional development.

Trond E. Hauge is Professor of Education at the Department of Teacher Education and School Development, University of Oslo, Norway. Prior to this he worked as a teacher in secondary schools and in a college of teacher education, as a consultant in the National Council for Primary and Lower Secondary Schools and in the National Council for Teacher Education in Norway. He has published books in Norwegian such as *Students' Well-Being in Schools*, *Youth and Religion* and *The Teacher as a Classroom Leader*. His main research interests include teachers' thinking and a practice teaching, teacher education and school effectiveness.

Gill Helsby is a Senior Researcher in the Centre for the Study of Education and Training at Lancaster University, England. Her research interests include the impact of recent curriculum initiatives on teachers' work practices and teachers' professional development.

Kirsti Klette is an Associate Professor at the University of Oslo, Institute of Educational Research. Her teaching, research and writings are in the areas of teaching and teachers' work, qualitative research methods and issues concerned with stability and change in schools.

David F. Labaree is Professor in the Department of Teacher Education at Michigan State University (East Lansing, Michigan, USA), where he co-ordinates the doctoral programme. His work focuses on the history and sociology of American education, educational policy, and educational reform. His first book was *The Making of an American High School* (Yale University Press, 1988), in which he explored the role of political and market pressures in shaping American education and the impact of conflicting goals on American schools. He continued these themes in his second book, in which he argues that schools are increasingly at the mercy of powerful consumer pressures that threaten to turn education into a game of *How to Succeed in School Without Really Learning*, which is the book's title (Yale, 1997). He shows that rampant consumerism is in the process of turning public education into a private good, while at the same time undermining the motivation of students to learn by focusing their attention on getting ahead rather than getting an education.

Lo Mun Ling is an Assistant Professor in the Department of Curriculum Studies, University of Hong Kong, where she has worked as a teacher educator since 1994. She has over fifteen years of teaching experience in secondary schools in Hong Kong and Australia. She is the co-author of *Integrated Science and Chemistry* textbooks used by many secondary schools in Hong Kong, and for the past three years, she has been the course director of the refresher training courses for serving secondary school teachers in Hong Kong. She is now Project Director of the Unified Professional Development Project, which is designed to enhance school–university partnerships. She is a member of a team evaluating the impact of the Target Oriented Curriculum which was introduced into Hong Kong primary schools in 1995.

Gary McCulloch is a Professor of Education at the University of Sheffield. His research interests are in the social history of education, teaching, the curriculum and education policy. His recent publications include *Failing The Ordinary Child? The Theory and Practice of Working Class Secondary Education* (Open University Press, 1998), *Teachers and the National Curriculum* (ed. with Gill Helsby, Cassell, 1997), and *Educational Reconstruction: The 1944 Education Act and the Twenty-First Century* (Woburn, 1994). He is currently working on the politics of teacher professionalism in England and Wales and on historical methodology in educational research. He is also editor of the *International Journal of the History of Education*.

Jorunn Møller is an Associate Professor in the Department of Teacher Education and School Development, University of Oslo, Norway. Her major interests are in the areas of educational administration, action research, supervision and school evaluation.

Paul Morris is a Professor in the Department of Curriculum Studies, University of Hong Kong, where he has worked as a teacher educator since

1976. Between 1988 and 1993 he was a member of the government's Education Commission and was involved with two major reports. He has published extensively in leading international journals, in the areas of curriculum analysis, teacher education and comparative education. His books include: *Education and Development in East Asia*, (co-edited with Anthony Sweeting), (New York, Garland, 1995) and *The Hong Kong School Curriculum: Development, Issues and Policy* (Hong Kong University Press 1996, 2nd edition). He is also editor of the series *Teaching in Hong Kong* (Longman), which consists of eleven volumes to date. He is currently leading a team of ten researchers who are evaluating the impact of the Target Oriented Curriculum which was introduced into Hong Kong primary schools in 1995.

Franz Rauch is a Lecturer at the Institute for Interdisciplinary Research and Continuing Education of the Universities of Innsbruck, Klagenfurt and Vienna, Department for School and Social Learning, and has been involved in research projects in curriculum and school development since 1991. In 1996 he was a research fellow at the University of Northumbria in Newcastle upon Tyne, England, in the course of the EC project 'Management and Organisational and Human Development'. In 1997 he was a Fulbright Scholar at the University of Missouri, St Louis. Before he started his career at university, he worked for several years as a teacher in vocational schools.

Judyth Sachs is Professor of Education in the School of Professional Studies at the University of Sydney. She is currently Pro-Dean (External and International Relations) within the Faculty of Education. She is past president of the Australian Association for Research in Education. Her research interests lie in the area of teacher professionalism, teacher professional development and women and leadership.

Index